THE G. STANLEY HALL LECTURE SERIES

Volume 2

G. STANLEY HALL, 1844–1924

THE G. STANLEY HALL LECTURE SERIES

Volume 2

Edited by
Alan G. Kraut

1981 HALL LECTURERS

Donn Byrne
Elizabeth F. Loftus
Carolyn Wood Sherif
Lee S. Shulman
Daniel Stokols

AMERICAN PSYCHOLOGICAL ASSOCIATION
WASHINGTON, D.C.

Published by the American Psychological Association, Inc.,
1200 Seventeenth Street, N.W., Washington, D.C. 20036
Copyright © 1982 by the American Psychological Association.
All rights reserved.

ISBN: 0-912704-60-8

Copies may be ordered from:
Order Department
American Psychological Association
1200 Seventeenth Street, N.W.
Washington, D.C. 20036

Printed in the United States of America

CONTENTS

PREFACE

This volume in the G. Stanley Hall Lecture Series is the second in an ongoing effort aimed at meeting the needs of introductory psychology teachers. Specifically, the series is designed to help teachers of introductory psychology courses refresh and update their knowledge in the many specialty areas within psychology. The chapters presented here provide a selective and recent literature review of five specialties that are likely to be covered in an introductory course; the selection within specialties highlights aspects the authors feel are most appropriate for introductory students.

These chapters were first presented as invited lectures at the 1981 American Psychological Association Convention at Los Angeles. A long process to select lecturers began over a year in advance. Criteria for selection included (a) expertise in a particular introductory content area, (b) a strong interest in teaching psychology, (c) experience in teaching introductory psychology and (d) an understanding of the special problems that an introductory survey course entails. The distinguished lecturers finally chosen reflect those qualities admirably: Carolyn Wood Sherif, Social Psychology; Lee Shulman, Educational Psychology; Elizabeth Loftus, Memory and Forgetting; Dan Stokols, Environmental Psychology; and Donn Byrne, Human Sexuality.

Carolyn Wood Sherif begins her chapter on social psychology by noting that "an awesome bulk" of research in social psychology has been produced in the past five years. Her task of organizing, explaining, and giving excitement to that "bulk" was perhaps the most difficult that any of the authors faced. She has succeeded in grand style. Even the experienced social psychologist will be provided with new insights as Sherif moves from an analysis of social situations to the impact of social situations on strangers and friends alike to the individual's view of self within the social context. Sherif makes a compelling case for her premise that there are both social and individual bases to social psychology.

Lee Shulman, like Sherif, has taken on a large job and has completed it in excellent fashion. After apologizing for not attempting to cover all there is to know about educational psychology, Shulman suggests an approach—telling what he calls "research stories"—that seems to cover (and make interesting) much of the field. The stories that he presents indicate a movement of scientific investigation back into the context of the classroom. There is enough of this cleverly written information both to delight any introductory student and to whet the appetite for more.

Elizabeth Loftus takes the traditional experimental literature on memory and places it in the midst of relevant societal concerns. Loftus calls the process putting "old wine in new bottles." Admirably, she loses not a drop of scientific integrity in the process. The conceptions that many societal activities involve memory in important ways, that memory can be studied in real-life settings, and that commonsense understandings about memory can be mistaken lead into the basic message that, if one wants to know why people remember (or misremember) as they do, one must study the mechanisms of memory in and out of the laboratory. Ebbinghaus would have been pleased.

Daniel Stokols discusses the "coming of age" of environmental psychology, a psychological specialty only recently recognized. Although he details the impressive scientific achievements that have already emerged from the field, his point is that environmental psychology is not yet a fully mature field. Stokols characterizes environmental psychology, rather, as an adolescent: sure of growth and adulthood but unsure of what that adulthood will be. He masterfully sets out the possible paths that environmental psychology may take and describes the theoretical implications of each. This type of presentation might well lead an introductory student to pursue environmental psychology and become part of the field's developmental process.

Finally, Donn Byrne reviews the area of predicting human sexual behavior. As a topic, sex appears to have a guaranteed predetermined appeal. Byrne both maintains that interest level and presents an undiluted and scientific review of the literature. He shows that early research in sex was largely descriptive and sets forth a convincing case for the desirability of having a theoretical perspective in one's research. In discussing different aspects of prediction, Byrne presents the field of psychosexology at its theoretical and empirical best.

These eminent psychologists are helping to build a tradition that began in March 1979 with a proposal for a lecture series from APA's Committee on Undergraduate Education (CUE), the group within APA charged with proposing policy to encourage excellence in the undergraduate psychology curriculum. The problem with which CUE had struggled during that winter was whether anyone could maintain an up-to-date working knowledge of the 20 to 25 fields typically covered in an introductory course. The committee concluded that, of course, no one could, particularly in this era of increasing specialization in and sophistication of psychological research fields. The real issue was what CUE could do to ease the problem. And so came the plan for a lecture series on the various specialties, to be geared toward teachers of introductory psychology, to be given annually at the APA Convention, and to be published in annual volumes.

More groups and individuals became involved and offered what was almost always helpful and welcome advice as the plan made its way through the APA governance structure. APA's Education and Training Board, the Committee on Continuing Education, the Board of Convention Affairs, the Division of Teaching of Psychology, and a number of prominent individuals long identified with undergraduate psychology education all had a say in shaping the proposal that was passed by APA's Board of Directors.

In addition, a number of individuals deserve special thanks for their contribution to this volume. Leonard Bickman, Charles Brewer, Douglas Candland, David Cole, Barbara Nodine, and Carl Thoreson composed the advisory committee that chose the 1981 Hall Lecturers. I also want to thank Sidney Arenson, E. Scott Geller, Vernon Hall, Martita Lopez, and Daniel Smothergill for commenting on earlier versions of these chapters. Finally, I want to thank former APA staff members Ludy Benjamin and Kathleen Lowman and current APA staff member Ann Rogers for their hard work on the Hall Series.

I regret to report that Carolyn Wood Sherif died on July 23, 1982, during the production of this volume. The final editing of Dr. Sherif's paper was done by Virginia O'Leary.

Alan G. Kraut

SOCIAL AND PSYCHOLOGICAL BASES OF SOCIAL PSYCHOLOGY

C arolyn Wood Sherif, Professor of Psychology at The Pennsylvania State University, also taught at the University of Oklahoma, Cornell University, and Smith College. Her continuing interest in instruction was represented by *Orientation in Social Psychology* (1976).

Before and after receiving her PhD (University of Texas at Austin, 1961), she collaborated with Muzafer Sherif in research on group formation and intergroup relations (*Groups in Harmony and Tension*, 1953; *Intergroup Conflict and Cooperation: The Robbers' Cave Experiment*, 1961; *Reference Groups*, 1964) as well as in writing two texts (1956, 1969). A National Sigma Xi Lecturer (1981–83), she was senior author of *Attitude and Attitude Change* (1965), a Citation Classic, which presents a theory basic to recent research on social judgment as reported in her chapter for the Nebraska Symposium (1980). Her chapter "Bias in Psychology," in J. Sherman and E. T. Beck's *Prism of Sex*, received the 1980 Distinguished Publication Award from the Association for Women in Psychology.

The world of psychology lost a valuable and beloved member when Carolyn Wood Sherif died on July 23, 1982.

CAROLYN WOOD SHERIF

SOCIAL AND PSYCHOLOGICAL BASES OF PSYCHOLOGY

T he title of this lecture and my emphasis in discussing recent social psychology may need clarification. Long ago James Mark Baldwin (1895) proposed that individuals and social context, including other individuals, are in a dialectic relationship that is indivisible. Human individuals are born into, live in, and participate in the creation of social environments quite distinct from natural environments without humans. Human beings are also capable of altering natural and social environments, especially when acting collectively. Thus social psychology has both social *and* psychological bases, as the title indicates, not one *or* the other. As F. H. Allport stated during the later years of his long career, the "master problem" of social psychology is working out the relationships between the social and psychological, not analyzing one or the other (Brooks & Johnson, 1978; Gorman, 1981).

In various phases of work on this paper, the following individuals provided helpful literature or counsel: Stewart Cook, Ted Huston, Michael Johnson, Arnold Kahn, Mel Mark, Merrill Noble, Virginia O'Leary, L. Ann Peplau, Thomas Pettigrew, Marylee Taylor, Muzafer Sherif, Daniel Stokols, and Barbara Wallston.

Guidelines for Exclusion and Inclusion

In 1977 Kelly Shaver estimated that over 90 percent of all research in social psychology was conducted within the previous 25 years. The past five years produced an awesome bulk. Therefore, guidelines for exclusion and inclusion were necessary in preparing this paper.

I started by surveying the social psychology chapters in 15 introductory psychology texts published between 1977 and 1981 (see the list preceding the references). I found that students in introductory psychology encounter chapters on different topics, cafeteria style, with social psychology at the end of the line (in all but one text). Although several texts included social-psychological concepts and research findings in other chapters (as indeed they should), the student was introduced to "social psychology" in these final chapters which, typically, did not include such clearly related topics as the development of "social motivations," "social learning," or "language and thought." Therefore, I reluctantly excluded such important topics in my review.

I tabulated the topics discussed in the social psychology chapters of the 15 texts, with some interesting results. First, with the exception of a few topics, what students are exposed to as social psychology in the introductory texts varies considerably from book to book. The only topics common to all, or to all but one or two, were attitudes, cognitive dissonance, attributions of causality, obedience to authority, and influence by an erroneous majority. Second, the most common and frequent topics in introductory texts concerned, on one hand, intrapsychic (intra-individual) concepts or, on the other, social influences *on* the individual by persons unacquainted with that individual. Sociocultural influences (including social stereotypes, discriminatory institutional practices, racist or sexist ideologies) were discussed in fewer than half of the texts. Social interactions, particularly those among previously acquainted persons, were even more neglected. To compensate for this neglect I decided to start here by enlarging on the social basis of social psychology and its importance for interpreting social behaviors.

Because the G. Stanley Hall lectures focus on the last five years, older works receive little more than a mention here. Instructors with a proclivity for oral history of earlier times will find valuable instructional materials in Richard Evans's *The Making of Social Psychology*

(1980). That book also provides some perspective on the self-proclaimed "crisis" in social psychology, which did not lead to its premature demise, as you may have heard. To the contrary, the crisis literature had several constructive implications for the directions social psychology has taken in recent years. These implications guided the organization of this paper.

First, the crisis literature pointed, by raising distressing questions, to a social vacuum in much social-psychological research studying single, unacquainted, often physically separated individuals in the laboratory. Where, in such research, were human groups (Steiner, 1974; M. Sherif, 1977)? Where were cultural institutions with their roles and rules (Triandis, 1975), status differentiations among people and groups (Moscovici, 1972; Tajfel, 1972), or social norms that affect both researcher and subjects (Pepitone, 1976)? Where was the historical context which bounded the research and might be influenced, in turn, by publishing the findings of that research (Gergen, 1973, 1976; Smith, 1976)? What of the cultural assumptions that guided researchers to formulate research problems for experiments in such a social vacuum (Archibald, 1978; Billig, 1976; Israel & Tajfel, 1972; Sampson, 1978)?

Such questions reflected a growing concern about whether research in social psychology had bearing on and relevance for social problems in everyday life (Ring, 1967; M. Sherif, 1970). They touched upon even earlier concerns about a general lack in psychology of systematic study of physical and human-made environments associated with much of the variance in social behavior (Barker, 1963; Sells, 1963; Sherif & Sherif, 1956, 1964). As the questions were asked, growing numbers of social psychologists began work under labels that pointed explicitly to that which was lacking—such labels as environmental social psychology (Stokols, 1981, and in this volume), cross-cultural psychology (Triandis, 1980; Triandis & Brislin, 1980), and applied social psychology (Bickman, 1980, 1981; Ellison & Buckhout, 1981; Kidd & Saks, 1980).

Second, the crisis literature, with precedents in the voluminous research on the "social psychology of the psychological experiment" (Adair, 1973), focused attention increasingly upon the individual's phenomenal experience in social situations and upon related cognitive processes. The growing interest in human consciousness and in cognitive processes in general psychology was both sparked by and reflected in social psychologists' research activities on social perception, social judgment, and attributional processes (Cartwright, 1979).

In this paper I have incorporated these two implications from the crisis literature by starting with the social basis of social psychology and then proceeding to recent studies of social cognition, making certain to relate these studies to the social context. Within that broad plan, I confess that the necessarily selective choice of topics reflects considerably my own interests.[1] In keeping with the constructive directions in the crisis literature, my preference is for integrative efforts, despite the ups and downs of fads to which social psychology, like other areas in the profession, is recurrently subject.[2]

Plan of the Paper

First, the social bases for social psychology are introduced through analysis of the social situations in which individuals participate. The "social realities" in such situations are discussed, with a rationale for their assessment independent of the ways in which the particular individuals studied in research perceive them. The impact of such social realities on behavior is illustrated first by research on the interactions of unacquainted individuals with different social positions in society at large, then by research on individuals with a history of previous interactions.

The second half of this paper concerns research on how individuals know about social realities, i.e., social cognition. General problems involved in relating social cognition to social realities are discussed, and a simple scheme is presented for the coordinated interaction of

---

[1] In part, my selective emphasis on social power and categorization in this paper reflects a counterreaction to G. S. Hall, for whom this series is named. His elitist and sexist chauvinisms were freely translated into recommendations on public policies aimed at providing healthy but docile workers, soldiers, and childbearers, as well as elite leaders. He once threatened "a new rape of the Sabines" if middle-class women would not cease attempts at family planning (see Degler, 1980). While the generous interpretation is that G. S. Hall reflected his times, his contemporaries did not all share his views.

[2] The crisis literature continues to grow, though at a more deliberate pace, with somewhat greater recognition that the problems are not new, having been faced and dealt with constructively by a number of leading social psychologists (e.g., Boutilier, Roed, & Svendsen, 1980; Doise, 1980a, 1980b; Smith, 1980; Tajfel, 1979; Taylor & Brown, 1979). The term "fads" was used by Shaw and Costanzo (1982) to characterize changing theories in social psychology.

situational and psychological determinants of psychological processes and behavior. Then the emphasis is upon research about one's reactions to other persons classified in the same social categories or groups as oneself and in categories or groups different from oneself. That topic leads to a discussion of current work on attitudes illustrative of social psychologists' conceptual interest in the cognitive-motivational-affective structures guiding and organizing individuals' definitions of the situation. Early concern with the distressingly low correlations between measured attitudes and subsequent actions has given way to research analyzing social situations as they relate to a person's attitudes and to growing interest in the personal importance of such attitudes. The revival of interest in the concept of a human self-system will be discussed from that perspective. The last section discusses certain problems of attitude change related to self-concerns in the social context.

Out of a Social Vacuum, Into Social Context

The current injunction, which is not new, is to study individual experience and behavior *in social context* (e.g., Pettigrew, 1981; Tajfel, 1979). But what is a social context?

In introductory psychology texts, a common definition of a social context is the presence, even the imagined presence, of other individuals. Others say that the social context is composed of interactions among individuals. As environmental psychologists remind us, however, individuals are located in some *place,* frequently in human-made locations with human-made objects, facilities, equipment, tools, books, and televisions, all of which are social. In those places, individuals engage by themselves, in pairs, in dyads, in quartets, or in larger groups in *activities.* Such activities are seldom random affairs without pattern. Individuals' encounters occur also within socially defined *time* frames and for varying periods.

There is more to a social situation than can be seen with a glance or even with careful measurement of its physical character and count of its participants, as important as these are. Certain locations go with some activities but not with others, as one will quickly find if one has the impulse to turn handsprings in a lecture hall. Certain people are not permitted to be in some locations or to engage in some activities.

What fills the social context by linking participants to the location, to the activities, and to one another? The answer is no more mysterious than observing that the individuals in the situation all speak to one another in Spanish rather than in English or Urdu. The social situation contains much of the culture and other aspects of the larger social organization, in the form of status and power differentials, social rules, or norms—all social values defining what is desirable, what one should want and should do. These social values developed historically, and they frame both the situation and the individuals at the moment the situation begins.

Interrelated Sets of Factors in a Social Situation

The need for independent assessment of a social context or situation prior to analyzing the experience and actions of particular individuals within it is illustrated by the scheme presented in Table 1. The table outlines five sets of factors or variables present in any social situation, with examples that include cultural factors. As an instructional device, it is useful for several purposes:

1. It serves as a framework for analyzing specific social situations, including the setups and procedures in laboratory experiments and field research when the relevant information is reported.

2. It serves as a basis for demonstrating that the various parts of a social situation are interrelated, i.e., that changing one set alters others. I use a classroom exercise with students for this demonstration. For example, at the opening of class, students are invited to have cookies while carrying out the task of meeting and learning the names of seven people they do not know. The lack of fit between the classroom, the task, the usual purpose of classroom activity, the class norms for staying seated, and the party norms for greeting others becomes strikingly evident in later discussion or reports.

3. It enables students to appreciate more readily, from research and first-hand experience, that the larger institutional context and cultural norms intrude into even the simplest social situation. Used in conjunction with the classroom exercise, for example, the table helps students become aware of the status differential between instructor and students; differences in gender or group affiliations of students;

Table 1
Scheme for Analysis of Social Situations: Interrelated Sets of Factors

I. Set of Factors Pertaining to Location
  For example:
    Human-made, human-altered, or natural; spatial dimensions, exits, lighting, temperature, and sound levels; artifacts, tools, objects; sociocultural rules for use; social value of location; relation to larger location (e.g., office in factory, area in city)

II. Set of Factors Pertaining to Other Individuals
  For example:
    (A) Number of individuals involved; (B) Individual and social characteristics, including signs of membership in sociocultural categories, group memberships, and gender; cultural norms and values related; (C) Homogeneity-heterogeneity with respect to individual and social characteristics and cultural norms; status differentials; (D) Absence or presence of prior relationships among individuals, formal or informal; relation as a social unit (group) or as two or more different groups

III. Set of Factors Pertaining to Activities
  For example:
    Instructed or not; goal made explicit or not; how initiated; communication permitted or not; highly structured or not; sequential or repetitive; individual requirements, e.g., singly, side-by-side, interactive task division (cooperative, competitive, etc.); social value of activity; norms for activity

IV. Set of Factors Pertaining to Temporal Organization (Or Lack Thereof)
  For example:
    Presence and type of temporal markers; length; culturally defined length (e.g., class period); scheduled or not; determined by task or participants; location within sleep-activity-eating cycles; cultural value of period; norms regulating

V. Set of Factors Pertaining to Individual Participant's Relation to Sets I, II, III, and IV
  For example:
    Familiarity-unfamiliarity; previous proficiencies; social standing; being "late" or "early"

the implicit rationale for a long narrow classroom with white walls, rows of chairs facing front, and lighting intense enough for open-heart surgery; and specific norms for conduct in a classroom. Students share their reluctance in approaching the instructor during the cookie party and discover the status differential. During one discussion a student was relieved to learn that others had shared his experience of wondering, during that party with an open door, whether it would be all right to get a drink at the water fountain just outside. The reality of norms that ordinarily lead each to remain seated, eyes glued on instructor or blackboard, become quite clear.

Important variables included within each set in the table are illustrative, not exhaustive. The inclusion of sociocultural variables can be expanded through the research reported in the six-volume *Handbook of Cross-Cultural Psychology* under the general editorship of Triandis (1980). For example, Volume 5 (Triandis & Brislin, 1980), includes a replication of the Asch experiment on majority influence in Japan, where its influence is less than in the United States. For examples within U.S. society, one might consult *Psychology and Criminal Justice* by Ellison and Buckhout (1981), which introduces the criminal justice system as the framework for understanding the successive social contexts for the victim, the police, the eye-witness, the jury, and so forth. Such background material could lead into the prison guard and prisoner role-playing study by Zimbardo and his collaborators (1977), which is presented in several texts.

Interrelationships among the sets of factors are readily illustrated through Altman's survey of research on crowding (1975). Whether or not one experiences being crowded, with associated stress, varies not only according to the density of persons in the location, but also according to what that location is customarily used for, the activities underway (e.g., an experiment versus a football game), the sociocultural arrangements and norms developed to regulate personal space (e.g., in Japan versus Montana), the genders of participants, and numerous relationships among these sets of factors.

Many realities in social contexts are structural. By "structure" I mean that the relationships among the parts of the situation are sufficiently stable that rules can be stated about how the parts relate. For example, in a lecture hall the instructor speaks while students sit quietly, and severe violations of this rule have consequences. Some of the rule-governed relationships or structures can be detected only in sequential interactions over time. I shall consider the rationale for discovering social structures in social situations.

Where is Social Structure in Social Situations?

The recent recognition that much social behavior is situationally guided has led several social psychologists to search for individuals' mental "templates" for different specific situations (e.g., Bem & Funder, 1978) or mental "scripts" for the sequence of activities and participants' roles (Abelson, 1981; Schank & Abelson, 1977). If individuals can report their perceptions and if these perceptions are not entirely different for different individuals, the aggregation of these perceptions could then aid in defining social situations. In fact, there is a large body of research showing differences between aggregated conceptions of different locations and organizations (reviewed by Stokols, 1981).

The limitations of such aggregated data should be recognized, however. Based on the philosophical tradition of Kant, this approach defines social reality solely in terms of how individuals perceive or reconstruct a social context. The limitations may be seen by asking two related questions:

1. Do individuals accurately perceive or conceive variables in a social situation that are in fact associated with alterations or differences in their behaviors in it? Recent research by Nisbett and Wilson (1977) and by Langer and Roth (1975) shows us once again that individuals may not.

2. Do aggregated individual conceptions indicate what changes in the social context might alter the ways individuals perceive that context? For example, it is fairly clear what changes might alter students' reports that college classrooms are "uncomfortable," "cramped," and "impersonal" (Sommer & Olsen, 1980); but what would change their reports that the classrooms are "sterile" and "bland"? Would flowered wallpaper alter those reports, or should what goes on in the classrooms also be considered?

With additional information derived independently of individual perceivers, a response to such troubling questions becomes possible. For example, in research on individuals' "cognitive maps" of cities, there is of course a cartographical map, carefully constructed by many individuals' efforts, with which to compare individually constructed maps or their aggregate composite. In Paris, Milgram and Jodelet (1976) found that the maps of individual Parisians were organized around landmarks (e.g., the Seine River, Notre Dame Cathedral, the Eiffel Tower, and the Etoile). Lomov (1979) reported that individuals constructed better maps of an historic section of Leningrad by working collectively on the task than by working individually.

In each of these findings, there is clear implication as to how individual cognitive maps could be changed. With apologies to Parisians, their maps would be changed if the cultural significance of Notre Dame Cathedral were changed or if a skyscraper were built on top of the cathedral. Individual maps can be made more accurate by allowing communication among individual map makers, in which case the social process through which the maps improve becomes interesting.

The general problem of finding objective indicators of social reality has arisen in discussions of "errors" in person perception (e.g., Schneider, Hastorf, & Ellsworth, 1979), of "errors" in attributional processes (e.g., Harvey, Town, & Yarkin, 1981), and of social cognition in general (e.g., Stroebe, 1980).

For example, Ross (1978) proposed that the tendency to attribute causality to internal dispositional factors *in* the individual is a "fundamental attributional error." The proposal that the tendency is fundamental, psychologically, has been countered by evidence that there may be a cultural norm in society favoring internal attribution (Jellison & Green, 1981). It has been countered by evidence that the error does not always occur (Monson & Snyder, 1977) but may depend on circumstances making particular individuals salient in the situation (S. Taylor, 1978) or upon other individuals' social position relative to the attributor (Wallston & O'Leary, 1981). The objection also has been voiced that one cannot speak of error when objective assessment of causality has not been made, though one might speak of preferences or aversions, i.e., bias (Harvey, Town, & Yarkin, 1981). Finally, it is possible that, in some of the research situations, the individual might have been unable, because of situational ambiguity, to find any reasons other than internal dispositions for the behavior in question.

There appears to be no way to settle such issues about error in knowing social realities except through serious study of the objective properties of the social structures and cultural norms *in* the context. The social psychologist who borrows from social science or studies the social realities is doing what any good psychologist does when studying perception or memory of physical reality. A good psychologist studying a visual illusion, such as the Müller-Lyer, measures the lines to be compared and the angles of the arrows. Then it is possible to specify, in advance of the individual's judgment of lines, the *stimulus* situation exposed to the perceiver. Similarly, social realities in a social context have to be studied, either by borrowing from the works on social science or by doing sociological tasks ourselves. In this sense, social psychology has to be both sociological and psychological. As a first example, recent research on status differentials among previously unacquainted persons is instructive.

Example: Preexisting Status Differentials According to Social Power

When the individuals in a social situation have never met, as is frequent in laboratory experiments and elsewhere, and are homogeneous with respect to gender, age, race, occupation, social class, etc., preexisting status differentials among them are no problem. Individuals heterogeneous as to gender, race, social class, or age status in the larger society are instantly categorized by each other in those social categories by a simple recognition process. When regularities appear in what happens among them at first encounter, it is parsimonious to refer those regularities to organizations and cultural norms in their larger society that were defined before their encounter started.

Every human society has an organized system for the use of social power. For a sociologist, the social categories of gender, race, or social class are also differentiations in the structure of social power. Sociologists point to data on access to core institutions; institutional discrimination (e.g., Feagin & Feagin, 1978); persistent income and occupational differentials between white men, black men, white women, and black women (e.g., Burstein, 1979); and differential treatments in the legal system as evidence that these social categories are also status differentials defined by relative social power. Do such status differentials according to social power predict what happens when individuals from these different social categories interact?

One way to tell is to observe what happens when individuals from the different social categories interact in problem-solving tasks, such as discussion tasks or the tasks used in research on "emergent leadership." Extensive research has shown that, when individuals homogeneous as to race or gender interact in such tasks over a fairly short time, differences among them appear in terms of total participation and effectiveness in initiating and controlling the interaction. The more effective participants in these respects acquire higher status in the situation and are regarded by others as more leaderlike. Will individuals differing by gender or race achieve status in such situations correlated with their relative power in the larger society?

Research shows that those who started and ended in the lower status ranks in such problem-solving tasks were blacks and women. The person achieving highest status was invariably a white male (Cohen & Roper, 1972; Lockhead & Hall, 1976). Thus it appears that the status differentials from the larger society become a part of the social structure in the immediate situation (Webster & Driskeel, 1978). How do such external status differentials affect individuals' behaviors in the situation? The answers lie in research on nonverbal interactions as well as in verbal and behavioral evidence.

Nonverbal Interactions Among Persons Asymmetrical in Power

Social psychologist Nancy Henley (1977) reviewed research findings on nonverbal interactions between status superiors and subordinates as well as between men and women. The use of space, the participants' demeanors, postures, eye contacts, and facial and emotional expressiveness, and the presence or absence of touching had been studied separately by many researchers. The review showed that such nonverbal communications invariably were differentiated for persons with superior and subordinate status in social power. When Henley then compared data on men and women in brief social interactions, typically as strangers, she found that these interactions were identical to those between superiors and subordinates of the same gender. Table 2 represents a list of the comparisons documented both for status superiors and subordinates and for interacting men and women. Lamb (1981) confirmed that, when women in positions of power interact with other women, they use the superior mode; therefore, these are not sex-related differences but power differences in our society. There should be no suggestion that these particular patterns are universal. For example, black-white differences in nonverbal eye-gaze patterns have been documented in homogeneous interac-

Table 2
Reciprocal Nonverbal Patterns of Interaction Between
Status Superiors and Subordinates and Between Men and Women

Class of Behavior	Used by Superiors and by Men	Used by Subordinates and by Women
Demeanor	Informal	Circumspect
Posture	Relaxed	Tense
Personal space	Closeness	Distance
Touching	Touch other	Do not touch
Eye contacts	Stare	Avert eyes
	Ignore	Watch other
Facial expression	Infrequent smiles	Frequent smiles
Emotional expression	Hidden	Revealed

Note. Data are based on social interactions between persons in column 1 and those in column 2. Thus typifications in columns need not characterize the individual's behaviors in another context (e.g., with status equality or gender homogeneity). The table is adapted by permission from N. M. Henley, *Body Politics: Power, Sex and Nonverbal Communication* (Englewood Cliffs, N.J.: Prentice-Hall, 1977), p. 181. Copyright © 1977 by Prentice-Hall, Inc.

tions (La France & Mayo, 1976). A recent cross-cultural study shows that a stern unsmiling countenance with slightly lowered brows is recognized as representing superior power only in western cultures (Keating, Mazur, Segall, et al., 1981).

The lower status of women and associated "watching" of the person with higher status clarifies the frequent finding that women are more sensitive to nonverbal behaviors and more accurate in interpreting them than are men (Noller, 1980, reviews the research). Such a finding would be expected if habitual lower status made careful watching functional in interactions with those of higher status.[3]

[3] A recent study also reported such differential sensitivity to nonverbal and paraverbal behaviors in married couples (Noller, 1980). The research procedures utilized independent judges to assess the wife's and the husband's effectiveness in conveying different intended meanings for ambiguous messages (e.g., "I'm cold, aren't you?") and required the spouse to interpret the intention. (For example, the above message could be interpreted as "it's a bit chilly" or "why don't you do something about it?"). Overall, wives were more effective in both sensing and interpreting their husbands' intentions. Most errors in women's messages to husbands were errors in men's interpretation. The wives and husbands in couples characterized as highest in marital adjustment differed least in sensitivity to the spouse's nonverbal behaviors.

*Ways in Which Status Differentials Are Maintained
in Interaction*

Both early and more recent research on interracial interactions among previously unacquainted individuals (Cohen & Roper, 1972; Cohen, Lockhead, & Lohman, 1976; Riordan & Ruggiero, 1980) has shown that the differential participation in and the effective initiation of activity between white and black participants were brought about by the behaviors of one or more white male participants who talked more, maintained distance, and paid less attention to lower status participants. These behaviors symbolized domination at the outset. Black participants reciprocated by participating less. This pattern resembles the "self-fulfilling prophecy" proposed by the sociologist Robert Merton (1948) as one social mechanism by which existing status differentials are preserved. The sequence confirms the belief shared by those with dominant status that lower status persons lack initiative.

Important recent experiments (Snyder, Tanke, & Berscheid, 1977; Word, Zanna, & Cooper, 1974; Zanna & Pack, 1975) have documented specific behaviors by the person with superior status that lead the person with lower status to reciprocate by complying. As Snyder and Swann (1978) have shown, generally interaction sequences are reciprocal, so that equals are more apt to reciprocate in kind, giving tit for tat. But when one person has superior status and acts in a dominating way, the person with lower status reciprocates by affirming the domination by his or her behaviors. When the lower status person is a member of an ethnic minority or a woman and is interviewed for a job, his or her behaviors are seen by the interviewer as evidence of lack of initiative and qualification. This sequence depends on both participants' recognition of and participation in the differential power structure. If one or the other were to dissent from the power structure, the outcomes would be quite different.

Darley and Fazio (1980), in a recent review of much of the literature, confirm that a power differential is the initial circumstance favorable to the "self-fulfilling prophecy." They also relate the recent findings on interpersonal interactions to the more complex phenomena of teachers' expectancies for different students which correlate with student achievements as well as to the phenomena of "experimenter bias" (Rosenthal & Rubin, 1978). The teacher or the researcher has much greater power in the situation than the subordinates (i.e., students or research subjects) to arrange the location, select the tasks, evaluate task performance, and determine who speaks, who is spoken to, and how they speak or are spoken to. Thus evidence on teachers' differential behaviors to different students, including those to boys and girls, continues to mount and to bear upon differential performance and behavior by students (e.g., Darley & Fazio, 1980; Dweck & Gilliard, 1975; Dweck, Goetz, & Strauss, 1980; Rosenthal & Rubin, 1978; Serbin & O'Leary, 1975; M. Taylor, 1979).

Unwitting experimenter bias is suggested by Eagly and Carli's recent statistical meta-analysis of all available experiments on gender differences in response to majority opinions or persuasive messages. The meta-analysis shows small mean differences between the genders but also a highly reliable tendency for male researchers, but not female researchers, to obtain results showing that women are more influenced than men (Eagly & Carli, 1981; see also Eagly, 1978; Sohn, 1980).

In studies of face-to-face, short-term interactions, the researcher may intend that the participants be initially equal in opportunity to participate in the task. Is it possible to equalize such opportunities when the participants' initial statuses, as defined by race or gender, differ?

Can the Status-Maintaining Sequence be Changed?

Two lines of research have been pursued: First, in a series of experiments, researchers have attempted preliminary equalization of status before interaction begins (Cohen, Lockhead, & Lohman, 1976; Cohen & Roper, 1972; Lockhead & Hall, 1976; Riordan & Ruggiero, 1980). Second, a series of laboratory and field experiments have been conducted utilizing interdependent tasks with superordinate goals, i.e., goals desired by all that can be achieved only by interdependent and more equitable participation by individuals from white, black, and Chicano status groups. Both attempt to disrupt the preexisting status differentials, the first by preparing participants to dissent from them and the second by making the differentials dysfunctional in activities which provide experience in cooperating as equals.

The preparatory procedures typically involve preliminary training of the lower status persons in a different but rather technical task, with a great deal of encouragement and praise, and then ensuring that the white males know about that preliminary task competence before interaction on the task of interest begins. A recent replication of preparatory training for black males and exposure of their competent performances to the newly arrived white males succeeded both in equalizing and in reversing the black-white participation patterns in a different task (Riordan & Ruggiero, 1980).

Equalized participations by young men and women are apparently more difficult to attain by preparatory procedures with women (Lockhead & Hall, 1976). Such stubborn gender-related differences in participation are more likely among young men and women than among white and black men but may not appear at all when the activity at hand requires active participation by everyone (e.g., Eskilson & Wiley, 1976; Nemeth, Endicott, & Wachtler, 1976). Such apparent discrepancies in research findings are only one example of the importance of the structural properties of the activity or task, which interact with other situational variables (in this case, the preexisting status differentials among participants). These discrepancies serve as an important warning against overgeneralizing about race or gender differences on the basis of brief encounters in a single task or situation.

Working with elementary schoolchildren in interethnic classrooms, Aronson and his collaborators (Aronson & Bridgman, 1979; Aronson, Bridgman, & Geffner, 1978; Aronson, Stephan, Sikes, Blaney, & Snapp, 1978; Blaney, Stephan, Rosenfield, Aronson, & Sikes, 1977) also found that preparatory work was necessary with some children, in this case with Chicano children, whose language differences initially placed them in double disadvantage with Anglo children.

Participation by mixed ethnic groups in interdependent interaction and in efforts toward superordinate goals has been studied by Cook and his collaborators with adolescents and adults (Blanchard, Adelman, & Cook, 1975; Cook, 1978; Weigel & Cook, 1975; Weigel, Wiser, & Cook, 1975) and by Aronson and his collaborators with children. These studies were intended to reduce social distance between participants, change customary interaction patterns, and alter the respective attitudes of white, black, and Chicano participants outside of the study situations. In this research, interaction typically continued over a long period of time and was officially encouraged and praised by authorities. When the superordinate goals were attained, remarkably successful results were reported in altering the interaction patterns, the attitudes, and the children's school achievement. The findings have important implications for social policies on interethnic contacts and associations in schools and elsewhere.

The importance of continuity in such collaborative and officially sponsored task structures was shown by Schofield (1979; Schofield & Sagar, 1977) in a naturally occurring field experiment. Neither official policies, interdependent tasks, nor experiences in informal interactions had lasting group effects when they were cancelled by other policies affirming the superior status of white students and separating the two races in fact. In this case, a track system making the academic track 80 percent white reduced social interactions between black and white students that occurred before the tracks were introduced.

Thus it is not surprising that Stephan (1978), reviewing research on desegregation in public schools, found that changed attitudes by white and black children were not frequent. A reduction in prejudice by white toward black children was reported in only 13 percent of the schools studied. When the children watch television after school, they see an overwhelmingly white world, where blacks and whites associate chiefly when their jobs bring them in contact (Weigel, Loomis, & Soja, 1980). The social realities children experience and see are hardly conducive to friendly, equal interethnic contacts or to lasting attitude changes. Similar analysis concerning boys and girls and television presentations of the genders leads to a similar conclusion.

Brief Encounters vs. Lasting Relationships

With the exception of the research interrupting the self-fulfilling prophecy, the foregoing examples of social structure in situations focused upon preexisting status differentials among comparative strangers who interacted briefly. Now, let us ask the following question: Is a social situation where individuals participate as strangers any different from one where participants have interacted with one another previously over some time? Intuitively, the answer is "yes, the two situations differ, for the acquainted individuals *know* one another." But what do they know? How does the knowledge affect their behaviors?

In the subsections that follow, research evidence will be presented that what acquainted individuals know includes expectations, stabilized in measurable degree, about how each other *will* behave and how each *should* behave in different locations, in different activities, at different times, and in relation to other people. Such stabilized and valued expectations of one another are formed only over time. When these expectations become mutual and reciprocal among the individuals, the behaviors of the participants in social interaction acquire a measure of regularity and predictability in different situations, so they may be studied as sociological properties of the relationship (role-status relationships and social norms).

Interpretive Issues in Generalizing from Research on Brief Encounters

Interpretive issues arise for the instructor of introductory psychology when the text chapter on social psychology presents research composing a static picture of human social behavior shaped by influence *from* others, often strangers, *upon* the individual during brief encounters. With the exception of studies of prosocial behavior introduced as counterpoint, such research often forms a wholly negative image of the effects of social influences from others upon the individual. Complaining of such a negative picture, one instructor wrote a parody of research he had been presenting to students, entitled "Humans Would Do Better Without Groups" (Buys, 1978). The gist of the parody was that other people make individuals become deindividuated and anonymous, diffuse responsibility to others, comply with the whims of an authority, err in response to a majority, imitate others, and find themselves prone to social contagion and swept up in mass movements.

Among several satirical replies to the instructor, two responses (Green & Mack, 1978; Shaffer, 1978) observed that none of the researchers cited had studied interactions among individuals over extensive periods of time or with known prior relationships, hence none had studied behavior in a "group" in the sociological meaning of that term. The lack of prior relationships among individuals makes the individuals particularly sensitive to any changes or variations in other aspects of the social situation, including the location, the task, the timing of events, and each other's actions or inactions.

For example, the structure and the purpose of the activity engaged in by research subjects is known to affect behaviors when individuals are together. Thus, if unacquainted individuals are asked to pull on a rope or to clap and shout as loudly as possible for no other reason than to comply with instructions, they put forth less effort when with others than alone, a phenomenon labeled "diffusion of effort" or "social loafing" by Latané (1981) which may also represent apprehension. But if the task is highly interdependent and is rewarded collectively, with an equal-sharing rule, individual effort and performance improve increasingly over time when others participate (French, Brownell, Graziano, & Hartup, 1977; Graziano, French, Brownell, & Hartup, 1976; Rosenbaum, Moore, Cotton, Cook, Hieser, Shovar, & Gray, 1980). Indeed, recent statistical meta-analyses of 122 such studies show that greater individual achievement occurs in interdependent task structures with correlative individual goals, over a variety of locations and specific tasks, than with individual or competitive task-goal structures (Johnson, Maruyama, Johnson, Nelson, & Skon, 1981). Clearly, the conclusion one draws about individual effort when others participate depends upon which task and social situation are studied.

There is no empirical or theoretical basis, however, for generalizing from findings on brief encounters among strangers to those on encounters among individuals with prior acquaintance and, particularly, with significant social ties. Things happen among individuals interacting in important activities over time which alter their reactions to the environment and to one another.

Environmental Changes Promoting New Social Relationships

Reciprocal influences among individuals in social interaction are a medium for changed experiences and behaviors responsive to other aspects of the social environment. A field experiment by Baum and Davis (1980) exemplifies such changes, indicating what does happen among interacting individuals over time. A long-corridor dormitory was modified simply by designating rooms in the middle of the corridor as lounge rooms. The investigators reported that the modification facilitated development of informal groups and of social rules governing the frequency and place of interactions among residents. The dormitory residents' enhanced personal control over privacy regulation and social encounters was, in turn, associated with fewer stress-like symptoms than among residents of unmodified long corridors.

Similarly, a two-year field experiment by Rodin and Langer (Langer & Rodin, 1976; Rodin & Langer, 1977; Wack & Rodin, 1978) showed that policy changes in a nursing home for the elderly were associated with more active socializing with staff and friends by the experimental sample, as well as with more frequent participation in sponsored activities, for example, movies and contests. The policy change had given certain responsibilities to residents (e.g., house-plants to care for) compared to the usual policy of assuring residents that the staff would care for them. The general alertness and health status of the experimental sample of residents improved during the study period.

Finally, recent research has compared helpfulness to a stranger in contrived situations in urban and nonurban locations. A recent large-scale study in Turkey (Korte, 1980) showed that the usual urban-nonurban contrast depends upon which urban locations are studied. Frequencies of helping exhibited by residents in crowded, poverty-stricken squatter settlements within large cities did not differ from those in Turkish towns with populations under 25,000, but help-ing was less frequent in other parts of the cities. The squatters in-cluded second- and third-generation residents. Their neighborhoods were periodically threatened by police, because the settlements are not legal. In the highly cohesive squatter areas, the residents devel-oped differentiated norms for treatment of threatening and non-threatening strangers in their midst.

The formation of new social relationships and new norms re-quires interaction over time. If we are to understand their beneficial or detrimental effects for individual participants, research studying specifically how they develop and relate to individual experience and behavior has to be included in our accounts of social psychology.

Lasting Relationships in Social Units

In the last several years, social psychologists have started serious study of the development of close interpersonal relationships, ranging from friends to sexual and married partners. New books on interpersonal attraction, liking, and loving are now expanded to include discussions of ongoing close relationships (e.g., Berscheid & Walster, 1978; Hus-ton & Levinger, 1978), and the gate is opening on what may be a flood of books specifically concerned with close relationships (e.g., Burgess & Huston, 1979; Cook & Wilson, 1979; Kelley, 1979).

Rands and Levinger (1979) reported an analysis of normative expectations by college students and by senior citizens for fourteen dyadic relationships varied in closeness (e.g., friends to married couples) and gender composition (e.g., homogeneous or heterogeneous). Striking generational differences were found. Where did they come from? Certainly, such differences reflect general changes in society at large affecting younger more than older generations. But do participating individuals in friendships, partnerships, or families also create new norms and patterns of relationships together?

Close unit relationships are difficult to investigate. Both researchers and participants share the cultural norm that they are private affairs, hence research data depends upon volunteers willing to discuss them. The privacy norm is particularly pervasive for heterosexual relationships. For example, in one study (Shotland & Straw, 1976) individuals witnessing a physical struggle between a man and woman were reluctant to help the woman on the assumed ground that the relationship was private, even though in actuality the man and woman were not acquainted. The study reporting this assumption showed that witnesses reasoned that the man would turn on them for interfering and that the woman was less likely to be hurt because the couple was related.[4]

Much of the research on close relationships is, therefore, based on self-description. What the partners describe are the social norms that govern joint activities, division of labor, self-disclosure, mutual support, physical contacts, and the usual techniques for influencing one another (Peplau, in press). The pictures that emerge are often very conventional.

For example, the power differentials between men and women are reflected in the techniques they typically use in trying to influence each other. Men report using quite direct means of influence that presume a cooperative or compliant partner, e.g., direct statements, appeals to expertise, persuasion, bargaining, or coercion (Falbo &

---

[4]The assumption of a personal relationship was in error in this research but was made unless the couple explicitly stated a lack of relationship. Statistics on rape and wife abuse, however, do not warrant the inference that a victim under attack is safer because the perpetrator is known to her. There is evidence, however, that participants in a social unit may resent and repel outsiders. Recent research also shows that only a few individuals are willing to intervene in a conflict putting them at physical risk. For example, the "Good Samaritans," who had secured compensation for injuries suffered during helpful interventions in violent emergencies under California law, were, in all but a single case, unusually large men with considerable experience in physical conflict (Huston, Ruggiero, Conner, & Geis, 1981).

Peplau, 1980). Women more frequently report the use of influence techniques used by less powerful persons (regardless of gender), e.g., indirect appeals to the unit relationship or fairness and unilateral withdrawal in the event of certain failure to influence the other. Interestingly, these gender differences did not appear when reports by lesbians were compared to those by homosexual males, nor were any typical patterns of influence found between individuals as partners with homosexual orientation (Falbo & Peplau, 1980). Do such couples develop their own role relationships and norms?

Peplau's study of college student couples (1979) suggests that the traditional asymmetry in power between men and women is being equalized by couples in which the women plan to pursue an advanced degree. Research on dual-career couples indicates that they face many problems imposed by institutional patterns (e.g., in employment) where guidelines from the larger culture lead only to traditional solutions; yet many appear to be making nonconventional and equalitarian choices (Wallston, Foster, & Berger, 1978). Are they creating new roles and rules? There is some evidence that they are (Bryson & Bryson, 1978).

What do we know about the development of new relationships among individuals? A response to that question has to start by re-examining the traditional model for studying social influence, which assumes a one-way flow from others *upon* the individual.

Reciprocal Influences Within and Between Developing Social Units

A static picture of one-way social influences acting upon the individual is frequently epitomized in introductory texts by presentations of Asch's classic experiments on the influence of erroneous majority judgments—presentations which neglect the several contextual variations that reduced or enhanced such influence (Asch, 1956). Notably, Asch reported a variation in which two naive subjects influenced one another to ignore the erroneous majority judgments.

Significantly extending the Asch variations, Moscovici and his collaborators (e.g., Moscovici & Faucheux, 1972; Moscovici & Nemeth, 1974) and Nemeth (1979) studied the reciprocal influences between minorities and majorities whose members initially disagree in judgments on a color perception task and, more recently, in simulated jury deliberations. They reported that an active minority, whose members take initiative and give confident and consistent opinions, can affect the opinions of the majority.

The findings show that an active minority's influence upon majority decisions in jury trials is accomplished only *over time*. According to Nemeth (1979), minority influence appears in late, rather than in early trial decisions. In the early stages of a deliberation, the minority raises alternatives that majority members had not considered previously; thus it is more effective in raising "reasonable doubt" of guilt than in establishing "guilt beyond reasonable doubt." When the jury decision goes in the minority direction, it is "always a group effect," that is, variance among individual decisions within the majority is reduced. Minority influence is never accomplished by liking or attraction to individuals in the minority, who come to be seen as "them"—a different social unit. In order to gain the decision, individuals in a jury minority are obliged to speak in favor of their proposal more than twice as frequently as those in a majority twice as large. Such a preponderance of remarks favoring one side or the other prefigured 97 percent of the jury decisions (Nemeth, 1979). Clearly, paths of social influence both within the majority and between the developing social units are determinants of the outcome. Such reciprocal and multiple paths of influence are characteristic, not exceptional, in developing relationships within and between social units.

The incipient formation of social units or groups and of relationships between such units was dramatically shown in a recent four-and-a-half-hour experiment by Insko, Thibaut, Moehle, Wilson, Diamond, Gilmore, Solomon, and Lipsitz (1980). In each session, three ad hoc units of four individuals each became recognizable groups with leader-follower relationships and social norms, and hierarchical relations developed among the three groups. Further, the "miniature cultures" of each group and their intergroup relations were transmitted to nine successive laboratory "generations." The generations were created by "retiring" one individual in each group after each trial and adding a new member, so that by the fifth generation, none of the original individual participants was present.

The study simulated conditions proposed by the anthropologist E. R. Service for the rise of institutionalized leadership and for a hierarchy among groups in prehistory. Thus, each ad hoc unit worked to produce paper products and to trade the products with other groups. One group had an advantage because of its central location in trading and of the other groups' need for its products. The three groups began to form, each with leadership based on seniority, which became increasingly effective over laboratory generations through nine generations when none of the individuals in the fifth generation was present. Thus, clearly, the groups did not form around an influential individual or leader but did develop a procedure for the exercise of leadership. The norms of their miniature cultures for in-group procedures and intergroup trading were also more firmly established. As anticipated, the advantaged group was recognized as predominant by its own members as well as by the others, who spontaneously cheered its every setback in trading. This important experiment clearly showed again that the arena of interaction among individuals *within* a group and the arena of interaction between members of *different* groups are distinguishable and different, both sociologically and psychologically.[5]

Developing Social Unit Relationships and Their Emerging Properties

The dialectical relationships between the sociological properties of a human group and the psychological functioning of participating individuals are evident most strikingly in the research on the formation of human groups (see Sherif & Sherif, 1969; C. Sherif, 1976, Chapter 3). When two or more individuals interact repeatedly over time in activities that jointly engage them, they invariably come to behave in many ways that reveal a unit relationship. They view themselves as "we." They come in time to regulate interactions with one another through mutual and expected role relationships, differentiated into status positions reflecting the individuals' relative effectiveness in initiating and controlling interaction in various activities of mutual importance.

[5] This experiment is sufficiently unusual and instructive to deserve further comment. Previous research had indoctrinated subjects with a social norm (for judging autokinetic movement) and then had traced the transmission of the norm across "generations" in which one subject was retired and was replaced by a new subject after each set of trials. That research had demonstrated the successful transmission of norms seen by new subjects as not too arbitrary, relative to the amount of apparent movement typically reported in the particular research setup (e.g., MacNeil & Sherif, 1976). In addition, Zucker (1977) had shown that structured relationships among participants (role playing, as in a model organization) enhanced successful transmission of the norm. But Insko et al. used no indoctrination; thus the development of groups and their norms were creations of the participants in the conditions established by the researchers for work and intergroup trading.

They form a set of social norms defining desirable and acceptable deeds, words, objects, and beliefs as well as a set of objectionable ones, at least in matters of consequence in the relationship.

These minimal properties in a developing social unit define a human group, which differs strikingly from a casual collection of individuals or a temporary unit relationship in task performance. Psychologically, such a sociological formation means that individuals are capable of creating new social units, new role relationships, and a host of social rules or norms which become part of the social context for individual experiences and action in any social situation where members interact.

The social psychologist Gary Fine (1979; Fine & Glassner, 1979; Fine & Kleinman, 1979) has recently called to the attention of sociologists the rich sources of culture that spring from the associations of human individuals in informal and formal social groups, such as teams, communes, and working committees. Their norms, labels, structures for personal relations, and policies frequently spread to others through social networks or, occasionally, through the mass media to the larger society. Such "cultural spread" through networks, recruitment, and the media is also striking in developing social movements seeking to expand their membership and messages, for example, the Black Civil Rights Movement or the Women's Movement (C. Sherif, 1976, Chapter 13).

Recent research into the concept of group cohesion and unit solidarity has shown that strictly interpersonal attraction or liking among members may be much less significant in defining the value attached to the individual-group relationship or to group performance than earlier research suggested (see Carron & Chelladurai, 1981; Widmeyer & Martens, 1978). The newer research shows that the cohesiveness and the solidarity of members as a unit are multidimensional products of interactions in activities of considerable personal and group importance. Cohesiveness is composed of a "sense of belonging" shared by the individuals, of the value of membership and enjoyment of the association, as well as of the group's level of coordination and the perceived "closeness" among members (Carron & Chelladurai, 1981).

The variables that contribute to group cohesiveness may differ depending upon the kind of activities typically engaged in, e.g., whether coordination or individual performance is emphasized. Similarly, the relationships between group cohesiveness and group performance vary. If coordination among individuals is essential to high performance, liking and closeness among members may be less important for performance than the value of membership.

As long as the unit relationship is valued, individual members comply with their role relations with others and with the group norms. Noncompliance has consequences, in the form either of sanctions from others or of disruption of the relations. But, to the extent that the unit relationship becomes a *reference group*, i.e., self-defining for the individual member, its influence extends beyond face-to-face encounters with the other members. Conformity occurs voluntarily in the absence of surveillance or sanctions. Such "internalization" implies a process of attitude formation, in which the boundaries defined in the group for individual action also frame definitions for the self. As we shall see, that process is basic for understanding certain problems of social cognition.

Knowing the Social Environment: Social Cognition

In contemporary psychology and especially in social psychology (Cartwright, 1979), cognitive approaches and the label "cognitive" have become fashionable. In a critique of "cognitive psychology as ideology," Sampson (1981) noted that the uncritical assumption that individuals "respond to how they define stimulus situations, not to the objective properties of those stimulus situations" can lead to ignoring the nature of social reality (p. 730). Such words of caution are particularly important when considering the problem of "knowing" about others in the same social categories as oneself and in different social categories or groups.

Which Social Realities are Relevant?

The label "cognition" is generic, referring to the various psychological processes involved in knowing which are traditionally covered in different chapters or sections of an introductory text. Social cognition covers perceiving, comparing or judging, evaluating, learning, remembering, inferring, and other forms of thinking. In ongoing social interaction, these cognitive processes tend to merge, a fact of tremendous importance since their relationships with social realities differ.

Thus we may stop the clock, as it were, and speak of perceiving when the question concerns how an individual construes an immediately present social situation. At another extreme, the situation and events occurred in the past; hence they are absent when the individual is called upon to recognize, recall, reconstruct, or construct them. In either case, scientific study of social cognition presumes that there are social realities to be apprehended by the individual. Otherwise the study of knowing becomes no more than documenting figments of individuals' imaginations, with the inevitable conclusion that social knowledge is impossible. Then organized social life would also be impossible.

In his classic book, *Remembering: A Study of Experimental and Social Psychology* (1932), F. C. Bartlett commented on the intermingling of various processes in the study of perception and their relationships with the stimulus situation:

> To perceive anything is one of the simplest and most immediate, as it is one of the most fundamental of all human cognitive reactions. Yet obviously, in a psychological sense, it is exceedingly complex. . . . Inextricably mingled with it are imaging, valuing, and those beginnings of judging which are involved in the response to plan, order of arrangement and construction of the presented material. It is directed by interest and by feeling, and may be dominated by certain crucial features of the objects and scenes dealt with. (p. 31)[6]

This quotation points to processes and to personal determinants that make perception more than simple reproduction of the stimulus situation; but it also emphasizes the "plan, order of arrangement and construction" as well as "crucial features" of the situation itself. Both emphases are useful in dealing with the large and growing research literature on attributional processes, i.e., the assignment of causality for behavior. For Heider (see Evans, 1980), such attributions of cause are part of the perceptual process when naive observers attempt to construe unexpected, puzzling, or ambiguous events. Indeed, Wong and Weiner (1981) reported that individuals are more likely to attempt to assign causality when events or behaviors are unexpected, ambiguous, and *negative*.

Only a part of the growing literature on attribution concerns perception. Schneider, Hastorf, and Ellsworth's *Person Perception* (1979) distinguishes two areas of study which clearly do: "reactive attribu-

---

[6] Copyright 1932 by Cambridge University Press, New York. Reprinted by permission.

tions" and "snap judgments." "Reactive attributions" are made when a person perceives one person act (say, with a blow to the head) and another individual immediately react (say, by falling while covering the head). The normal course of action, reaction, and interaction among individuals would not be possible if such observations were always or even frequently faulty. In short-term interactions (as in the laboratory), however, ambiguity may be great. Typically, cause is assigned to the initiator of action, even when the initiation consists of no more than taking the most visible seat at a table (S. Taylor, 1978; Nemeth, 1979). The relevant social reality here is not intuitively obvious in the situation. It lies in the well-documented finding that the central position in seating is a status symbol; persons of power or authority typically occupy it, and it enables control in interaction.

Reactive attributions by observers of a quiz game were studied when the questioner was selected by chance and was able to select the topic of the quiz (Ross, Amabile, & Steinmetz, 1977). Their perception was accurate that the questioner in fact posed questions that gave the contestant difficulty. But observers later judged that the questioner had more general knowledge than the contestant. The bias favoring the questioner was an inference based upon accurate perception of a situation too limited to warrant the later comparative judgment requested by the researchers.

Such bias may also enter the perceptual process early, in the form of "snap judgments" about individuals based on the individuals' belonging to a social category. Thus, in repeating the Ross et al. procedures (1977), Pettigrew, Jemmott, and Johnson (reported in Pettigrew, 1981) found that "good" performances by the black questioners in the quiz game were attributed not to their greater general knowledge but to "luck"; hence these performances were only accidentally the cause of contestant failures. Poor performances by the black contestants were attributed to their lesser general knowledge and poorer college preparation—another inference which, however, reflects social ideology and stereotyped beliefs to which the white observers had been exposed before the experiment.

The distinctions made by Schneider et al. (1979) among reactive attributions, snap judgments in forming impressions of persons, and inference processes are useful in attempting to relate contemporary research on attributional processes to general problems of social cognition, particularly the relations of these processes to social realities. A great deal of the research on attribution assumes perceptual and judgmental processes but studies inferences made after a single event or after a sequence of events. Research inspired by the different attributional models associated with the writings of E. E. Jones, H. H. Kelley, and B. Weiner and their collaborators concerns such inference processes.[7] M. B. Smith (1980) sees these models as "grappling with fundamental symbolic processes by which people assign and therefore create meaning—in the crucial realm of the self and the interpersonal world" (p. 321). Such explorations are likely to flourish and to clarify these important problems when attributional processes are linked firmly with social realities, as well as with ideological beliefs, values, and social actions. As Wallston and O'Leary (1981) remarked in a review of one part of the literature, such linkages are still sorely needed.

Coordinative Interaction Among Psychological and Situational Determinants

In analyzing an individual's social cognitions, most social psychologists would, I believe, recognize the contribution of Kurt Lewin's famous formula: $B = f(P, E)$, i.e., behavior is a function of the person-environment relationship (Lewin, 1935, 1951). Today growing numbers insist, however, that the social context defining social reality must be studied independently of the particular perceiving person, if that per-

---

[7] Since these attributional models are presented in several texts, they will not be discussed here. The fact that the three models often focus on different problems and use differing terminology makes the research literature difficult for the reader not thoroughly familiar with each. As Wallston and O'Leary (1981) remark in reviewing attributions to women and men, each model proposes mechanisms whereby observers might arrive at different causal explanations for the same behaviors by women and by men. The research, however, infrequently permits choice between one or the other, since different research models are used to test the different theories. Irene Frieze (University of Pittsburgh) has recently completed a meta-analysis of a set of studies using one model for attributions in achievement situations, a practice that may help researchers focus on critical variables (see Frieze, Whitley, Hansen, & McHugh, 1982). There have been efforts to clarify and to reconcile the models as well as to note their overlapping or common predictions (e.g., Schneider, Hastorf, & Ellsworth, 1979; Shaver, 1975). In addition to the distinctions noted by Schneider et al., distinctions between attributions of cause and the individual's intentions or "reasons" for behaving in certain ways may be useful (Buss, 1978). At times the literature is also unclear in distinguishing between attribution of cause to a person and attribution of personal responsibility for actions, which is likely to be contingent upon moral codes and institutional and cultural norms, including those of the legal system (e.g., Hamilton, 1980; Myers, 1980).

son's cognition and behavior are to be analyzed in social context. In final analysis, such independent study of the social situation is the basis for learning what the person contributes in cognitive processes and what is presented by the social situation.

Through several student generations, the diagram in Figure 1 has proved helpful to illustrate the formula that behavior is a function of coordinative interactions among interrelated sets of factors in the social situation (see Table 1) and of internal factors within the person at a given time. The diagram represents the frame of reference for analyzing behavior. It conveys in one glance the joint determination by stimulus factors impinging at the moment and by states of the organism, motives and attitudes orienting the person at the time, and self-other schemata. The sequence is indicated by the arrows, those with dashed lines suggesting possible sequence once behavior has occurred.

Phenomenal experience or awareness, which is not represented in the diagram, is assumed in a unit relationship with behavior, not divorced from behavior. Cognitive processes are included in the more general term psychological processes and are not equated with phenomenal experience of consciousness, the span of which is limited at a given time; they need not include awareness of the factors influencing psychological processes in a complex situation. Organizing concepts, such as attitude, schema, or script, are on the internal side, but they relate to the social situation. They do not substitute for social reality, unless the latter is lacking. They may be self-defining in varying degrees and in different circumstances.

On one hand, the diagram makes clear that the analysis of social cognition cannot be divorced from social realities in the situation nor from the individual's past experiences, preferences, or aversions, as Zajonc (1980) also pointed out recently. The notion of "purely cognitive" processes is perhaps best understood as a polarized reaction against excessively psychodynamic models suggesting that behavior is a direct outcome of internal impulses, a possibility ruled out by the diagram. On the other hand, the diagram is similarly critical of those behavioristic formulations which suggest direct connection between a stimulus and a response.

The diagram serves in teaching certain general principles about the relationship between external realities, social or otherwise, and psychological determinants, such as past experiences, affect, attitudes, and so forth. Such general principles include the following:

1. Both phenomenal awareness and social cognition are bounded by clearcut physical and social structures in the context, as well as by salient objects or events.

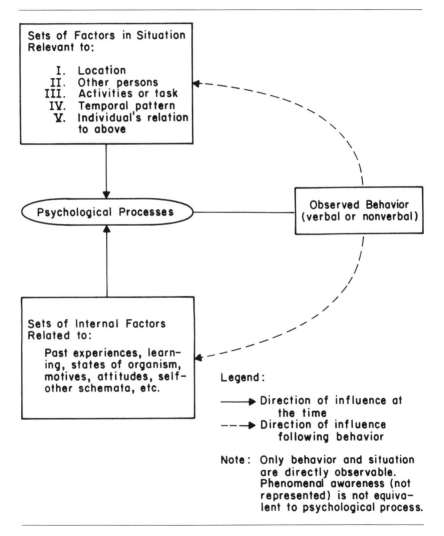

Figure 1. Frame of Reference for Analyzing Behavior in a Social Situation at a Particular Time.

2. When external circumstances lack clear physical and social structure, i.e., are ambiguous in respects related to social actions or their consequences, cognitive activity is increasingly affected by the individual's past experiences with social reality, by enduring attitudes incorporating preferences and aversions as well as beliefs, and by temporary organismic states.

3. In part, such personal contributions to psychological processes reflect a general expectation, built from childhood onward, for a fairly stable and regular world, even if it is not one to the individual's liking.

4. Always a selective perceiver, the individual in ambiguous circumstances becomes particularly selective, on the basis of past experiences, of the behaviors of others who can be trusted. That is why the action or the inaction of others in a highly ambiguous situation become such important influences in the individual's experience and behavior. The influence from judgments of others in the autokinetic situation or the silent inaction of bystanders in the face of an unexpected event, which might or might not be an emergency, are both examples of this general principle.

5. Psychological processes are not only selective but, from one's infancy onward, typically proceed at a conceptual level of functioning, in which discrete stimuli and events are classified or categorized relative to past experiences.

Such categorical processes are prominently involved in recognition, impression formation, and snap judgment attributions (Schneider et al., 1979). Insofar as the categories correspond with social categories used in society, they reflect differentiated life circumstances of people, their relative power, and the ideology in that society. Thus social categories are linked with social realities, processes, and beliefs experienced by the individual in the past.

People Categorized as "Us" and "Them"

Recently a great deal of social-psychological research has concerned the age-old problem that individuals react differently to people in social categories defined as "us" or "we"—those classified like oneself in socially significant ways—and to people classified as "them" or "those other kind of people" in different categories.

The psychological importance of social categorizations defining "us" and "them" is tacitly assumed when students are told that interpersonal attraction is most likely among individuals who are "similar" in some socially important way, such as attitudes, values, beliefs, or social category. That empirical generalization, however, contains no hint of why the following contrasting phenomena are all to be found in reactions to people who are "different": on one hand, friendly approaches, alliances, and desire to associate with some "different" people; but, on the other hand, discriminatory treatment, maintenance of social distance even in geographical proximity, oppression, aggression, hostile attitudes, consensual and highly unfavorable attributions to others.

The introductory student is sometimes given a theory of interpersonal attraction based on similarity to explain how "we" react to each other, then theories of aggression to explain treatments of "them." Or differential treatment of dissimilar persons is explained as "irrational human behavior" stemming from equally irrational prejudices and social stereotypes acquired as part of personality dynamics aberrant from the "normal" (Allport 1954, p. 515; also Adorno, Frenkel-Brunswick, Levinson, & Sanford, 1950). The implicit assumption appears to be that reactions to persons in different social categories are inevitably hostile.

That assumption was explicit in William Graham Sumner's sociological doctrine of "ethnocentrism" (1906). His catchall description of "this view of things in which one's own group is the center of everything and all others are scaled and rated with reference to it" (p. 13) was coupled with the thesis that a human group can exist in internal peace and order only through "correlative hostility and war towards others-groups." Thus the thesis implied that in-group preference and the recognition of differences lead necessarily to negative attitudes toward other groups.

We know that Sumner's theory is wrong on several counts. Groups can form with high solidarity and in-group preference in the absence of any other group (Sherif, Harvey, White, Hood, & Sherif, 1961). Analysis of a monumental survey of social distance, stereotypes, and preferences or rejections of other groups in East Africa by Brewer and Campbell (1976; Brewer, 1979a) showed that members of in-groups do not regard out-groups in the uniformly hostile ways that Sumner's theory would predict. Nor were his specific speculations on proximity upheld, though a history of past conflicts between the groups "was reflected in mutual attributions of traits associated with conflict and distrust" (Brewer, 1979a, p. 77). Nor can the theory deal with the undeniable fact that some groups and categories of people exist as socially different but are not hostile.

Some older theorizing defined social categories for "other" social groups as irrational, based on "nonessential and 'noisy' attributes" encapsulated into "faulty and inflexible generalizations" that were seen as the cause of the "antipathy" of social prejudice (Allport, 1954, pp. 9, 176). More recent writers have observed that the frequency of social categorization and of stereotyped attributions to others suggests that they are not "abnormal" and that defining a phenomenon as "bad" can prevent its scientific analysis (cf. Ashmore & Del Boca, 1981). The attribution of personal qualities or traits to other individuals is not confined to those in "different" social categories. On one hand, calling such attributions "implicit theories of personality" when they apply to "us" and "stereotypes" when they apply to "them" can confuse understanding of the psychological processes involved in both (Ashmore, 1981; Ashmore & Del Boca, 1979; Grant & Holmes, 1981). On the other hand, dealing with the processes involved solely in cognitive terms, divorced from relevant social realities (e.g., as probability statements), runs the risk of equating stereotyped images of others with a statement on the probability of rain today (e.g., McCauley, Stitt, & Segal, 1980). Categorical and attributional processes are normal in cognitive functioning, but they cannot explain differential reactions to in-group and out-group members unless relevant social realities and processes are also explained.

One of the most active researchers on cognitive aspects of the problem made a similar point by comparing the individual's normal categorical functioning with a "do-it-yourself kit." In Tajfel's words (1979), the fact that a person has such a kit does not

> inform us whether, when, how and for what purposes he [or she] will use it. We only know that there are some things he [or she] can do with [the kit] . . . and some constructions that are definitely impossible because of the limitations of this particular box of tricks. (p. 184)

In order to explain what the individual actually does with it, Tajfel concluded that it is necessary to know how "groups are constructed in a particular system . . . and how the constructions and their effects depend upon, and relate to, forms of social reality" (p. 184).

Social Realities and Social Cognition in Group Relations

A theory developed by the Sherifs (Sherif & Sherif, 1953, 1969; C. Sherif, 1976) emphasized such social realities. Since others have labeled that theory "realistic conflict theory" (e.g., Brewer, 1979a, 1979b; LeVine & Campbell, 1972), it is important to note that the theory deals with both conflicting and nonconflicting relationships between groups. The theory starts with social realities, namely the formation of social units (groups or social categories), and then continues with the consequences as members become psychologically linked with the social units as reference groups or categories (i.e., as social units that are self-defining). One such consequence is the attribution of at least some positive qualities to one's own group by its "good" members.

A second set of social realities, which does not follow directly from the first, pertains to the historical relationships between groups, which may be friendly, cooperative, dominant-subordinate, or directly in conflict in relation to desired resources, prestige, or other social values. The history of these relationships is reflected in the norms and social myths of the respective groups related to one another. "Good" members of each group form their attitudes within bounds of the group norms and social myths (e.g., stereotyped attributions) and thus tend to retain them through social processes among members, even when the original sources of friendship, superiority-subordination, or conflict in relations with other groups are long past. Geographical or socially developed distance between groups strengthens in-group maintenance of the past. Nonconforming members are sanctioned for attitudes or actions not conforming to the group's. When the circumstances of interaction between the groups change substantially, then such nonconforming members can make their voices heard or their actions approved with less threat of punishment or separation from their own groups. Thus the ongoing circumstances and relations between the groups are also social realities of importance.

Therefore, in this theory, it is not psychologically aberrant (even though undesirable) that new members of the groups form unfavorable attitudes and attributions to those in other groups or categories if their past relationships have been characterized by conflict, rivalry, or dominance-subordination. Such attitudes and attributions mirror the history of intergroup relationships from the singular perspective of members within each group. The question of whether there is a kernel of truth in their stereotyped attributions to one another is not to be sought in individual differences among persons in the separate groups, even though such differences may be striking. (If they are not, they may be socially created.) The social reality of stereotyped attributions lies in the relationships *between* the groups or social categories in the past. The stereotypes attributed to the other group define what the relationships with its members *should* be and assign causes for past and ongoing intergroup interactions with them.

Recent research on stereotyped attributions to those persons within one's social category and to those in other categories shows that the attributed traits within each are patterned (intercorrelated), constituting "implicit theories of personality" to be applied to persons in those categories (Ashmore, 1981). Unfavorable stereotypes are not negative "halos" consisting of every bad trait members can imagine about others but are selective attributions pertinent to maintaining particular relationships to persons in that category (Doise, 1978). If intergroup or intercategory relationships have been symbiotic, cooperative, or mutually beneficial, the norms of the respective participants and their attributions to one another reflect that past history.

Research on "Minimal Differentiation or Intergroup" Situations

A series of three experiments in summer camps on group formation, intergroup conflict, and cooperation developed from the foregoing theory, the last being the experiment at Robbers' Cave (Sherif, Harvey, White, Hood, & Sherif, 1961). Later, researchers began to use procedures called the "minimal intergroup situation" or, more recently, the "minimal differentiation" situation, in an effort to bring the problem of in-group versus out-group bias into the laboratory. Procedures in the minimal differentiation and minimal intergroup situations differ substantially, hence the research findings also differ in important respects. Each will be considered briefly, in turn.

As developed by Tajfel (1970), the minimal differentiation experiment amounts to the study of individual decisions and attributions to two categories of subjects among whom there is no interaction, no knowledge of who else is in either category, and no direct implication by the researcher of the possibility for personal reward. The categories are created arbitrarily by the research, e.g., by telling a subject that he or she is an "over-estimator" or "under-estimator," prefers pictures by artist X or Y, or simply is an X or Y. The subject is then asked to allocate rewards, using prepared matrices or a sliding scale, to other subjects in category X and to those in category Y. No rewards to oneself are mentioned.

The repeated finding in such research has been that the most frequent allocation of rewards has favored others in one's own category. Such own-category preference does not maximize the gain of those in one's own category but does maximize the difference between rewards to categories X and Y, even when that difference means lowering rewards to those in one's own category (Brewer, 1979b; Tajfel & Turner, 1979). Because maximization of difference between categories is a general psychological phenomenon, the findings have at times been interpreted as confirming Sumner: Any differentiation between individuals, even separation into arbitrary categories, breeds in-group preference *and* out-group hostility and stereotyping. That interpretation is not accurate.

As Brewer's review of the evidence (1979b) shows, there is no evidence that individuals in the other category are derogated or attributed significantly unfavorable traits. In fact, Brewer regards the evidence as indicating that social categorization can serve the positive functions of encouraging in-group preference and mobilizing members to action without danger of out-group hostility. The findings show contrast between categories but not necessarily out-group derogation or hostility.

But what of the discriminatory in-group preference in allocating rewards? Tajfel and Turner (1979) have argued that it reflects the individual's efforts to maintain self-esteem through group membership. As Billig (1976, p. 352) observed, however, that proposal extrapolates far beyond the data in the minimal differentiation situation. Brewer (1979b) reported on the difficulties in such a situation of removing expectations for competition from subjects accustomed to competitive rewarding when two groups are together. The differential rewards to one's own category disappeared when subjects' expectations for reward from others in their own category were explicitly removed, and the expectation of reward from those in the other category reversed the preferential rewards to that category (Locksley, Ortiz, & Hepburn, 1980). Since differential rewarding to best friends is no greater than to randomly assigned pairs (Vaughan, Tajfel, & Williams, 1981), situationally aroused expectations about personal reward or competition appear to be the clearest explanation for own-category preferences in reward in the minimal differentiation situation.

The other procedure, the "minimal intergroup situation" (Ferguson & Kelley, 1964), typically requires task performance and interaction among individuals in ad hoc groups, whose members then compete with another such group for exclusive recognition or reward. In those experiments where interactions have been permitted to continue for a time and the activities are motivationally relevant, the accumulated findings are quite clear: Not only in-group preference but also more favorable attributions to one's own group and the beginnings of unfavorable attributions to the other group are found (Austin & Worchel, 1979; Brewer, 1979a, 1979b). Continuing competition is associated with greater cohesion within each group, provided that there is realistic possibility of success (Blake & Mouton, 1979; Dion, 1979). Performance by members of one's own group is overestimated, particularly if it is successful and the appraisals are made in public, as a show of solidarity with other members (Hinkle & Schopler, 1979). Social reality is recognized, however, in the form of a more accurate estimate of the opposition's performance when that performance has been observed. In this research, the other, competing group is not typically underestimated but is downplayed relative to one's own group.

Finally, as Doise (1978) has shown, if different groups are composed of already differentiated social categories (such as Swiss boys or girls; Swiss students or apprentices; Swiss speakers of French, German, or Italian), the direction of differential judgments and attributions follows the existing status differentials between their members. For example, composing groups of Swiss boys and girls led to both groups' overestimating the boys' performance. Forming mixed gender groups, called the "reds" and the "blues," resulted in higher appraisals for one's own group, red or blue; but attributions of personal qualities to boys or girls were not affected by the short-term cross-classification. These attributions arose from traditional stereotypes of boys and girls in the society. Wilder and Thompson (1980), studying women attending rival colleges, found that the strength of category differentiation and unfavorable attributions to the other group in the situation varied with the amount of experience members had in the experimental situation with each other as in-group and as out-group members.

Superordinate Goals

Like the Robbers' Cave experiment, considerable other research shows that hostility and negative attributions to the out-group and its members are reduced and are replaced by favorable views when the two groups interact cooperatively toward valued goals neither can attain singly, i.e., superordinate goals. Blake and Mouton (1979), using various procedures to reduce conflict and hostile attitudes between groups in industrial situations, reported that "superordinate goals developed by the participants themselves as members of intact groups are the soundest approach to replacing competition with cooperation" (p. 31). They had extensive practical experience intervening in such conflicts as "third party" negotiators, and they documented the third party's limitations. From the viewpoint of the conflicting parties, third-party intervention is often an unwelcome intrusion. It may actually exacerbate conflict if the conflict level is already quite high, as Rubin (1980) reported in surveying the research evidence. Such findings provide the rationale, either to those in power or to consenting groups eager to avoid disastrous conflict, for mandatory and binding arbitration.

Laboratory studies by Worchel and his collaborators (1979) stress that positive changes following cooperation between groups occur when the cooperative efforts attain success, not failure, and when the cooperative interaction is repeated, rather than occurring only once. Members of groups in conflict must learn how to cooperate as social units. Failure of cooperative efforts retards conflict reduction, particularly if members of the different groups are marked by visible differences (e.g., laboratory coats of different colors). Worchel and Norvell (1980), however, reported that failure does not severely disrupt already developing attraction between the groups when the failure can correctly be blamed on environmental circumstances beyond the groups' control.

These findings are congruent with the research reviewed previously on the reduction of preexisting status differentials among children and adults by Cook, Aronson, and their collaborators. The changes in attitudes, attributions, and actions that occur when intergroup or category relationships change are significant, for they show relationships between psychological and social processes. The relevant social realities are different, and the consequences of social categorization also differ psychologically.

Social Categorization and Attitudes

Some of the cognitive phenomena when individuals construe others in different social categories can be understood as consequences of using a simple categorical system for designating what is similar and what is different, as one might in sorting squares from circles. Thus the work of S. E. Taylor and her collaborators (S. E. Taylor, 1981; Taylor, Fiske, Etcoff, & Ruderman, 1978) has confirmed the theory proposed by Kanter (1977) that exaggeration or accentuation of gender or ethnic differences is a contextual phenomenon, occurring when a minority of women or of nonwhite males appears in an otherwise all white-male context. Those in one's own category are assimilated, hence less distinguishable in mixed interactions, while those in the other category are contrasted, their differences being emphasized. Thus the individual makes more errors of remembering within one's own category than in the other category (S. E. Taylor et al., 1978). The fewer the individuals in one gender category, the more their behavior in social interaction is seen by those in the other gender category as distinctive, compared to similar behavior by someone in the majority category (S. E. Taylor, 1981).

The minority is affected also by the majority context. In one study, women conformed to the views of a male majority on traditionally masculine topics (Feldman-Summers, Montano, Kasprzyk, & Wagner, 1980). In the presence of a male majority, but not when with other women, women judges of articles attributed to male or female authors discriminated against the women authors, as did the men (Toder, 1980). There are evaluative components in the categorical schema as well as an interaction with contextual circumstances. The limitations of a strictly categorical approach are seen when one looks at the fate of proposals in social life to reduce contrast by equalizing the number of men and women at work, of blacks or whites in a neighborhood, or of men and women of any ethnic category in the care of home and children. Such proposals not only bear on social realities but also arouse great emotional reactions, in the form of strong acceptances and strong objections. Thus the categorical schema related to important social categories has to be seen as motivated and affective as well as cognitive, in short, as an attitudinal structure (Pettigrew, 1981).

A recent review of studies of person perception and judgment of men and women by Wallston and O'Leary (1981) reveals highly differentiated attitudes toward men and women in varying social contexts. The traditional gender categories in society are linked with different activities, men's status in paid work and public life being higher and the category "women" being tied to traditional women's activities, not to the activities in the male sphere. The psychological selectivity of both researchers and other perceivers is revealed by an extraordinary concentration of the research on women's physical attractiveness and on men's judged competence in task performance. The differing categorical and attributional schemata for men and women are revealed when men and women are appraised in different social situations, particularly when women are appraised in nontraditional contexts.

In nontraditional activities, women's performances are often judged as less competent than men's, unless one woman reaches very high competence levels. Then, in a meritocratic system, women are praised as more competent than comparable men (a clear case of contrast or maximization of difference) relative to the restricted activity categories in which women's performances are ordinarily assessed. A similar contrast was reported by Linville and Jones (1980) in appraisals of a black candidate highly qualified for law school and of an equally qualified white candidate.

Physical attractiveness has usually been studied in dating situations and has been particularly prized for women. But, in nontraditional work contexts, a highly attractive and competent woman is judged less qualified than one less attractive. Physical attractiveness is a much less salient anchor for judgments of men's work competence. Incompetence for men is the worst judgment that can be made and tends to be exaggerated (Wallston & O'Leary, 1981).

The Wallston-O'Leary review emphasizes the importance of studying differential reactions to others through coordinating data on their cognitive, affective, and behavioral correlates in social contexts.

That emphasis is congruent with recent work on social attitudes, some of which is neglected in many introductory psychology texts.

Attitudes Defining Self-Other Relationships

Historically, the attitude concept became central in social psychology in dealing with individuals' reactions to social objects (e.g., persons, groups, institutions, and social issues) with characteristic affect (positive or negative), entrenched beliefs about those objects, and consistent behaviors toward them. Over the years, the development of a variety of self-report techniques for attitude measurement, the popularity of opinion surveys, and the operational definition of "attitude" as "what my test measures" led to neglect of the issue of how important or personally salient the attitude objects were for individuals. As a consequence, both the affective and the behavioral aspects of the concept were neglected (see C. Sherif, 1980).

Recently, researchers have conceived and studied social attitudes related to the individual's actions as complex categorical structures (schemata) incorporating beliefs, attributions, and affect. Understanding the person's actions involves analysis of attitudinal structures and of social context. The work by Fishbein and Ajzen (1975) on attitudes and intentional behavior in a specific situation clarified the problems in studying attitudes and linked the concept firmly with actions. This work is summarized in a formula for predicting the individual's intention to act in a specific situation. Fishbein and Ajzen prefer to restrict the term "attitude" to a measure of the individual's "affect toward behavior"; but the formula represents other affective as well as cognitive components located within the person, relating the person to the attitude object in social context. Designating the entire formula as an attitudinal structure or schema is not out of line with the typical characterization of an attitude as having both cognitive and affective components related to behavior.

Fishbein's recent presentation of the model (Figure 2) is shown here with slight adaptations for ease of interpretation. The model has been used with considerable success in predicting large portions of the variance in declared intentions to act, which are highly predictive of actions in the foreseeable future. Although the model has been criticized as overly specific in focusing on particular actions, it includes beliefs and the category of individuals whose norms are personally

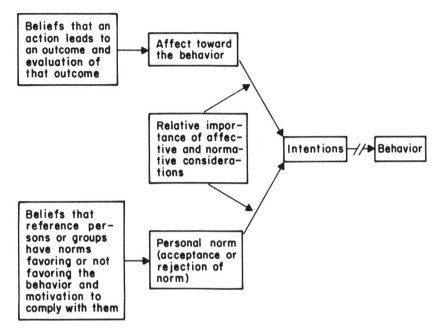

Figure 2. Representation of Attitudinal Schema Related to Behavior in Social Context. Adapted from M. Fishbein, "A Theory of Reasoned Action," in H. E. Howe, Jr., and M. M. Page (Eds.), *1979 Nebraska Symposium on Motivation* (Lincoln: University of Nebraska Press, 1980), p. 69. Copyright © 1980 by University of Nebraska Press. Adapted by permission.

important to the individual, i.e., reference persons or groups, which are assuredly conceptual. Thus the model implicates a complex of self-other relationships, including their relative importance to the person (see arrows) compared to the individual's affective evaluations of acting in the situation.

A recent test of the model (Smetana & Adler, 1980) found that when the personal norm ("how I should act") is internalized (in Kelman's, 1980, sense of that term), it correlates highly with the individual's affective evaluations of acting, i.e., does not contribute independently to the person's intentions. Other research shows that the more the beliefs about the attitude object are self-defining the greater is their relationship with the individual's intentions and actions (see C. Sherif, 1980). Although Fishbein and Ajzen's explicit focus has been on predicting social action, their work and the work inspired by their model also hold promise for greater understanding of the complex attitudinal structures related to social action in social contexts.

An even more obvious relationship between the concepts of attitude and of cognitive schema is found in the work of the Sherifs and their collaborators (C. Sherif, 1976, 1980; Sherif & Sherif, 1969). Coordinate with their theory of intergroup attitudes, their conception of the person's attitude structure is that person's own categories, which relate him or her to social objects and other people and include beliefs about and attributions to others, with characteristic positive and negative affect. The categories are simultaneously cognitive and affective, delineating what is acceptable and objectionable to the person. The extent or degree to which acceptable categories are self-defining for the person is crucial in understanding how a situation is construed and in predicting whether or not action will occur (C. Sherif, 1980).

Figure 3, based on Helen Kearney's research on active advocates and opponents of legalized abortion, illustrates this concept of attitude (see C. Sherif, 1980). As the top bar indicates, the individual's attitude is formed in relation to social realities, in this case the various positions actually taken by different groups of people on the issue, as determined by prior sociological study and ranked from one extreme to the other by consensual judges. The attitude is composed of the person's categories for differentiating these positions as well as for evaluating these positions as acceptable or objectionable. In addition, the possibility is allowed that some categories are neither acceptable nor objectionable to the person, who is noncommittal toward them. The two bars at the bottom of the figure summarize data on the attitudes of active advocates and opponents of legalized abortion, indicating their latitudes of acceptance, rejection, and noncommitment.

The two bars in the middle of the figure typify experimental samples selected to agree on the same acceptable positions on the issue but to differ in their degree of involvement with the issue. They exemplify the general finding that highly involved persons exhibit a greater latitude or range of rejection than acceptance, and much less noncommitment than less involved persons.

In line with predictions from social judgment-involvement theory (Sherif, Sherif, & Nebergall, 1965; M. Sherif & Hovland, 1961), individuals with the same acceptable positions on abortion, but differing in involvement, made significantly different judgments of the same communication, which was moderately opposed to their acceptable positions. Individuals highly involved in their acceptable positions,

Eleven Ordered Public Positions on Issue (Abortion)

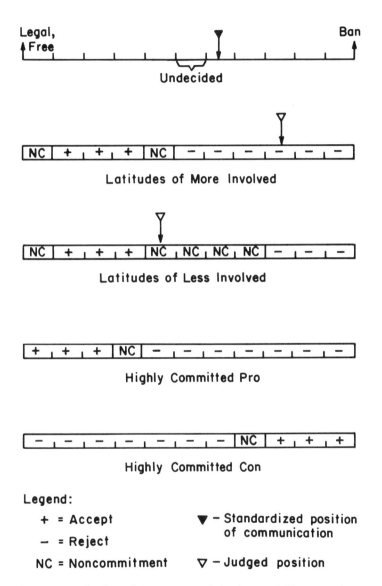

Figure 3. Latitudes of Acceptance, Rejection and Noncommitment on the Abortion Issue. Data from H. Kearney, in C. W. Sherif, "Social Values, Attitudes, and Involvement of the Self," in H. E. Howe, Jr., and M. M. Page (Eds.), *1979 Nebraska Symposium on Motivation*, (Lincoln: University of Nebraska Press, 1980).

personally and in their reference groups, used their own positions as anchors in making the judgment, thereby maximizing the difference, i.e., contrasting the message in relation to their position. Less involved judges assimilated the moderate message toward their own position, i.e., minimized the differences from their acceptable positions. In fact, the less involved individuals judged the message moderately opposing their positions to be on their own side of the issue.

Granberg and Brent (1980) have analyzed survey research data on recent presidential elections, data showing strong assimilative tendencies by supporters of presidential candidates in making judgments of their candidate's positions on various issues, i.e., one's candidate was seen as closer to the voter's own position on those issues. Granberg and Brent also reported contrast effects in judging opponents who differed greatly from their preferred candidate on the issues.

Such assimilation-contrast effects are to be expected chiefly when there is some ambiguity in the social context. Moderate views are frequently more ambiguous than unequivocally extreme positions. Thus Judd and his collaborators (Judd & Harackiewicz, 1980; Judd & Kulik, 1980) reported contrast effects in judgment but found that subjects judged more quickly and remembered better extreme positions on social issues than moderate positions. Subjects also judged more quickly and remembered better those positions with which they strongly agreed or disagreed than with those they found moderately acceptable or unacceptable.

In short, individuals respond both to social realities and to their own evaluative categorizations of realities which are affect laden. Judd and Kulik (1980) summarize the latter findings as follows: "Information that is highly consistent or highly contradictory to one's attitudes is judged more easily and is more likely to be remembered than information that is only moderately consistent or contradictory" (p. 576). They regard this tendency as a clear functional advantage in dealing with social realities, since it aids in identifying others in one's reference group as well as one's opponents.

Involvement of Self in Social Cognition

The trend in social psychology toward revitalizing the concept of the human self-system reflects, in part, the demonstrable differences in social cognition and in behavioral consistency obtained as a function of the involvement of self-defining categories (ego involvement), both in the laboratory and in field research (Kelman, 1980; C. Sherif, 1980; Smith, 1980). The general problem of why individuals perceive and react differently to others located in the same category and to those in different categories from themselves is clarified by a theory of a self-system, developing in social contexts and relating the individual to past experiences, personal capacities, and attributes as well as to others in the social environment (Greenwald, 1981; C. Sherif, 1980; Wegner & Vallacher, 1980).

Much of the recent literature concentrates on what Greenwald (1981) calls "intrapersonal self-tasks," that is, maintenance of self-esteem, feelings of self-control or efficacy, and other subjective experiences of self (see Wegner & Vallacher, 1980). A large research literature has demonstrated that the extent to which the individual's self is involved in ongoing social contexts is a critical determinant of behavior in a variety of problem areas. The degree to which self is involved is assessed through several techniques, most desirably by some combination of the following: public commitments to action, active participation in relevant activities in the past, self-ratings of consistency, ratings of personal importance, certainty and confidence in judgments or opinions, and, indirectly, the latitudes of acceptance-rejection-noncommitment. (As stated, more frequent rejections than acceptances and little noncommitment are typical of highly involved individuals on bipolar social realities, such as intergroup conflicts.)

The following list summarizes comparisons between persons with higher and lower levels of involvement which are supported both by older literature and the recent research noted. When individuals are more involved, the following research findings are reported:

Greater consistency in behavior across situations (Bem & Allen, 1974);

Shorter reaction time and greater confidence in judgments (Markus, 1977, 1980);

Better recall (Smith & Jamieson, 1972; Spiro & Sherif, 1975);

Greater selectivity in perception and recall (Spiro & Sherif, 1975; Kendzierski, 1980), though not always for what is consistent with or enhancing to one's self;

Less likelihood of being influenced by others to adopt highly discrepant opinions (C. Sherif, 1976);

Greater difficulties in reaching agreement in discussions with others who oppose one's views (see C. Sherif, 1980);

Greater consistency between attitude and personal intentions, and greater likelihood of actions congruent with attitude (C. Sherif, 1980).

As this list of findings suggests, the continuing study of what is personally important to individuals and in what degree it is important will contribute to better understanding of attitude stability and change. For example, Wicklund and Frey (1980) report that heightening the individual's self-awareness in a social situation through exposure to a mirror or television camera also heightens consistency between stated values and social actions. Confirming that finding, Scheier and Carver (1980) also found that, if the techniques heightening awareness occur as the individual anticipates interacting with others whose attitudes disagree, the resulting behavior is more congruent with the attitudes of the others. Reminiscent of the "presentation of the self" to others as analyzed by Goffman (1959), this finding underlines the importance of knowing how involved the individual is in an attitude position and what or who else is personally important in the situation. The self-system is not a simple affair. Unless a value of great importance to the person is tapped, congeniality with others can readily override personal consistency in other respects.

Similarly, the issue of selectivity in perception and memory will be clarified when researchers systematically study the person's degree of personal involvement with the varied sets of factors in relevant social situations (Table 1). The research findings that information about persons in a different social category which is atypical or unfavorable is remembered better than the same information about persons in one's own category are suggestive of functional mechanisms maintaining unfavorable social stereotypes (Hamilton & Gifford, 1976; Howard & Rothbart, 1980). Similarly, the demonstration of selective perception and memory favoring stereotypically consistent over stereotypically inconsistent information would operate toward stereotype maintenance (Cohen, 1981). There is considerable research data, however, showing *proportionally* greater recall of attitudinally inconsistent materials than that of attitudinally consistent materials (Wyer, 1980), a tendency that is increased by heightened involvement (Spiro & Sherif, 1975).

Comparatively little memory research relates selectivity to the functional utility of memories in situations involving the self. In some social contexts, recalling contradictory information can prevent "blind

imperialism" in action, a luxury that one can enjoy in reminiscing about oneself privately over long periods of time (Greenwald, 1980). The evidence is not all gathered concerning the degree of involvement, the circumstances, and the utility of selective recall in maintaining or altering attitudes.

Attitude Change in Larger Context

Many years ago Hovland (1959) remarked upon the greater amount of attitude change obtained in laboratory experiments in contrast to the small amount that seemed to occur in survey research on cross sections of the American public over time. One suggested reason for this difference was that survey research typically studied attitudes of personal and social importance, attitudes which were self-defining for individuals on their own social contexts, while laboratory research did not.

Today the importance of the person's involvement in an attitude position is better recognized in research on attitudes and attitude change (e.g., Kelman, 1980; Petty & Cacioppo, 1981; C. Sherif, 1980; Smith, 1980). There is still a bifurcation in the literature, however, with those studying communication focusing on attitude change in less involving issues (cf. Petty & Cacioppo, 1981) and those concerned with more involving issues studying changes in the social context that must precede and accompany efforts in attitude change (e.g., Cook, 1978). That bifurcation is reflected in some introductory psychology texts where the general topic of attitude change is presented through laboratory research varying the message and the communicator, but the change of ethnic attitudes is discussed through research on the conditions for "equal status" contact.

Over a longer period than that available to Hovland (1959), survey research data show unmistakable trends for increasingly higher proportions of the white U.S. public to accept positions and beliefs about blacks and other minorities, and about women of all ethnic backgrounds, that only small fractions would accept in the 1950s (Taylor, Sheatsley, & Greeley, 1978; Thornton & Freedman, 1979). The more recent analyses contain panel data concerning opinions toward both minorities and women, making clear that the changes are not simply generational shifts with intransigents dying off. The data also include changes by the same individuals over time. During the same period, certain changes occurred in patterns of association among minority and majority individuals in educational and other public settings, as well as among men and women in work settings, that are striking to those who recall the earlier period. Despite their limitations, to be noted shortly, these changes in associations and opinions are important.

The changes in associational patterns were preceded and accompanied by demographic and other larger social changes. They were ultimately achieved by changes in the legal system, enforced by governmental power. Neither changed associations nor the opinion changes, however, were initiated by legal authorities, and they were by no means inevitable outcomes of the larger social changes. They were initiated by individuals forming groups directed toward change which coalesced into social movements, agitating and pushing for change, at times confronting opponents sharply in intergroup conflict (C. Sherif, 1976). Real-life events confronted consumers of the mass media with dramatic actions by proponents, opponents, and the federal government. The significance of these events is suggested by Riley and Pettigrew's analysis (1976) of survey research data collected before and after the desegregation of public schools in Little Rock and before and after Martin Luther King's murder in 1968.

The greatest changes in verbal opinions following those events occurred among groups and regions already more favorable or more unfavorable than others to interracial contacts. The immediate effect was that those divergent groups differed more than they had before, i.e., they were more polarized. Such attitude changes typically involved the individual's increased agreement with positions already acceptable in some degree or toward which the person was previously noncommittal. They occurred among individuals with personal involvement in the issue (Petty & Cacioppo, 1981). Even when the changes involved moderation of opponents' and intensification of proponents' positions, increased polarization was the outcome.

Such polarization of attitudes, coupled with the formation over time of active counter-movement groups, accounts for the pockets of resistance to public desegregation, civil rights for minorities and women, and the Equal Rights Amendment. The mobilization of previously inactive but now highly involved groups opposing busing, legal aid to the poor, extension of civil rights legislation, freedom of choice in matters of religion and reproduction, "secular humanism," and international friendship, while proclaiming their "moral majority," belies the earlier claims by politicians and journalists that these were "single issues."

Political scientists refer to individuals most directly affected by a social change as "self-interested." In terms of this definition of self-interest, such individuals do not constitute the major opposition to the single issues, for example, the busing of school children as a last ditch means for desegregating public schools (Kinder & Sears, 1981; Sears, Hensler, & Speer, 1979). Those most strongly opposed to busing were not those whose children were bused or most likely to be bused but those willing to respond to a survey by endorsing unfavorable beliefs about minorities. Such findings lead to enquiry about other possible "self-interests" of such "symbolic racists."

Symbolic racism, as studied by Sears and his collaborators, represents racist ideology, i.e., a system of beliefs and attributions to others that define those in one's own social category as superior to those in other categories. (Sexist ideology is similarly defined.) In reference groups upholding such a doctrine, self-esteem derives not only from being a good and accepted participant but also from seeing one's group as superior to others. Change which threatens that alleged superiority becomes a threat to members' own self-interest. This analysis owes much to Tajfel and Turner's extension (1979) of social comparison theory to include intergroup comparisons; however, their analysis also assumes that the maintenance of self-esteem by group members requires another group to whom one's own group may be seen as superior. If one carried the argument a step further, one might ask whether some form of superiority doctrine is necessary for the maintenance of one's self-esteem associated with group membership.

To the contrary, members of the social movements pushing for changes now being actively resisted wanted to become equal, not superior, to the categories in society most unlike them, viz. whites or white men. The difference in ideology has important social-psychological implications, for it divides people into groups with very different directions concerning whether the concepts of social power and social justice should be sharply differentiated or equally applied. One can gain self-esteem by finding group identity in a movement toward equitable use of social power and justice. It is not necessary, psychologically, to have an inferior comparison group.

Issues of differential social power among groups and social categories of people in society are bound to enter into problems of attitude change among their participants. The social realities are that the great bulk of privileged white Americans live out of contact with the ethnic minority. Improvement in working and living conditions of a small proportion of minority individuals has not been accompanied by striking improvements in the lives of the larger proportion. Over three fourths of white Americans of all ages agree that blacks should "not push themselves in where they're not wanted" (S. Taylor et al., 1978), which is exactly the language used toward "intruders," not to "our kind." Higher proportions of women working outside of the home and seeking higher education have not been accompanied by striking improvements in women's economic status but have added outside work to women's responsibilities in home and child care.

Students today come from a generation in which the norms make knowingly expressing racist or sexist beliefs unacceptable, at least in academic settings. The recent survey by Crosby, Bromley, and Saxe (1980) of research using unobtrusive methods to detect racist discrimination is instructive. Their review of research on helping, spatial behavior, aggressive shock-giving in the laboratory, and other indirect techniques for studying attitudes led them to conclude that, despite the verbal conformity to nonracist beliefs in social research, "antiblack prejudice is still strong among white Americans" (p. 546). Verbal compliance with widely accepted, normative beliefs does not necessarily imply individual attitudes and actions in line with those norms.

The accumulated research data suggests that attitudes have changed in those public areas of interpersonal and intergroup interactions where actual social changes have occurred but not in other areas. If attitudes toward other categories or groups are to change more, our relationships with those others have to change correspondingly. Social psychologists have found that discriminatory attitudes can be changed through repeated experiences of interacting as equally important participants across category lines toward superordinate goals.

Students are likely to label the proposal for change of attitudes through such participations as highly impractical. They point to the few opportunities for ethnic minority and majority members, or for women and men, to cooperate as equals in the real world. An instructor faces a choice. It is easy to agree. An alternative is to ask why there are so few opportunities for interacting as equals and why changes in existing relationships are "impractical."

Asking the question "why" leads to recognition that psychology is dependent upon knowledge from historians, sociologists, economists, and political and other social scientists for understanding the social realities that limit opportunities, that define what is "practical" at the moment, and that relate to prevailing beliefs about what "should be." It may lead some students to wonder about a psychology of human beings that assumes a fixed, unchanging social environment, when that social environment was created and is populated by human beings. Can there be a valid social psychology which does not deal with a changing social environment or with human problems in changing society?

In conclusion, social psychology has bases lying in the study of social realities that form the context for individual experiences and actions. The major and enduring problems in social psychology concern individuals' participation in their social contexts, their psychological relationships with others in social contexts, and the human capacity to act individually and with others to change a social context, even to create with others new social forms, new social rules, and new groups. The study of social cognition necessarily is framed within those social contexts, the attitudes that form within them, and the human self-systems that lend continuity to experience and social behavior. When both the social and psychological bases of social psychology are utilized, we move toward a psychology of the human individual that is "valid social psychology" and a social psychology that "is valid individual psychology" (M. Sherif, 1936, p. 4).

Selected Introductory Psychology Texts Surveyed

Bourne, L. E., Jr., & Ekstrand, B. R. *Psychology: Its principles and meanings* (3rd ed.). New York: Holt, Rinehart & Winston, 1979.

Darley, J. M., Glucksberg, J., Kanin, L. J., & Kinchla, R. A. *Psychology*. Englewood Cliffs, N.J.: Prentice-Hall, 1981.

Fernald, L. D., & Fernald, P. S. *Introduction to psychology* (4th ed.), Boston: Houghton-Mifflin, 1978.

Gewitz, J. *Psychology: Looking at ourselves* (2nd ed.). Boston: Little, Brown, 1980.

Hilgard, E. R., Atkinson, R. L., & Atkinson, R. C. *Introduction to psychology* (7th ed.). New York: Harcourt Brace Jovanovich, 1979.

Kagan, J. *Psychology*. New York: Harcourt Brace Jovanovich, 1980.

Kimble, G. A., Garmezy, N., & Zigler, E. *Principles of general psychology* (5th ed.). New York: Wiley, 1981.

Lindsay, P. H., & Norman, D. A. *Human information processing: An introduction to psychology* (2nd ed.). New York: Academic Press, 1977.

Lindzey, G., Hall, C. S., & Thompson, R. F. *Psychology* (2nd ed.). New York: Worth, 1978.

McConnell, J. V. *Understanding human behavior* (3rd ed.). New York: Holt, Rinehart & Winston, 1980.

Mischel, W., & Mischel, H. N. *Essentials of psychology* (2nd ed.). New York: Random House, 1980.

Morgan, C. T., King, R. A., & Robinson, N. M. *Introduction to psychology* (6th ed.). New York: McGraw-Hill, 1979.

Rubin, Z., & McNeil, E. B. *The psychology of being human* (3rd ed.). New York: Harper & Row, 1981.

Wortman, C. B., Loftus, E. F., & Marshal, M. *Psychology.* New York: Knopf, 1981.

Zimbardo, P. G. (from the earlier editions by F. L. Ruch). *Psychology and life* (10th ed.). Glenview, Ill.: Scott, Foresman, 1979.

References

Abelson, R. P. Psychological status of the script concept. *American Psychologist,* 1981, *36*, 715–729.

Adair, J. G. *The human subject.* Boston: Little, Brown, 1973.

Adorno, T. W., Frenkel-Brunswick, E., Levinson, D. J., & Sanford, R. N. *The authoritarian personality.* New York: Harper & Row, 1950.

Allport, G. W. *The nature of prejudice.* Reading, Mass.: Addison-Wesley, 1954.

Altman, I. *The environment and social behavior: Privacy, personal space, territory and crowding.* Monterey, Calif.: Brooks/Cole, 1975.

Archibald, W. P. *Social psychology as political economy.* Toronto: McGraw-Hill Ryerson Ltd., 1978.

Aronson, E., & Bridgman, D. Jigsaw groups and the desegregated classroom: In pursuit of common goals. *Personality and Social Psychology Bulletin,* 1979, *5,* 438–466.

Aronson, E., Bridgman, D., & Geffner, R. The effects of a cooperative classroom structure on students' behavior and attitudes. In D. Bar-Tel & L. Saxe (Eds.), *Social psychology of education: Theory and research.* Washington, D.C.: Hemisphere, 1978.

Aronson, E., Stephan, C., Sikes, J., Blaney, N., & Snapp, M. *The jigsaw classroom.* Beverly Hills, Calif.: Sage, 1978.

Asch, S. E. Studies of independence and conformity: I. A minority of one against a unanimous majority. *Psychological Monographs,* 1956, *70* (9).

Ashmore, R. D. Sex stereotypes and implicit personality theory. In D. L. Hamilton (Ed.), *Cognitive processes in stereotyping and intergroup relations.* Hillsdale, N.J.: Erlbaum, 1981.

Ashmore, R. D., & Del Boca, F. K. Sex stereotypes and implicit personality theory: Toward a cognitive-social psychological conceptualization. *Sex Roles,* 1979, *5,* 219–248.

Ashmore, R. D., & Del Boca, F. K. Conceptual approaches to stereotypes and stereotyping. In D. Hamilton (Ed.), *Cognitive processes in stereotyping and intergroup behavior.* Hillsdale, N.J.: Erlbaum, 1981.

Austin, W. G., & Worchel, S. (Eds.). *The social psychology of intergroup relations.* Monterey, Calif.: Brooks/Cole, 1979.

Baldwin, J. M. *Mental development in the child and the race.* New York: Macmillan, 1895.

Barker, R. G. On the nature of the environment. *Journal of Social Issues,* 1963, *19* (4), 17–38.

Bartlett, F. C. *Remembering: A study in experimental and social psychology.* New York: Cambridge University Press, 1932.

Baum, A., & Davis, G. E. Reducing the stress of high density living. An architectural intervention. *Journal of Personality and Social Psychology,* 1980, *38* (3), 471–481.

Bem, D., & Allen, A. On predicting some of the people some of the time: The search for cross situational consistencies in behavior. *Psychological Review,* 1974, *81,* 506–519.

Bem, D. J., & Funder, D. C. Predicting more of the people more of the time: Assessing the personality of situations. *Psychological Review,* 1978, *85,* 485–501.

Berscheid, E., & Walster, E. H. *Interpersonal attraction* (2nd ed.). Reading, Mass.: Addison-Wesley, 1978.

Bickman, L. (Ed.). *Applied social psychology annual* (Vol. I). Beverly Hills, Calif.: Sage, 1980.

Bickman, L. (Ed.). *Applied social psychology annual* (Vol. II). Beverly Hills, Calif.: Sage, 1981.

Billig, M. *Social psychology and intergroup relations.* New York: Academic Press, 1976.

Blake, R. B., & Mouton, J. S. Intergroup problem solving in organizations: From theory into practice. In W. G. Austin & S. Worchel (Eds.), *The social psychology of intergroup relations.* Monterey, Calif.: Brooks/Cole, 1979.

Blanchard, F. A., Adelman, I., & Cook, S. W. Effect of group success and failure upon interpersonal attraction in cooperating interracial groups. *Journal of Personality and Social Psychology,* 1975, *32,* 519–530.

Blaney, N. T., Stephan, C., Rosenfield, D., Aronson, E., & Sikes, J. Interdependence in the classroom: A field study. *Journal of Educational Psychology,* 1977, *69,* 139–146.

Boutilier, R. G., Roed, J. C., & Svendsen, A. C. Crisis in the two social psychologies: A critical comparison. *Social Psychology Quarterly,* 1980, *43* (1), 5–17.

Brewer, M. B. The role of ethnocentrism in intergroup conflict. In W. G. Austin & S. Worchel (Eds.), *The social psychology of intergroup relations.* Monterey, Calif.: Brooks/Cole, 1979. (a)

Brewer, M. B. In-group bias in the minimal intergroup situation: A cognitive-motivational analysis. *Psychological Bulletin,* 1979, *86,* 307–324. (b)

Brewer, M. B., & Campbell, D. T. *Ethnocentrism and intergroup attitudes: East African evidence.* New York: Halsted, 1976.

Brooks, G. P., & Johnson, R. W. Floyd Allport and the master problem of social psychology. *Psychological Reports,* 1978, *42,* 295–308.

Bryson, J., & Bryson, R. (Eds.). Dual career couples. *Psychology of Women Quarterly* (Vol. 3, No. 1). New York: Human Science Press, 1978.

Burgess, R. L., & Huston, T. L. (Eds.). *Social exchange in developing relationships.* New York: Academic Press, 1979.

Burstein, P. Equal employment opportunity legislation and the income of women and nonwhites. *American Sociological Review,* 1979, *44,* 367–391.

Buss, A. R. Causes and reasons in attribution theory: A conceptual critique. *Journal of Personality and Social Psychology,* 1978, *36,* 1311–1321.

Buys, C. J. Humans would do better without groups. *Personality and Social Psychology Bulletin,* 1978, *4,* 123–125.

Carron, A. V., & Chelladurai, P. The dynamics of group cohesion in sport. *Journal of Sport Psychology,* 1981, *3,* 123–139.

Cartwright, D. Contemporary social psychology in historical perspective. *Social Psychology Quarterly,* 1979, *42,* 83–93.

Cohen, E. Person categories and social perception: Testing some boundaries of the processing effects of prior knowledge. *Journal of Personality and Social Psychology,* 1981, *40,* 441–452.

Cohen, E. G., Lockhead, M. E., & Lohman, M. The center for interracial cooperation: A field experiment. *Sociology of Education*, 1976, *49*, 47–58.

Cohen, E. G., & Roper, S. S. Modification of interracial disability: An application of status characteristic theory. *American Sociological Review*, 1972, *37*, 643–657.

Cook, M., & Wilson, G. (Eds.). *Love and attraction*. Oxford, England: Pergamon, 1979.

Cook, S. W. Interpersonal and attitudinal outcomes in cooperating interracial groups. *Journal of Research and Development in Education*, 1978, *12*, 97–113.

Crosby, F., Bromley, S., & Saxe, L. Recent unobtrusive studies of black and white discrimination and prejudice: A literature review. *Psychological Bulletin*, 1980, *87*, 546–563.

Darley, J. M., & Fazio, R. H. Expectancy confirmation processes arising in the social interaction sequence. *American Psychologist*, 1980, *35*, 861–866.

Degler, C. H. *At odds: Women and the family in America from the revolution to the present*. New York: Oxford University Press, 1980.

Dion, K. L. Intergroup conflict and intergroup cohesiveness. In W. G. Austin & S. Worchel (Eds.), *The social psychology of intergroup relations*. Monterey, Calif.: Brooks/Cole, 1979.

Doise, W. *Groups and individuals: Explanations in social psychology*. Cambridge: Cambridge University Press, 1978.

Doise, W. Levels of explanation in the European Journal of Social Psychology. *European Journal of Social Psychology*, 1980, *10*, 213–231. (a)

Doise, W. *Cours de psychologie sociale II: L'explication en psychologie sociale*. Geneve: Université de Geneve, Centrale universitaire des polycopiés, 1980. (b)

Dweck, C. S., & Gilliard, D. Expectancy statements as determinants of reactions to failure: Sex differences in persistency and expectancy change. *Journal of Personality and Social Psychology*, 1975, *32*, 1077–1084.

Dweck, C. S., Goetz, T. E., & Strauss, N. L. Sex differences in learned helplessness: IV. An experimental and naturalistic study of failure generalization and its mediators. *Journal of Personality and Social Psychology*, 1980, *38*, 441–452.

Eagly, A. H. Sex differences in influenceability. *Psychological Bulletin*, 1978, 86–116.

Eagly, A. H., & Carli, L. Sex of researchers and sex-type communications as determinants of sex differences in influenceability: A meta-analysis of social influences studies. *Psychological Bulletin*, 1981, *90*, 1–20.

Ellison, K. W., & Buckhout, R. *Psychology and criminal justice*. New York: Harper & Row, 1981.

Eskilson, A., & Wiley, M. G. Sex composition and leadership in small groups. *Sociometry*, 1976, *39*, 183–194.

Evans, R. I. *The making of social psychology: Discussions with creative contributors*. New York: Gardner Press, 1980.

Falbo, T., & Peplau, L. A. Power strategies in intimate relationships. *Journal of Personality and Social Psychology*, 1980, *38* (4), 618–628.

Feagin, J. R., & Feagin, C. B. *Discrimination American style: Institutional racism and sexism*. Englewood Cliffs, N.J.: Prentice-Hall, 1978.

Feldman-Summers, S., Montano, D. E., Kasprzyk, D., & Wagner, B. Influence attempts when competing views are gender-related: Sex as credibility. *Psychology of Women Quarterly*, 1980, *5* (2), 311–320.

Ferguson, C. K., & Kelley, H. H. Significant factors in overevaluation of own-group's product. *Journal of Abnormal and Social Psychology*, 1964, *69*, 223–228.

Fine, G. A. Small groups and culture creation: The idioculture of Little League baseball teams. *American Sociological Review*, 1979, *44*, 733–745.

Fine, G. A., & Glassner, B. Participant observation with children: Promise and problems. *Urban Life,* 1979, *8,* 153–174.

Fine, G. A., & Kleinman, S. Rethinking subculture: An interactionist analysis. *American Journal of Sociology,* 1979, *85,* 1–20.

Fishbein, M. A theory of reasoned action. In H. E. Howe, Jr., & M. M. Page (Eds.), *Beliefs, attitudes and values.* Nebraska Symposium on Motivation, 1979. Lincoln: University of Nebraska Press, 1980.

Fishbein, M., & Ajzen, I. *Belief, attitude, intention, and behavior: An introduction to theory and research.* Reading, Mass.: Addison-Wesley, 1975.

French, D. C., Brownell, C. A., Graziano, W. G., & Hartup, W. W. Effects of cooperative, competitive, and individualistic sets on performance in children's groups. *Journal of Experimental Child Psychology,* 1977, *24,* 1–10.

Frieze, I. H., Whitley, B. E., Jr., Hansen, B. H., & McHugh, M. C. Assessing the theoretical models for sex differences in causal attributions for success and failure. *Sex Roles,* 1982, *8,* 333–343.

Gergen, K. Social psychology as history. *Journal of Personality and Social Psychology,* 1973, *26,* 309–320.

Gergen, K. Social psychology, science and history. *Personality and Social Psychology Bulletin,* 1976, *2,* 373–383.

Goffman, E. *The presentation of the self in everyday life.* Garden City, N.Y.: Doubleday, 1959.

Gorman, M. Pre-war conformity research in social psychology: The approaches of Floyd H. Allport and Muzafer Sherif. *Journal of the History of the Behavioral Sciences,* 1981, *17,* 3–14.

Granberg, D., & Brent, E. Perceptions of issue positions of presidential candidates. *American Scientist,* 1980, *68,* 617–625.

Grant, P. R., & Holmes, J. G. The integration of implicit personality theory: Schemas and stereotype images. *Social Psychology Quarterly,* 1981, *44,* 107–115.

Graziano, W., French, D., Brownell, C. A., & Hartup, W. W. Peer interaction in same- and mixed-age triads in relation to chronological age and incentive conditions. *Child Development,* 1976, *47,* 707–714.

Green, R. B., & Mack, J. Would groups do better without social psychologists? A response to Buys. *Personality and Social Psychology Bulletin,* 1978, *4,* 561–563.

Greenwald, A. G. The totalitarian ego: Fabrication and revision in personal history. *American Psychologist,* 1980, *35,* 603–618.

Greenwald, A. G. Ego task analysis: An integration of research on ego-involvement. In A. Hastorf & A. Isen (Eds.), *Cognitive social psychology.* New York: Elseiver North Holland, 1981.

Hamilton, D. L. Intuitive psychologist or intuitive lawyer? Alternative models of the attribution process. *Journal of Personality and Social Psychology,* 1980, *39,* 767–772.

Hamilton, D. L., & Gifford, R. K. Illusory correlations in person perception: A cognitive basis of stereotypic judgments. *Journal of Experimental Social Psychology,* 1976, *12,* 392–407.

Harvey, J. H., Town, J. P., & Yarkin, K. L. How fundamental is "the fundamental attribution error"? *Journal of Personality and Social Psychology,* 1981, *40* (2), 346–349.

Henley, N. M. *Body politics: Power, sex and nonverbal communication.* Englewood Cliffs, N.J.: Prentice-Hall, 1977.

Hinkle, S., & Schopler, J. Ethnocentrism in the evaluation of group products. In W. G. Austin & S. Worchel (Eds.), *The social psychology of intergroup relations.* Monterey, Calif.: Brooks/Cole, 1979.

Hovland, C. I. Reconciling conflicting results derived from experimental and survey studies of attitude change. *American Psychologist*, 1959, *14*, 8–17.

Howard, J. W., & Rothbart, M. Social categorization and memory for in-group and out-group behavior. *Journal of Personality and Social Psychology*, 1980, *38*, 301–310.

Huston, T. L., & Levinger, G. Interpersonal attraction and relationships. In M. R. Rosenzeig & L. W. Porter (Eds.), *Annual review of psychology* (Vol. 29). Palo Alto, Calif.: Annual Reviews, 1978.

Huston, T. L., Ruggiero, M., Conner, R., & Geis, G. Bystander intervention into crime: A study based on naturally occurring episodes. *Social Psychology Quarterly*, 1981, *44* (1), 14–23.

Insko, C. A., Thibaut, J. W., Moehle, D., Wilson, M., Diamond, W. D., Gilmore, R., Solomon, M. R., & Lipsitz, A. Social evolution and the emergence of leadership. *Journal of Personality and Social Psychology*, 1980, *39* (3), 431–448.

Israel, J., & Tajfel, H. (Eds.). *The context of social psychology. A critical assessment.* New York: Academic Press, 1972.

Jellison, J. M., & Green, J. A self-presentation approach to the fundamental attribution error: The norm of internality. *Journal of Personality and Social Psychology*, 1981, *40*, 643–649.

Johnson, D. W., Maruyama, G., Johnson, R., Nelson, D., & Skon, L. Effects of cooperative, competitive, and individualistic goal structures on achievement: A meta-analysis. *Psychological Bulletin*, 1981, *89*, 47–62.

Judd, C. M., & Harackiewicz, J. M. Contrast effects in attitude judgment: An examination of the accentuation hypothesis. *Journal of Personality and Social Psychology*, 1980, *38*, 390–398.

Judd, C. M., & Kulik, J. A. Schematic effects of social attitudes on information processing and recall. *Journal of Personality and Social Psychology*, 1980, *38* (4), 569–578.

Kanter, R. M. *Men and women of the corporation.* New York: Basic Books, 1977.

Keating, C. F., Mazur, A., Segall, M. H., et al. Culture and the perception of social dominance from facial expressions. *Journal of Personality and Social Psychology*, 1981, *40* (4), 615–626.

Kelley, H. H. *Personal relationships: Their structures and processes.* Hillsdale, N.J.: Erlbaum, 1979.

Kelman, H. C. The role of action in attitude change. In H. E. Howe, Jr., & M. M. Page (Eds.), *Beliefs, attitudes and values.* Nebraska Symposium on Motivation, 1979. Lincoln: University of Nebraska Press, 1980.

Kendzierski, D. Self-schemata and scripts: The recall of self-referent and scriptal information. *Personality and Social Psychology Bulletin*, 1980, *6* (1), 23–29.

Kidd, R. F., & Saks, M. J. *Advances in applied social psychology.* Hillsdale, N.J.: Erlbaum, 1980.

Kinder, D. R., & Sears, D. O. Prejudice and politics: Symbolic racism versus racial threats to the good life. *Journal of Personality and Social Psychology*, 1981, *40*, 414–431.

Korte, C. Urban-nonurban differences in social behavior and social psychological models of urban impact. *Journal of Social Issues*, 1980, *36* (3), 29–51.

LaFrance, M., & Mayo, C. Racial differences in gaze behavior during conversations: Two systematic observational studies. *Journal of Personality and Social Psychology*, 1976, *33*, 547–552.

Lamb, T. A. Nonverbal and paraverbal control in dyads and triads: Sex or power differences? *Social Psychology Quarterly*, 1981, *44*, 49–53.

Langer, E., & Rodin, J. The effects of choice and enhanced personal responsibility for the aged: A field experiment in an institutional setting. *Journal of Personality and Social Psychology,* 1976, *34,* 191–198.

Langer, E., & Roth, J. Heads I win, tails it's chance: The illusion of control as a function of the sequence of outcomes in a purely chance task. *Journal of Personality and Social Psychology,* 1975, *32,* 951–955.

Latané, B. The psychology of social impact. *American Psychologist,* 1981, *36,* 343–356.

LeVine, R. A., & Campbell, D. T. *Ethnocentrism: Theories of conflict, attitudes and group behavior.* New York: Wiley, 1972.

Lewin, K. *A dynamic theory of personality.* New York: McGraw-Hill, 1935.

Lewin, K. *Field theory in social science.* New York: Harper & Row, 1951.

Linville, P. W., & Jones, E. E. Polarized appraisals of outgroup members. *Journal of Personality and Social Psychology,* 1980, *38* (5), 689–703.

Lockhead, M. E., & Hall, K. P. Conceptualizing sex as a status characteristic: Applications to leadership training strategies. *Journal of Social Issues,* 1976, *32,* 111–124.

Locksley, A., Ortiz, V., & Hepburn, C. Social categorization and discriminatory behavior: Extinguishing the minimal intergroup discrimination effect. *Journal of Personality and Social Psychology,* 1980, *39,* 773–783.

Lomov, B. F. Mental process and communication. In L. H. Strickland (Ed.), *Soviet and western perspectives in social psychology.* New York: Pergamon Press, 1979.

MacNeil, M. K., & Sherif, M. Norm change over subject generations as a function of arbitrariness of prescribed norms. *Journal of Personality and Social Psychology,* 1976, *34,* 762–773.

Markus, H. Self-schemata and processing information about the self. *Journal of Personality and Social Psychology,* 1977, *35,* 63–75.

Markus, H. The self in thought and memory. In D. M. Wegner & R. R. Vallacher (Eds.), *The self in social psychology.* New York: Oxford University Press, 1980.

McCauley, C., Stitt, C. L., & Segal, M. Stereotyping: From prejudice to prediction. *Psychological Bulletin,* 1980, *87,* 195–208.

Merton, R. K. The self-fulfilling prophecy. *Antioch Review,* 1948, *8,* 193–210.

Milgram, S., & Jodelet, D. Psychological maps of Paris. In H. Proshansky, W. Ittelson, & L. Rivlin (Eds.), *Environmental psychology* (2nd ed.). New York: Holt, Rinehart & Winston, 1976.

Monson, T. C., & Snyder, M. Actors, observers, and the attribution process. *Journal of Experimental Social Psychology,* 1977, *13,* 89–111.

Moscovici, S. Society and theory in social psychology. In J. Israel & H. Tajfel (Eds.), *The context of social psychology: A critical assessment.* New York: Academic Press, 1972.

Moscovici, S., & Faucheux, C. Social influence, conformity bias and the study of active minorities. In L. Berkowitz (Ed.), *Advances in experimental social psychology* (Vol. 7). New York: Academic Press, 1972.

Moscovici, S., & Nemeth, C. Social influence II: Minority influence. In C. Nemeth (Ed.), *Social psychology: Classic and contemporary integrations.* Chicago: Rand McNally, 1974.

Myers, M. A. Social contexts and attributions of criminal responsibility. *Social Psychology Quarterly,* 1980, *43,* 405–419.

Nemeth, C. The role of an active minority in intergroup relations. In W. G. Austin & S. Worchel (Eds.), *The social psychology of intergroup relations.* Monterey, Calif.: Brooks/Cole, 1979.

Nemeth, C., Endicott, J., & Wachtler, J. From the '50's to the '70's: Women in jury decisions. *Sociometry,* 1976, *39,* 293–304.

Nisbett, R. E., & Wilson, T. D. Telling more than we can know: Verbal reports on mental processes. *Psychological Review,* 1977, *84,* 231–259.

Noller, P. Misunderstandings in marital communication: A study of couples' nonverbal communication. *Journal of Personality and Social Psychology,* 1980, *39,* 1135–1148.

Pepitone, A. Toward a normative and comparative social psychology. *Journal of Personality and Social Psychology,* 1976, *34,* 641–653.

Peplau, L. A. Power in dating relationships. In J. Freeman (Ed.), *Women: A feminist perspective* (2nd ed.). Palo Alto, Calif.: Mayfield, 1979.

Peplau, L. A. Women and men in love: Sex differences in close relationships. In V. E. O'Leary, R. K. Unger, & B. S. Wallston (Eds.), *Women, gender and social psychology.* Hillsdale, N.J.: Erlbaum (in press).

Pettigrew, T. F. Extending the stereotype concept. In D. Hamilton (Ed.), *Cognitive processes in stereotyping in intergroup relations.* Hillsdale, N.J.: Erlbaum, 1981.

Petty, R. F., & Cacioppo, J. *Attitudes and persuasion: Classic and contemporary approaches.* Dubuque, Iowa: Wm. C. Brown, 1981.

Rands, M., & Levinger, G. Implicit theories of relationship: An intergenerational study. *Journal of Personality and Social Psychology,* 1979, *37,* 645–661.

Riley, R. T., & Pettigrew, T. F. Dramatic events and attitude change. *Journal of Personality and Social Psychology,* 1976, *34,* 1004–1015.

Ring, K. Experimental social psychology: Some sober questions about some frivolous values. *Journal of Experimental and Social Psychology,* 1967, *3,* 113–123.

Riordan, C., & Ruggiero, J. Producing equal-status interracial interaction: A replication. *Social Psychology Quarterly,* 1980, *43* (1), 131–136.

Rodin, J., & Langer, E. Long-term effects of a control-relevant intervention with the institutionalized aged. *Journal of Personality and Social Psychology,* 1977, *35,* 897–902.

Rosenbaum, M. E., Moore, D. L., Cotton, J. L., Cook, M. S., Hieser, R. A., Shovar, M. N., & Gray, M. J. Group productivity and process: Pure and mixed reward structures and task interdependence. *Journal of Personality and Social Psychology,* 1980, *39,* 626–642.

Rosenthal, R., & Rubin, D. B. Interpersonal expectancy effects: The first 345 studies. *The Behavioral and Brain Sciences,* 1978, *3,* 377–415.

Ross, L. D. The intuitive psychologist and his shortcomings: Distortions in the attribution process. In L. Berkowitz (Ed.), *Cognitive theories in social psychology.* New York: Academic Press, 1978.

Ross, L. D., Amabile, T. M., & Steinmetz, J. L. Social roles, social control, and biases in social perception process. *Journal of Personality and Social Psychology,* 1977, *35,* 485–494.

Rubin, J. Z. Experimental research on third-party intervention in conflict: Toward some generalizations. *Psychological Bulletin,* 1980, *87,* 379–391.

Sampson, E. E. Scientific paradigms and social values: Wanted—A scientific revolution. *Journal of Personality and Social Psychology,* 1978, *36,* 1332–1343.

Sampson, E. E. Cognitive psychology as ideology. *American Psychologist,* 1981, *36,* 730–743.

Schank, R. C., & Abelson, R. P. *Scripts, plans, goals, and understanding.* Hillsdale, N.J.: Erlbaum, 1977.

Scheier, M. F., & Carver, C. S. Private and public self-attention, resistance to change and dissonance reduction. *Journal of Personality and Social Psychology,* 1980, *39* (3), 390–405.

Schneider, D. J., Hastorf, A. H., & Ellsworth, P. C. *Person perception.* Reading, Mass.: Addison-Wesley, 1979.

Schofield, J. W. The impact of positively structured contract on intergroup behavior: Does it last under adverse conditions? *Social Psychology Quarterly*, 1979, *42*, 280–284.

Schofield, J. W., & Sagar, H. A. Peer interaction patterns in an integrated middle school. *Sociometry*, 1977, *40*, 130–138.

Sears, D. O., Hensler, C. P., & Speer, L. K. Whites' opposition to "bussing": Self-interest or symbolic politics? *American Political Science Review*, 1979, *73*, 369–384.

Sells, S. B. (Ed.). *Stimulus determinants of behavior*. New York: Ronald Press, 1963.

Serbin, L. A., & O'Leary, K. D. How nursery schools teach girls to shut up. *Psychology Today*, 1975, *9*, 56–58 ff.

Shaffer, L. S. On the current confusion of group-related behavior and collective behavior: A reaction to Buys. *Personality and Social Psychology Bulletin*, 1978, *4*, 564–567.

Shaver, K. G. *An introduction to attribution processes*. Cambridge, Mass.: Winthrop, 1975.

Shaver, K. G. *Principles of social psychology*. Cambridge, Mass.: Winthrop, 1977.

Shaw, M. E., & Costanzo, P. R. *Theories of social psychology* (2nd ed.). New York: McGraw-Hill, 1982.

Sherif, C. W. *Orientation in social psychology*. New York: Harper & Row, 1976.

Sherif, C. W. Social values, attitudes, and involvement of the self. In H. E. Howe, Jr., & M. M. Page (Eds.), *Beliefs, attitudes and values*. Nebraska Symposium on Motivation, 1979. Lincoln: University of Nebraska Press, 1980.

Sherif, C. W., Sherif, M., & Nebergall, R. E. *Attitudes and attitude change: The social judgment-involvement approach*. Philadelphia: W. B. Saunders, 1965.

Sherif, M. *The psychology of social norms*. New York: Harper, 1936.

Sherif, M. On the relevance of social psychology. *American Psychologist*, 1970, *25*, 144–158.

Sherif, M. Crisis in social psychology: Some remarks towards breaking through the crisis. *Personality and Social Psychology Bulletin*, 1977, *3*, 368–382.

Sherif, M., Harvey, O. J., White, B. J., Hood, W. R., & Sherif, C. W. *Intergroup conflict and cooperation: The Robbers' Cave experiment*. Norman, Oklahoma: Institute of Group Relations, 1961.

Sherif, M., & Hovland, C. I. *Social judgment: Assimilation and contrast effects in communication and attitude change*. New Haven: Yale University Press, 1961.

Sherif, M., & Sherif, C. W. *Groups in harmony and tension*. New York: Harper & Row, 1953.

Sherif, M., & Sherif, C. W. *An outline of social psychology*. New York: Harper & Row, 1956.

Sherif, M., & Sherif, C. W. *Reference groups: Exploration into conformity and deviation of adolescents*. New York: Harper & Row, 1964.

Sherif, M., & Sherif, C. W. *Social psychology*. New York: Harper & Row, 1969.

Shotland, R. L., & Straw, M. K. Bystander response to an assault: When a man attacks a woman. *Journal of Personality and Social Psychology*, 1976, *34*, 990–999.

Smetana, J. G., & Adler, N. E. Fishbein's value x expectancy model: An examination of some assumptions. *Personality and Social Psychology Bulletin*, 1980, *6*, 89–96.

Smith, M. B. Social psychology, science and history: So what? *Personality and Social Psychology Bulletin*, 1976, *2*, 438–444.

Smith, M. B. Attitudes, values and selfhood. In H. E. Howe, Jr. & M. M. Page (Eds.), *Beliefs, attitudes and values*. Nebraska Symposium, 1979. Lincoln: University of Nebraska Press, 1980.

Smith, S. S., & Jamieson, B. D. Effects of attitude and ego-involvement on the learning and retention of controversial material. *Journal of Personality and Social Psychology*, 1972, *22*, 303–310.

Snyder, M., & Swann, W. B. Behavioral confirmation in social interaction: From social perception to social reality. *Journal of Experimental Social Psychology,* 1978, *14,* 148–162.

Snyder, M., Tanke, E. D., & Berscheid, E. Social perception and interpersonal behavior: On the self-fulfilling nature of social stereotypes. *Journal of Personality and Social Psychology,* 1977, *35,* 656–666.

Sohn, D. Critique of Cooper's meta-analytic assessment of the findings on sex differences in conformity behavior. *Journal of Personality and Social Psychology,* 1980, *39* (6), 1215–1221.

Sommer, R., & Olsen, H. The soft classroom. *Environment and Behavior,* 1980, *12,* 3–16.

Spiro, R. J., & Sherif, C. W. Consistency and relativity in selective recall with differing ego-involvement. *British Journal of Social and Clinical Psychology,* 1975, *14,* 351–361.

Steiner, I. Whatever happened to the group in social psychology? *Journal of Experimental Social Psychology,* 1974, *10,* 94–108.

Stephan, W. G. School desegregation: An evaluation of predictions made in *Brown vs. Board of Education. Psychological Bulletin,* 1978, *85,* 217–238.

Stokols, D. The environmental context of behavior and well-being. In D. Perlman & P. Cozby (Eds.), *Social psychology: SPSSI's perspective.* New York: Holt, Rinehart & Winston, 1981.

Stroebe, W. The critical school in German social psychology. *Personality and Social Psychology Bulletin,* 1980, *6* (1), 105–111.

Sumner, W. G. *Folkways.* New York: Ginn, 1906.

Tajfel, H. Experiments on intergroup discrimination. *Scientific American,* 1970, *223,* 96–102.

Tajfel, H. Experiments in a vacuum. In J. Israel & H. Tajfel (Eds.), *The context of social psychology: A critical assessment.* New York: Academic Press, 1972.

Tajfel, H. Individuals and groups in social psychology. *British Journal of Social and Clinical Psychology,* 1979, *18,* 182–189.

Tajfel, H., & Turner, J. An integrative theory of intergroup conflict. In W. G. Austin & S. Worchel (Eds.), *The social psychology of intergroup relations.* Monterey, Calif.: Brooks/Cole, 1979.

Taylor, D. G., Sheatsley, P. B., & Greeley, A. M. Attitudes toward racial integration. *Scientific American,* 1978, *238,* 42–49.

Taylor, D. M., & Brown, R. J. Towards a more social social psychology? *British Journal of Social and Clinical Psychology,* 1979, *18,* 173–180.

Taylor, M. Race and sex of experimenter in self-fulfilling prophecies in a laboratory training situation. *Journal of Personality and Social Psychology,* 1979, *37,* 897–912.

Taylor, S. E. Salience, attention and attribution: Top of the head phenomena. In L. Berkowitz (Ed.), *Advances in experimental social psychology* (Vol. 11). New York: Academic Press, 1978.

Taylor, S. E. A categorization approach to stereotyping. In D. L. Hamilton (Ed.), *Cognitive processes in stereotyping and intergroup relations.* Hillsdale, N.J.: Erlbaum, 1981.

Taylor, S. E., Fiske, S. T., Etcoff, N. L., & Ruderman, A. J. Categorical and contextual bases of person memory and stereotyping. *Journal of Personality and Social Psychology,* 1978, *36,* 778–793.

Thornton, A., & Freedman, D. Changes in the sex role attitudes of women, 1962–1977: Evidence from a panel study. *American Sociological Review,* 1979, *44,* 831–842.

Toder, N. L. The effect of sexual composition of a group on discrimination against women and sex-role attitudes. *Psychology of Women Quarterly,* 1980, *5* (2), 292–310.

Triandis, H. C. Social psychology and cultural analysis. *Journal of the Theory of Social Behavior,* 1975, *5,* 81–106.

Triandis, H. C. (Ed.). *Handbook of cross-cultural psychology* (Vols. 1–6). Boston: Allyn & Bacon, 1980.

Triandis, H. C., & Brislin, R. W. (Eds.). *Social psychology.* In H. C. Triandis (Ed.), *Handbook of cross-cultural psychology* (Vol. 5). Boston: Allyn & Bacon, 1980.

Vaughan, G. M., Tajfel, H., & Williams, G. Bias in reward allocations in an intergroup and an interpersonal context. *Social Psychology Quarterly,* 1981, *44,* 37–42.

Wack, J., & Rodin, J. Nursing homes for the aged: The human consequences of legislation-shaped events. *Journal of Social Issues,* 1978, *34,* 6–21.

Wallston, B. S., Foster, M. A., & Berger, M. I will follow him: Myth, reality, or forced choice—Job-seeking experiences of dual-career couples. *Psychology of Women Quarterly,* 1978, *3,* 9–21.

Wallston, B. S., & O'Leary, V. E. Sex makes a difference: Differential perceptions of women and men. In L. Wheeler (Ed.), *Review of personality and social psychology* (Vol. 2). Beverly Hills, Calif.: Sage, 1981.

Webster, M., & Driskeel, J. Status generalization: A review and some new data. *American Sociological Review,* 1978, *43,* 220–236.

Wegner, D. M., & Vallacher, R. R. (Eds.). *The self in social psychology.* New York: Oxford University Press, 1980.

Weigel, R. H., & Cook, S. W. Participation in decision-making: A determinant of interpersonal attraction in cooperating interracial groups. *International Journal of Group Tensions,* 1975, *5,* 179–195.

Weigel, R. H., Wiser, P. L., & Cook, S. W. The impact of cooperative learning experiences on cross-ethnic relations and attitudes. *Journal of Social Issues,* 1975, *31,* 219–244.

Weigel, R. H., Loomis, J. W., & Soja, M. J. Race relations in prime time television. *Journal of Personality and Social Psychology,* 1980, *39,* 884–893.

Widmeyer, W. N., & Martens, R. When cohesion predicts performance outcome in sport. *Research Quarterly,* 1978, *49,* 372–380.

Wicklund, R. A., & Frey, D. Self-awareness theory: When the self makes a difference. In D. M. Wegner & R. R. Vallacher (Eds.), *The self in social psychology.* New York: Oxford University Press, 1980.

Wilder, D. A., & Thompson, J. E. Intergroup contact with independent manipulations of in-group and out-group interaction. *Journal of Personality and Social Psychology,* 1980, *38,* 589–603.

Wong, P. T. P., & Weiner, B. When people ask "why" questions and the heuristics of attributional search. *Journal of Personality and Social Psychology,* 1981, *40,* 650–663.

Worchel, S. Cooperation and the reduction of intergroup conflict: Some determining factors. In W. G. Austin & S. Worchel (Eds.), *The social psychology of intergroup relations.* Monterey, Calif.: Brooks/Cole, 1979.

Worchel, S., & Norvell, N. Effect of perceived environmental conditions during cooperation on intergroup attraction. *Journal of Personality and Social Psychology,* 1980, *38* (5), 764–772.

Word, C. O., Zanna, M. P., & Cooper, J. The nonverbal mediation of self-fulfilling prophecies in interracial interaction. *Journal of Experimental Social Psychology,* 1974, *10,* 109–120.

Zajonc, R. B. Feeling and thinking. Preferences need no inferences. *American Psychologist,* 1980, *35,* 151–175.

Zanna, M. P., & Pack, S. J. On the self-fulfilling nature of apparent sex differences in behavior. *Journal of Experimental Social Psychology,* 1975, *11,* 583–591.

Zimbardo, P. G., Haney, C., Banks, W. C., & Jaffe, D. The psychology of imprisonment: Privation, power and pathology. In J. C. Brigham & L. S. Wrightsman (Eds.), *Contemporary issues in social psychology* (3rd ed.). Monterey, Calif.: Brooks/Cole, 1977.

Zucker, L. G. The role of institutionalization in cultural persistence. *American Sociological Review,* 1977, *42,* 726–743.

LEE S. SHULMAN

EDUCATIONAL PSYCHOLOGY RETURNS TO SCHOOL

L ee S. Shulman is Professor of Education and Affiliate of Psychology at Stanford University. At the time of this address, he was Professor of Educational Psychology and Medical Education and Co-Director of the Institute for Research on Teaching at Michigan State University, where he had been a member of the faculty since 1963. He holds bachelor's, master's, and doctoral degrees from the University of Chicago.

Dr. Shulman has done extensive research on the problem-solving patterns of teachers and physicians and has written on the psychology of instruction in mathematics, science, and medicine. His publications include *Medical Problem Solving: The Analysis of Clinical Reasoning* (Harvard University Press, 1978; with Elstein and Sprafka) and the *Handbook of Teaching and Policy* (Longman, in press; with Sykes). His publications have appeared in the *Handbook of Research on Teaching*, the *Review of Educational Research*, the *Journal of Medical Education*, *Child Development*, and the *Review of Research in Education*. He served as editor of the *Review of Research in Education* from 1976 to 1978.

Dr. Shulman is an APA Fellow (Division 15) and has been a Guggenheim Fellow and a Fellow of the Center for Advanced Study in the Behavioral Sciences. He was elected to the National Academy of Education in 1979.

LEE S. SHULMAN

EDUCATIONAL PSYCHOLOGY RETURNS TO SCHOOL

My purpose in this lecture is to provide an overview, moderately critical and occasionally integrated, of much of contemporary educational psychology. The scope of educational psychology is vast, extending from research on classroom motivation to studies of cognitive and social development, from behavior modification for classroom management to the cognitive psychology of school subjects, from basic research in support of theory development to applied studies in the service of practical problem solving. I have made no attempt to review this entire field of study. Certainly another reviewer would have made other choices, both of breadth and of emphasis. The reader should thus beware that this paper is consciously selective and limited; there is much important educational psychology omitted from its pages. That omission is neither an evaluation of the quality of the work nor a commentary on its importance to the field.

Educational psychology is not a single coherent field. It is a set of loosely related topics, problems, issues, and investigations. All of these elements share a concern for learning and teaching, but they have emerged from divergent corners of psychology, from other social sciences, and from the controversies and challenges of educational practice. To provide an adequate description of educational psychology, I will ask what are its topics, its questions, and its persistent dilemmas. More specifically, what are the stories of the inquiries educational psychology pursues and of the findings it values?

In order to appreciate the special character of contemporary educational psychology, one must understand this field from the perspective of its recent past. The changes that have overcome educational psychology have been dramatic. During the past two decades, when many of us were trained, theories of learning were ostensibly the psychological basis for education. But what form did those theories take? On what sorts of evidence were they grounded? They were typically based on research with rats, monkeys, pigeons, and human beings engaged in tasks that demanded such complex performances as eye blink conditioning, the learning of paired associates with nonsense syllables, and the attainment of concepts represented as abstract figures. The inferential bridge between that psychology and the problems of education would make the Golden Gate look like a modest covered bridge over a country creek. Studies of teachers were practically nonexistent, and nearly all that were available were studies of teacher traits or characteristics. The Piagetians were growing in influence among educational scholars, but they seemed obsessed with the timing and trainability of conservation, an accomplishment that bore little resemblance to anything found in classrooms. And when anyone did make reference to schools or teachers, it was typically to assert that neither made any difference in the achievement of students. The problems, topics, and issues of educational psychology were remarkably remote from the world of education.

These conditions have now changed. Educational psychology has returned to its roots in the psychology of school subjects, a tradition initiated in the early efforts of John Dewey, E. L. Thorndike, and Charles Judd. The pioneer in our profession, G. Stanley Hall (after whom these lectures are named), also saw education as a central focus for the emerging field of psychology. It was no coincidence that his first journal, one of the earliest in our field, was named *The Pedagogical Seminary.* Unquestionably, education and schools, rather than clinical psychology and psychopathology, originally constituted the applied field of psychology. Perhaps only the genius and charisma of Freud and the seductiveness of the medical model made clinical psychology as central to our discipline as it is now.

School subjects, curricula, classrooms, teaching, and schools are once again at the heart of investigations in educational psychology. A renascence of the psychology of school subjects is occurring in the work of contemporary cognitive scientists who are enriching and even supplanting Piaget's general theory of intellectual development with more school- and subject-specific cognitive models. Direct investigations of classroom teaching and learning, including both the cognitive and motivational processes, of participants are being pursued. In such research, the boundaries among psychological, sociological, and anthropological inquiries are eroding, thus providing frequent glimpses of the emerging domain of educational social/behavioral science.

Therefore, I will here discuss the return of educational psychology to both classroom and school. It is a dual return—to the main streets of education and to the mainstreams of psychology. Ironically, even when the learning of school subjects was central to psychology, rarely did even educational psychologists venture inside the walls of classrooms. The contemporary contextualization of educational psychology is thus an important innovation, not merely a return to earlier wisdom.

Educational Psychology: A Topography

If I am to organize my discussion of educational psychology in terms of its major topics, then beginning with an examination of its topography is appropriate. A topic is a place, a location for discourse. The topography of educational psychology should be understood not only in terms of its internal organization but also with reference to its location in relation to the rest of psychology and, equally important, to its neighboring fields. Topics are places—commonplaces. This lecture will therefore bear some resemblance to a tour of the topics of educational psychology.

Educational Psychology is a border province. It lies on the periphery of the nation of Psychology, and its character reflects all the virtues and liabilities of border provinces elsewhere. Educational Psychology shares a longer border with the adjoining nation of Education—a loose confederation of often warring, rarely cooperative states, much like pre-Bismarck Germany—than with our own country of Psychology. In fact, over the years there have been frequent disagreements over which of the two countries Educational Psychology is properly a part.

Like dwellers in border provinces elsewhere, educational psychologists are required to speak the languages of both countries. Ignorance of either language would risk problems in conducting that commerce which is the very heart of the economy of a border province. Inevitably, the speech community of the border state develops its own dialect which incorporates features of each of the major languages. Nevertheless, the speakers of the language of Education continue to regard those who use Educational Psychology as speakers of a weird and technical jargon unsuited to the practical enterprise of education, while those fluent in Psychology find the hybrid dialect corrupt and inelegant.

The inhabitants of Educational Psychology are typical border provincials. Because commerce is a major enterprise, the inhabitants of their realm are not only citizens of Psychology and Education but also a mixed multitude of stateless persons from the neighboring nations of Sociology, Anthropology, Linguistics, Computer Science, Statistics, and even the remote and mysterious Teacher Education. This array contributes even further to the polyglot character of the language community and to the uncertain identities of the citizens. In fact, many of the citizens are themselves recent immigrants attracted by the bright lights and promise of the promised land of Psychology but hardly integrated into its social structure. Thus, on one hand, the border provincials tend to be marginal, of low prestige, and continually asking, "Who am I?" On the other hand, they are also likely to be receptive to new ideas from adjoining lands and to serve as sources of innovation and change for the larger nation. They are insecure and yet, paradoxically, have little to lose. Ironically, because of the contrasting economic and social status of Education and Psychology, those citizens of lowest prestige in Psychology become the holders of highest social rank when they venture into Education.

This tour of the current state of Educational Psychology will be a topical one. I will visit major places but make no attempt to visit all. Moreover, no attempt will be made to incorporate the many facets of the field into a single theoretical framework because no such scheme exists. Nevertheless, when useful connections among the topics can be made, I will take the opportunity.

A field is defined, in large measure, by the research sites deemed strategic (Merton, 1957) or the research programs either pursued or declared moribund (Lakatos, 1970). What are these strategic research sites or research programs for the psychology of education? The sites we shall visit are

1. The psychology of school subjects
2. Studies of ability and intelligence
3. The psychology of classroom teaching and learning
4. The psychology of pupil responses to teaching
5. The psychology and psychoethnography of classroom tasks and settings.

Before embarking on this tour, however, I offer some general observations about the history of relations between psychology and education.

Stories of Research

To be most effective, an introductory psychology course should have stories to tell, stories that will capture the attention of students and render concrete the abstract concepts and principles on which a course places its emphasis. In the same fashion, this lecture will be populated with such stories, both to hold the attention of its audience and to exemplify that very principle of instruction. It is no accident that many of us in educational research have come to develop a new and more complex conception of how research ideas come to influence the behavior of educational practitioners. While we may still believe that particular findings of research can often be translated into specific prescriptions for pedagogical practice, more often we have come to understand that research influences and shapes the prevailing views of practitioners, whether policymakers or pedagogues. These views or climates of opinion, in A. N. Whitehead's (1925) preferred phrase, can sometimes be shaped by the systematic presentation of carefully organized scientific evidence. But, even more frequently, prevailing views are shaped by vivid narratives, stories which convey an image of the educational enterprise and thus help participants in the enterprise make better sense of the world in which they live. At its best, the image also contributes to an enlightened form of common sense.

The psychologist after whom these lectures are named,

G. Stanley Hall, was the center of a bitter and long-term controversy regarding the relative merits of "science" and "commonsense" in the development of the child-study movement and the "new educational psychology." Hall was seen as too eager to involve teachers and parents in the collective interpretation of data, in the creation of a commonsense psychology. The scientistic proponents, exemplified by H. Münsterburg and E. L. Thorndike, argued that such a commonsense approach diminished the new science, although Thorndike was infected with substantial ambivalence in this matter. As Hall passed from center stage in the educational psychology controversies, he was replaced by C. H. Judd as Thorndike's major antagonist.

In his most virulent attack on Hall, Münsterburg (1899, cited in Ross, 1972, pp. 341–342) stated:

> Progress in our science has depended upon the most laborious, patient work of our laboratories and the most subtle and refined methods, and . . . all this seductive but rude and untrained and untechnical gathering of cheap and vulgar material means a caricature and not an improvement of psychology.

At an early stage in his career, Thorndike (1898, cited in Ross, 1972, p. 346) defended Hall and the child-study movement against Münsterburg's onslaughts.

> Everyone, even in normal schools and child study societies [must] go ahead making judgments about mental facts. . . . [V]ery poor psychology it may be . . . but they can do work as good for the purposes of mental science as much of the work of naturalists has been for biology. . . . [A]ny attempt to improve the judgments of common sense about any sort of facts may prove fruitful.

Nevertheless, in the preface to the first edition of his *Educational Psychology,* Thorndike (1903, cited in Grinder, 1981, p. 356) expressed reservations in the spirit of Münsterburg regarding the proper foundations for a psychology of education.

> This book attempts to apply to a number of educational problems the methods of exact science. I have therefore paid no attention to speculative opinions and very little attention to the conclusions of students who present data in so rough and incomplete a form that accurate and quantitative treatment is impossible.

Twelve years later, Thorndike's continuing antagonist, Charles Judd, echoed the older child-study philosophy of Hall.

> If teachers could be induced to begin systematic observation in their special lines and report their findings, the science of educational psychology would flourish. (Judd, 1915, cited in Grinder, 1981, p. 363)

He also observed that such an approach might reduce

> an acrimonious dispute that has been carried on in some quarters between practical school people and the so-called scientific experts. . . . [M]any a teacher is alienated and refuses to become party to the scientific study of education because he does not sympathize with the expert's demand for rigid, scientific exactness. (Judd, 1915, cited in Grinder, 1981, p. 363)

This concern reflected by Judd about the value placed on research by educational practitioners highlights a continuing dilemma among members of this border state. The persistent struggle between the inclination to study with precision almost anything that will stay put and the improbable dream of becoming smarter about the broad central questions of human existence is perhaps best captured in William James's observations more than ninety years ago regarding the contemporaneous work of the German experimental psychologists of sensation.

> Within a few years what one may call a microscopic psychology has arisen in Germany, carried on by experimental methods, asking of course every moment for introspective data, but eliminating their uncertainty by operating on a large scale and taking statistical means. This method taxes patience to the utmost, and hardly could have arisen in a country whose natives could be *bored.* Such Germans as Weber, Fechner, Vierordt and Wundt obviously cannot; and their success has brought into the field an array of younger experimental psychologists, bent on studying the *elements* of the mental life, dissecting them from the gross results in which they are embedded, and as far as possible reducing them to quantitative scales. The simple and open method of attack having done what it can, the method of patience, starving out, and harassing to death is tried; the Mind must submit to a regular *siege,* in which minute advantages gained night and day by the forces that hem her in must sum themselves up at last into her

overthrow. There is little left of the grand style about these new prism, pendulum, and chronograph-philosophers. They mean business, not chivalry. What generous divination, and that superiority in virtue which was thought by Cicero to give a man the best insight into nature, have failed to do, their spying and scraping, their deadly tenacity and almost diabolic cunning, will doubtless some day bring about. (James, 1890, I, pp. 192 ff.)

His observations regarding Fechner and psychophysics are perhaps equally well known:

> But it would be terrible if even such a dear old man could saddle our Science forever with his patient whimsies, and, in a world so full of more nutritious objects of attention, compel all future students to plough through the difficulties, not only of his own works, but of the still drier ones written in his refutation. (James, 1890, I, p. 549)

While we are not here to reminisce about the ancient past of our discipline, these are not irrelevant concerns for educational psychologists. Educational psychologists must not only satisfy the canons of inquiry of their disciplinary home, but they must also work until the fruits of those scientific labors have been successfully incorporated into the lives of the educators who dwell alongside. The work, which is couched in terms terribly remote from the lives and concerns of educators, may never achieve application. Moreover, terminology aside, studying what really matters is important if it matters that one's studies matter. A modern dilemma for psychology is to find a way to rediscover or invent the commonsense psychology necessary to inform practical action yet not to dismiss the important role of disciplined inquiry. As we shall see, to resolve this dilemma is a continuing challenge for those of us in educational psychology.

It is, therefore, no accident that both information-processing psychology and many aspects of anthropology have recently taken hold in the work of educational psychologists. Both fields place great emphasis upon the importance of coming to understand the world as the subject of our research sees it. For the information-processing psychologist, the emphasis is upon understanding the manner in which the task environment of the subject is transformed into a problem space, a framework or scaffolding within which the problem-as-presented becomes the problem-as-addressed. For the more sociologically or anthropologically inclined, the focus is on the definition of the situation, the manner in which participants in a social situation define its essential elements, its figure, and its ground. As we shall see in the comments that follow, these perspectives are quite central to the emerging educational psychology.

Studies of Learning and Problem Solving: Psychology of School Subjects

Educational psychology traditionally begins with school learning, where some of the most exciting recent research has transpired. It is unclear whether instructional psychology has expanded to incorporate cognitive science, whether cognitive science in its rapid development has swallowed up instructional psychology or perhaps has given birth to a new psychology of instruction and learning, or whether these two multinational corporations have simply merged. But the coalescence of the two fields has been remarkable. And in this marriage, the birth of a psychology of school subjects has been the most exciting occurrence. Resnick has well expressed the excitement in the introduction to her recent review of the research in instructional psychology (Resnick, 1981):

> An interesting thing has happened to instructional psychology. It has become part of the mainstream of research on human cognition, learning and development. . . . Instructional psychology is no longer basic psychology *applied* to education. It is fundamental research on the processes of instruction and learning. (p. 660)

Resnick identifies three major trends in cognitive psychology of particular relevance to instructional psychology.

> First, there is a shift towards studying more and more complex forms of cognitive behavior. This means that many of the tasks and processes of interest to cognitive psychologists are ones that can form part of a school's curriculum. Psychological work on such tasks is naturally relevant to instruction. Second . . . is a growing interest in the role of *knowledge* in human behavior. Much effort is now directed at finding ways to represent the structure of knowledge and at discovering the ways in which

knowledge is used in various kinds of learning. . . . Finally, to-day's assumptions about the nature of learning and thinking are interactionist. We assume that learning occurs as a result of mental constructions of the learner. These constructions respond to information and stimuli in the environment, but they do not copy or mirror them. This means that instruction must be designed not to put knowledge into learners' heads but to put learners in positions that allow them to construct well-structured knowledge. (p. 660)

Resnick organizes her review of the field of instructional psychology around these three attributes of recent work in the field. Her emphasis on the increased complexity, and thus relevance to schooling, of the tasks employed in the study of human cognition is very important. A number of things have stimulated the change. Among them has been the recognition that the ostensibly simple elementary processes have turned out to be as complex and as difficult to study as are those more relevant to schooling. Moreover, cognitive psychologists have come to appreciate how domain and subject specific is most learning and problem solving. As long as so much of the psychology of learning and cognition is domain specific, thus reducing the likelihood of broad generalizability, and as long as simple processes turn out upon inspection to be just as involved as seemingly more complex ones, one might as well study areas of obvious usefulness, such as reading, mathematics, or science. This has meant that, by and large, educational psychologists need to strain somewhat less to make inferences between the experimental tasks of cognitive psychology and the curricular tasks of education. The tasks are frequently the same.

Resnick also has emphasized the new importance placed on the role of knowledge as an attribute of the human learner and problem solver. No longer is the empty organism the starting point for our experiments. Instead of inventing experimental tasks so remote from the likely experiences of subjects that individual differences in their knowledge and experience can be effectively ignored as potential influences on their behavior, cognitive psychologists now have begun to emphasize the careful representation of those forms of preexisting knowledge and their influence on the manner in which problems are solved or bungled.

The third feature of the new cognitive psychology is its interactionist perspective, which posits active learners who not only respond to their environment but also act upon, transform, and shape it.

Moreover, not only do these active learners transform their setting, they also are capable of being self-conscious about the methods and strategies they employ in that endeavor. The extent to which that self-consciousness occurs is an important aspect of the ability to learn and to solve problems. As we shall see, this interactionist perspective has important implications for our understanding of teaching and learning in classrooms.

In general, consistent with the traditions of information processing psychology, these investigations study and attempt to document how experts in the solving of particular problems go about their work. Expertise is defined in the broadest sense, ranging from that of first graders who have become expert in subtraction to experienced physicians who have become expert in diagnosis. Distinctions between experts and novices has become a topic of great educational significance. Once those attributes distinguishing experts from novices are clearly identified and understood, then the objectives of instruction in those areas can be more explicitly defined and pursued.

Several examples may serve to characterize the current research in this field. Beginning approximately ten years ago, Resnick, Groen, and their associates at Pittsburgh's Learning Research and Development Center (e.g., Groen & Parkman, 1972) began the study of how young children learn the computational algorithms of elementary arithmetic. They studied children who were able to perform elementary addition and subtraction and developed models which accounted for the processes the children employed in those activities. One of the most exciting findings from these studies was the demonstration that pupils did not merely learn what they were taught. Indeed, they could be counted upon to transform what they had been taught into new algorithms when needed (Groen & Resnick, 1977). In particular, Resnick observed that

> even when children are taught a simpler to learn (but less efficient to perform) procedure for addition, they are likely to invent the [more efficient] procedure for themselves after a number of weeks of practice. This is reminiscent of the process Krutetskii (1976) called "curtailment," in which children (especially the more mathematically able) develop short-cut procedures that are more efficient than the ones taught. (Resnick, 1981, pp. 675–676)

This example is from a growing body of studies demonstrating the active manner in which learners transform the contents of instruction into procedures that they can use more effectively.

Work in this field is paralleled by an enormous body of research on reading comprehension, in which the active organizing capacity of learners is central. Studies of reading comprehension are not only proving useful in our understanding of instruction in this critical domain, they are also serving as entry points for our understanding of "understanding" as a psychological process. In this manner, cognitive theories of understanding are becoming far more sophisticated, and appreciation of the factors which make a text more or less readable to a youngster is growing.

Davison (1981) presents the translation of such basic research into matters of immediate practical relevance to authors of reading series and teachers of reading. One of the continuing interests of reading specialists has been to establish the "readability" of instructional materials and to calibrate the difficulty level of textbooks to the grade level of students. To establish this calibration, readability indices have been devised. In general, the indices associate text difficulty with the length of words, the frequency of long words in written discourse, and the length of sentences. Thus efforts to make texts more readable generally have led to shortening words and sentences and to replacing less familiar words with more familiar ones.

Research at the University of Illinois Center for the Study of Reading has now demonstrated that such attempts to make materials more readable have frequently resulted in their becoming less so. Richard Anderson, director of the center, gives the example of a story, *The Elves and the Shoemaker,* which can be found in one basal reader. One begins to sense the difficulties engendered by the quest for readability when finding that this story contains neither the word "elf" nor the word "shoemaker." Simpler but less semantically appropriate words have been put in their place. The sentences for the story are quite short. But how does one take a fairly complex narrative and present it in short sentences?

The typical strategy is to break up longer sentences through removal of a variety of conjunctions or other connectives. The words most frequently deleted are "before," "after," "if," "then," "because," and the like. Thus those very words which provide cues to the reader regarding some of the most critical features for understanding a narrative—namely, matters of sequence and causation—are removed from the text in the interests of readability. Needless to say, studies have demonstrated that such editing increases rather than decreases the difficulty of comprehending the written text. Ironically, the pupils most seriously disadvantaged by these deletions are those whose entering abilities and schemata require the greatest dependence upon textual cues. Thus those students already more able can construct the missing cues for themselves while the less able are left to flounder. Anderson and his colleagues have already begun to meet with the publishers of major reading series to share the results of such research and, one hopes, to influence the manner in which future books are written.

This study is but one example of how research in educational psychology frequently documents that theory-based attempts to facilitate the acquisition of understanding occasionally produce results exactly the opposite of those intended.

Greeno (1977, 1980) has devoted several years to studies of geometry problem solving among high-school students. We all can recall the frustration of staring at a geometry theorem we have been assigned to prove, believing we know all that is needed and yet being stymied about where to begin and how to proceed. Greeno has identified the critically important cognitive strategies or executive routines which appear to distinguish the students who are capable of solving such problems from those students who are not. Here again, typical instruction has focused on elements of knowledge but has been inexplicit or silent about strategies of solution. Thus only those students who can invent the strategies of solution themselves or infer them from the unarticulated models of their instructors are able to acquire these skills successfully. Work in geometry as well as in physics problem solving has demonstrated that experts possess schemata or conceptual frames which allow them rapidly to classify the problems set before them into categories with which they have associated solution strategies. The less expert problem solver appears unable to perform these critical preliminary classification and planning steps.

It has been important not only to study expertise but also to understand *in*expertise. Students are capable not only of inventing correct approaches to solving problems which they have never been taught, they are equally adept at inventing consistently incorrect procedures. J. S. Brown and his collaborators (e.g., Brown & Van Lehn, 1981) have called those procedural errors "buggy algorithms" because of their similarity to "bugs" in computer programs.

The study of incorrectly invented procedures becomes more

complex and interesting when the setting for the research moves from the psychological laboratory to the typical school classroom. In the classroom, the social context changes the meaning of instructional tasks in significant ways. Students not only seek to solve the problem as presented, they also aspire to complete the task as assigned. That is, the problem now becomes embedded in the pedagogical and social context of an "assignment." Thus, to prefigure an idea that will be discussed in greater detail later, an important distinction one must learn to make as one looks at the relationship between the cognitive psychology of school subjects and the pedagogical psychology of school teaching and learning is between a problem-to-be-solved and an assignment-to-be-completed. These tasks are psychologically quite distinct, even if the specific exercise and its attendant solution are identical in both instances.

Only when such activities are studied in the context of classrooms observed over time can the cumulative effects of student invention be observed adequately. A particularly vivid example of this phenomenon is the case study of Benny, conducted by Stanley Erlwanger (1975) several years ago. Benny was a participant in an elementary school classroom in which mathematics was studied under an individualized curriculum, which is a type of instructional system widespread in America today. In such a system pupils move at their own pace. The individualized instruction is built around modular instructional units which begin with a diagnostic pretest, followed by self-instructional materials and concluded with a criterion referenced posttest. Each modular unit is fairly short and can be completed in a matter of a few days.

From the records of the classroom, Benny appeared to have been progressing nicely over the course of the year in his arithmetic program. Erlwanger began a series of rather intensive clinical interviews with Benny using arithmetic problems as the basis for their dialogue. He found that Benny had managed to pass through the units of instruction while developing an idiosyncratic and consistently erroneous set of principles of mathematical computation and understanding. While these erroneous principles somehow allowed him to "succeed" with unit after unit, they cumulated to a mathematically impossible understanding of the materials. How had this situation occurred? Apparently Benny had done whatever was needed to complete his assignments, but the strategies needed to accomplish that goal were not synonymous with those intended by the teacher or the constructors of the curriculum. Doyle (1977) has represented this distinction by reminding us of Becker's (Becker, Geer, & Hughes, 1968) definition of a classroom as a setting in which, in the manner of a marketplace, students exchange performance for grades. I will present another vivid example of this phenomenon when, later in this paper, I examine more specifically current studies of pupil responses to teaching.

The best story I can tell which exemplifies the critical role played by the knowledge and understanding brought to a problem situation by the problem solver comes from the work which Elstein, Sprafka, and I (Elstein, Shulman, & Sprafka, 1978) have conducted on the problem solving of specialists in internal medicine. This example will also move our tales of expertise from the third-grade classroom to the physician's office. When we began our studies of medical diagnosis more than 10 years ago, we were much influenced by the body of research in strategies of concept attainment active at that time. The pioneering efforts of Bruner, Goodnow, and Austin in *A Study of Thinking* (1956) had prepared us to examine the alternative strategies of information acquisition available to physicians in terms of the levels of cognitive strain which each engendered. It was clear from the literature of concept attainment that the most conservative information acquisition strategies, those dubbed "conservative focusing," placed the least cognitive strain on problem solvers; approaches which required the generation and simultaneous testing of multiple hypotheses had been clearly demonstrated to exceed the information processing capacities of the human problem-solver.

Thus it was with initial alarm and growing disbelief that we observed physician after physician consistently employ a strategy of medical diagnostic thinking in which the earliest stages involved the generation of multiple competing hypotheses. These multiple hypotheses were then held in memory simultaneously to serve as the intellectual scaffolding under which the medical history, physical examination, and laboratory testing were conducted. At first blush, at least in light of what was established psychological wisdom at the time, the physicians were doing the impossible. (Interestingly, our observations also flew in the face of established medical lore; but that story is for another setting.)

Only when the consistency of our data forced us to confront the clear contradiction between our finding and that of the experimental psychology of concept attainment were we able to comprehend the meaning of our results. Information-processing capacities and cognitive strain are a function of what is already in the head of the problem solver. The experimental tasks of classical concept attainment research were constructed in a manner that purposely rendered meaningless the knowledge and experience individuals brought to the psychological laboratory. They were constructed for that purpose and were successful in achieving it. Under conditions in which an individual possesses no prior knowledge regarding the organization and content of a problem domain, strategies of conservative focusing and their equivalents are preferred; however, when individuals are working in semantically rich domains where they possess high levels of knowledge and experience, simultaneous multiple hypothesis testing is not only possible, it is the only intelligent way to proceed. Thus the move from semantically poor to semantically rich problem solving requires not merely an increase in the complexity of the theoretical model; indeed, it requires a radically different set of principles.

Another important finding in the medical problem-solving studies was that there was very little transfer from problem solving in one domain of internal medicine to another. This work thus lent further support to findings in other areas of the psychology of school subjects confirming Thorndike's (1903) argument for specific transfer of training. Although the possibility remains that broad transfer of cognitive strategies or of higher order, metacognitive awareness or even of broad general conceptual schemes may yet be demonstrated, evidence for such claims remains currently weak.

These have been but a few examples of the currently exciting field of the cognitive psychology of school subjects. It is important to appreciate the overall image of learners conveyed by such research: active, inventive, transforming, knowledge-bearing, comprehending, and self-conscious. They not only actively engage in the processes of learning, they also are capable of thinking about what it means to be so engaged. And their capacity to be self-conscious about these processes appears to make them even more effective as they employ the processes.

A number of years ago, Elstein and I (Shulman & Elstein, 1975) suggested that a proper history of research in cognitive psychology could be represented in a Broadway musical titled *From Würzburg to*

Pittsburgh. The continued activity of this research in the University of Pittsburgh's Learning Research and Development Center and by the psychologists at Carnegie-Mellon University adds strength to that conviction.

Ability and Intelligence

We are witnessing renewed interest in the psychology of ability and intelligence. The roots of this body of work are distinctively educational, tracing back to the original commissioning of Binet's work by the schools of the city of Paris, passing through the important contributions of Terman and his associates at the Stanford University School of Education in the development of the individual intelligence test in America and including the work of Jensen based at the Berkeley School of Education.

There are at least three streams of work in this area on which I would comment. First, there are the contemporary approaches to a redefinition and reconceptualization of the components of ability in terms consistent with the cognitive psychology of information processing. Sternberg's (1977) componential analysis of intelligence is a good example of this effort. The current attempt to replace a psychometric definition of intelligence, the criteria of which are predominantly the degree to which measures can discriminate precisely among individuals and groups, with a process definition of intelligence, which attempts to be consistent with current conceptions of cognition, brings the domains of learning and intelligence much closer together. This body of work can be expected ultimately to have its effects on the design of tests of various kinds of ability.

Second, there are the more clearly pedagogical studies of aptitude-treatment interaction (ATI) stimulated both by Cronbach's (1957) quest for a rapprochement between correlational and experimental psychology and by the more practical search for effective means of designing instruction for all types of learners. This work was initiated, in large measure, from the frustration of educational researchers confronting the recurring finding of "no significant difference" in comparative instructional research, as reviewed by such scholars as Stephens (1967). How could it be possible that differences in instruction made no difference in what individuals learn? In principle, there had to be some methods of instruction that were superior to others. Finding consistently powerful main effects for instruction was difficult only because particular forms of instruction interacted with specific individual differences and thus masked the effects if these differences were not properly distinguished. This account not only seemed to make good psychological sense, it also corresponded closely to the pedagogical intuitions of most teachers.

Although the recent history of ATI research has somewhat dampened the expectations of rapid educationally relevant applications, the research program progresses slowly and carefully. Consistent findings are beginning to emerge (Snow, 1976). Meanwhile, the findings for powerful instructional main effects have become much more encouraging as have our conceptions of learners' abilities to transform and adapt situations and treatments to their own goals and approaches. Thus it is beginning to appear that the need to develop differential instructional treatments for large groups of learners may not exist. Instead, broadly powerful instructional treatments may be effective for high proportions of school learners, and the results of ATI research may be more useful in the fine tuning of instruction for smaller subgroups of students and for more complex objectives.

In the early 1960s, a third approach to conceptualizing ability and intelligence developed: John Carroll's model of ability and school learning. Such central variables in the model as "aptitude," "opportunity to learn," and "perseverance" were all couched in a language and metric readily translatable into instruction—*time* for learning and teaching. Influenced by this model of aptitude have been such successful educational innovations as Benjamin Bloom's (1976) mastery learning, which has stimulated much research and demonstration from first grade through the university all over the world.

Teaching

Teaching is the central enterprise of education, and the past decade has been the decade of research on teaching. No single area of educational psychology has grown so rapidly, attracting new investigators, producing and refining its findings in ways increasingly relevant to the practice of education, and extending the range of conceptual schemes and methodological approaches employed in its inquiries.

Four bodies of work are germane to this topic: (1) general studies, whether pursued using correlational or experimental designs, linking the behavior of teachers to the achievement of pupils, or process/ product research; (2) studies stimulated by the Carroll (1963) model, focusing on the manner in which time is employed both by teachers and students or time-on-task, academic learning time, mastery learning research; (3) studies on teachers' differential treatment of individual pupils, emanating originally from the work on teacher expectations and extending to examination of patterns of grouping, pacing, feedback, and correction; and (4) studies of teacher thought, judgment, and decision making as teachers assess students formally and informally, select instructional experiences for students, and evaluate or explain students' successes and failures.[1]

Studies of Teacher Behavior

Studies in the process/product tradition have attempted to answer the question, What are those things teachers do in classrooms that correlate with and can bring about higher student achievement? The goal of this research has been to identify and organize sets of teacher behavior that can be said to produce student achievement gains reliably and consistently. Such work takes two forms. In the main, systematic observation instruments are used in classrooms to observe teachers who have been identified as either more or less effective in promoting achievement gains among students. Then those behaviors which consistently distinguish the more from the less effective teachers are identified and examined. The second form of research is the field experiment. In this type of study the kinds of behavior that have been identified as effective are transformed into teacher education approaches, and groups of teachers are trained in their use. The effects of such teacher training on the subsequent achievements of their students are then contrasted with the effects of teachers not so trained in order to establish a causal link between what the teachers do and how well the students perform.

I will examine one specific example of this large body of work. One of the teacher behavior variables that has been investigated in studies of reading instruction in the early elementary grades is the

---

[1] Space limitations preclude treatment of this last topic, though it is the one closest to my own work. A comprehensive review can be found in Shavelson and Stern (1981).

order in which turns are assigned to pupils. A perennial question for teachers is in what order to call on students to perform. Traditional pedagogical lore has generally followed the admonition I found recently in *Stoddard's American Intellectual Arithmetic,* a textbook published over 120 years ago (Stoddard, 1860). In the "Suggestions for Teachers," which opens the textbook, the author advises, "pupils should be called upon promiscuously, and not in rotation, to take part in the recitation." The goal of this strategy is to maintain the attention of all the pupils. Never have I seen the suggestion of promiscuity in the classroom made so convincingly. When discussing turn taking recently with several groups of teachers, I have found that they, too, agree with Stoddard that assigning turns at random is a far better approach than always calling on students in order. But what does the research in the process/product tradition tell us about this decision?

Anderson, Evertson, and Brophy (1979) found in their first-grade reading studies that those teachers who employed ordered turns achieved far greater gains in reading performance than did those teachers who assigned turns in other ways. This counter-intuitive finding has subsequently been replicated and appears to be stable. Moreover, when the use of ordered turns is included in experimental teacher-training approaches and subsequently employed by the experimental teachers, student performance improves. Although disentangling the influence of one particular teacher tactic, such as turn ordering, from the complex of 30 or more included in the field experiments is impossible, I am prepared to assert that for early elementary reading instruction, especially with working-class children, the evidence strongly supports superiority of ordered turns over the promiscuous alternative.

Two explanations for this finding can be advanced, each of which draws upon the logic of other approaches to the study of teaching and thus prefigures subsequent topics in this account. First, careful examination of the turn assignments of teachers purporting to distribute opportunities randomly reveals that random turns do not exist. Instead, when no ordering is imposed, certain pupils receive an inordinately high proportion of turns, and others receive few if any. Thus opportunity to learn (from turns) and, hence, time available to invest in the academic task, is less available to many pupils.

A second explanation derives from studies of student responses to teaching. When members of a reading group are confronted with an unclear turn-allocation policy, they frequently devote a substantial amount of attention to attempts at discerning the basis for the teacher's behavior. That is, they work at "psyching out" the teacher's actions rather than attending exclusively to the reading materials and the substance of the teacher's communications.

Findings are accumulating impressively with respect to the causal connections between a variety of teacher behaviors and pupil achievement. These have been summarized by Gage (1978; Gage & Giaconia, 1980), Rosenshine (1979), Brophy (1979), Good (in preparation), Berliner (1979), and others in a model of "direct teaching." It is important to understand that the model has been validated with respect to elementary level instruction in the basic skills with an emphasis on decoding or computation. Nevertheless, these are important findings, especially during a time when, for a variety of reasons, direct instruction has fallen out of favor. Not only are such findings encouraging both researchers and practitioners regarding the stronger link being forged between educational research and practice, but also older studies and their generalizations are undergoing reexamination.

Barr and Dreeben (1978) have reanalyzed the data collected by Flanders (1968) in the late 1950s from which a generation of teachers learned that indirect forms of instruction were superior to those direct forms of instruction in which the teacher controlled the classroom discourse. They have concluded that the key to the earlier findings was that "direct" and "indirect" were both defined as ratios rather than as absolute values. Those teachers who had a higher ratio of indirect to direct teaching also happened to be the teachers who spent the most time teaching overall. The secret of their success was not necessarily their ratio of indirect to direct teaching. Instead, and thoroughly consistent with contemporary findings, teachers who spent more time in instructional interaction of almost any kind with their students produced better outcomes in the basic skills than did teachers who spent less time teaching.

Findings such as these highlight a potential paradox in the comparison of the research on learning reviewed earlier with the research on teaching. Although the research on learning has taught us the importance of the active, transforming role of the learner, the research on teaching continues to demonstrate the importance of direct instruction, an approach which seems to suggest a passive view of the learner. But it is important to recognize that direct instruction does not put knowledge in the heads of learners but creates the conditions under which students will use their academic learning time fruitfully. It is to the research which emphasizes time-on-task and academic learning time to which I shall now turn.

Time and Learning

The work of the California Beginning Teacher Evaluation Study (BTES) (Denham & Lieberman, 1980; Fisher et al., 1978) has made the phrase "time-on-task" part of every teacher's working vocabulary. This study confirmed that the key to effectiveness in teaching was the ability of some teachers to increase the amount of academic learning time used by students. Some have criticized those studies for having demonstrated the obvious. But, as Whitehead (1925, p. 6) observed: "Familiar things happen, and mankind does not bother about them. It takes a very unusual mind to undertake analysis of the obvious." Moreover, the studies have gone far beyond that single accomplishment. Fisher and his co-workers identified the importance of academic learning time—time actively engaged in tasks of appropriate difficulty. Appropriate difficulty was not always simple to define because what was appropriate for some kinds of tasks did not appear to be appropriate for others. Nevertheless, the work of this research program helped focus the attention of both teachers and researchers on the variety of ways in which time was spent in classrooms, some productively and some not. The researchers drew directly from Carroll's (1963) model of school learning as elaborated by Harnischfeger and Wiley (1976) among others.

The importance of time and timing in instruction was not limited to the work of the Beginning Teacher Evaluation Study. Time allocation also became a phenomenon of interest to another group of researchers within the research-on-teaching community—those concerned with the effects of teacher expectations.

Teacher Expectations

There were probably two major sources for the currently active field of research on teacher expectations. The first and most obvious source was the book by Rosenthal and Jacobson (1968) on the Pygmalion effect. Their claim that teachers' expectations for students could influence their subsequent scores on intelligence tests met with serious criticisms from methodologists within educational psychology. Nevertheless, the hypothesis was intriguing and even compelling, at least for school achievement as a criterion. The critical question for most researchers on teaching became, not whether there was an expectation effect, but whether differences could be demonstrated in the ways teachers behaved toward students for whom they had high rather than low expectations.

A second source of this work was the research of Philip Jackson (1968). In his *Life in Classrooms,* Jackson had documented the different ways in which teachers treated individuals within the same classroom. Hence, although characterizing the teaching behavior in a classroom monolithically was possible, it was clear that instruction was directed differentially to students and subgroups within a given classroom. Thus after having teachers specify which were the children in their classrooms for whom they had high and low expectations, Brophy and Good (1974) conducted studies of teacher behavior in relation to those students. Among their more dramatic findings were the following: Low-expectation students received behavioral criticisms from the teacher two and a half times more frequently than did high-expectation students. High-expectation students received praise nearly three times as often as did low-expectation students, while interactions involving criticism were two and a half times as frequent for low-expectation students as for high-expectation students. The wrong answers of low-expectation students were followed by criticism three times as often as the equally wrong answers of high-expectation students. The correct answers of high-expectation students were praised more than twice as often as the correct answers of low-expectation students. Although in the classroom-based teacher expectation studies there were nagging questions of chicken and egg, of whether the teacher behavior followed the formation of the expectations or was simply correlated with the behavior which produced the expectation in the first place, it was clear that the two groups were not receiving the same instruction from the teachers.

Although expectations can be demonstrated as sources of teacher behavior that contributes to deficits in student performance, different kinds of expectations can produce formidable student achievement gains. Thus, in studies of school effects, teacher expectations for student achievement have been among the most important variables under analysis. For example, Michael Rutter, a London psychiatrist, conducted a large-scale study of the effects of inner-city London secondary schools on their students (Rutter et al., 1979). He had been following a group of inner-city London youngsters longitudinally for a number of years as part of his study of the effects of environment on mental health. When his large cohort reached secondary-school age, Rutter began to study the impact of the differing environments of twelve inner-city London schools on the students in his sample as they progressed through the programs.

As summarized in his recent book, *Fifteen Thousand Hours,* Rutter discovered that these schools had widely differing effects on the academic achievement, behavior, and rates of delinquency and of school attendance of students, controlling for entering differences. When the attributes of the schools and classrooms were analyzed to identify the features of those settings which contributed most to the observed differences, the key variables were clustered by Rutter into a construct he called "school ethos." Central to the school ethos were the expectations that teachers in the schools had developed with respect to the performance of their students. In those schools where expectations were high, the life of the school was very different from that in schools where expectations were low. Work was taken more seriously, far more teacher and student time was devoted to serious academic pursuits, and homework was both assigned and completed; and the resulting performances of the students reflected those emphases.

Research on teacher expectations has not demonstrated that merely manipulating teacher expectations can infinitely influence the development of students. When teacher expectations are sufficiently positive, however, teachers are led to perform the sorts of instructional activity that are far more likely to engage students productively in academic tasks and, therefore, to produce greater achievement gains. We are not speaking of miracles or of action at a distance but rather of documentable differences in how schools and classrooms are conducted (see also Brookover et al., 1979; Edmonds, 1979).

Pupil Responses to Teaching

Investigations of the effects of teaching on individual pupils, whether or not emphasizing the role of time, have discovered that the differences in effects of teaching cannot be ascribed entirely to differences in the ways teachers treat individual pupils. Therefore, researchers have been motivated to engage in studies that promise to reconnect the psychology of teaching with the psychology of learning—studies of the manner in which individual pupils mediate and transform teaching. These studies have taken at least two forms. The first type of study focuses on how individual pupils redefine or interpret the instructional task in the course of participating in the classroom. The second approach focuses on the classroom group or subgroups and examines the properties of interaction, negotiation, role assignment, and the like which transform the task-as-presented into the task-as-performed.

In the first of these approaches, one finds studies of teaching articulating with the currently exciting work in cognitive science with which we began our discussion—studies of expertise in which the emphasis is on the learner's transformation of the task environment into a workable problem space; the special role of executive routines in the organization and deployment of intellectual skills; the importance of metacognitive processes (e.g., Brown, Campione, & Barclay, 1979; Flavell, 1979) in how students learn from teaching and in what they learn; and the interaction of individual aptitudes with instructional treatments, the ATI phenomenon.

Doyle's (1977, 1979) work originally alerted the field to the need to focus on two aspects of the role of the student in learning. One aspect was the manner in which student behavior was the stimulus for, and not merely the response to, teacher behavior. The other aspect was the way in which students defined the instructional situation and mediated the effects of instruction. Doyle's first admonition was a straightforward one. How justifiable were the claims that, when teachers spent more time with students, students learned more or that, when teachers praised students increasingly, the students achieved at higher levels? Was it not equally plausible to claim that students who performed well caused teachers to spend more time with them and that students who achieved correctly elicited more praise from teachers? The implicit direction of causation in the process/product correlational studies was thus brought under critical scrutiny by Doyle.

Doyle's emphasis on the student mediation hypothesis can be exemplified by the ongoing work of Linda Anderson (1981) at the Institute for Research on Teaching at Michigan State University. Large-scale classroom observation studies, such as the California BTES discussed earlier, emphasized the importance of pupil engagement with academic tasks. Such research also documented that in the typical American classroom a high proportion of student time was spent individually in seatwork. The critical question was what was going on in the student's head as he or she sat, apparently engaged, working with individual materials. The observor might quite understandably judge that the student was engaged with the task. But is the task as construed by the student identical to the task as construed by the teacher? What is being learned during seatwork? How is the student mediating the ostensible instruction? The experimental psychologist will rapidly see that in this case researchers on teaching are asking whether there is a difference between the nominal and the functional stimulus in the instructional setting.

Anderson has been observing target pupils intensively as they engage in seatwork in first-grade classrooms. Seatwork in such classrooms generally revolves around workbook pages which provide students with practice in the subskills of reading and writing. Although the work is still in progress, Anderson has already identified distinctive differences between the manner in which high achieving pupils deal with seatwork and the manner in which low achieving pupils do the same. First, for both types of pupil, the major goal of seatwork is to get done. Both types seem relatively insensitive to the educational or instructional goals of the different exercises in which they are engaged. It is clear that success for students is completion rather than accuracy.

Even more important, however, are the strategies which low achievers use to complete work they find difficult. Low achieving students have been observed to employ any strategy available to complete an assignment irrespective of whether the completed paper makes sense or not. They seem not to have developed strategies for self-monitoring or self-appraisal which can be used to identify for themselves whether the work they have done is appropriate. They are so often confused that they appear to assume that confusion is a property of almost all academic work. In contrast, when high achieving students encounter difficulty, they tend to sense their problem immediately and seek help. As Anderson (1981) has observed, when something does not make sense or seems confusing, it is an unusual event to a high achiever, and therefore more salient and likely to trigger action to reduce confusion and/or add necessary information. This highlighting of unexpected misunderstanding may help further the development of metacognitive skills (which could aid in information seeking to reduce confusion), even though formal instruction seldom is focused on the development of such skills.

On the other hand, low achievers, whom we have seen more often with assignments that seem difficult for them, may be less likely to expect their work to "make sense." That is, "sense" is not predictable, and so a lack of sense (i.e., recognizing that you do not understand) is not unusual. . . . Over time, this approach may prevent the development of metacognitive skills that allow students to become better guides of their own learning. (pp. 16–17)

This sort of work is also helping to document the relationships between, on the one hand, the kinds of metacognitive strategies that have been identified in laboratory studies of reading comprehension and in solution strategies for arithmetic word problems and, on the other hand, the sorts of metacognitive strategies actually developed by students when such problems are presented as assignments in classroom contexts. It has become extremely instructive to understand how the manner in which a classroom context is organized can, irrespective of the structure of the cognitive task itself, foster the development of cognitive strategies far different from those intended by designers and implementers of the instruction.

The focus of research in educational psychology thus appears to be coming full circle. If the purpose of instruction is to put the learner in a position to be actively constructive, one now finds researchers on teaching asking what the learner is doing as he or she is being taught. Thus, instead of looking at student cognitive processes as students work on instructional tasks per se, we are now examining the cognitive processes of students engaging interactively in classroom learning experiences. This coordination of research on teaching with research on learning is still very new. But it shows promise of producing a generation of research in educational psychology that will have high relevance to the problems of practice.

Fitting Teaching to Learners

Studies investigating the fit between teaching and learning consistently advise the same strategy: When children are experiencing difficulty in learning, one should identify the source of the problem and intervene accordingly. However, what constitutes proper diagnosis or wise intervention may not always be obvious. Carew and Lightfoot (1979), in *Beyond Bias,* have identified the problem of the teacher who attempts to "meet the needs" of disadvantaged children through tailoring instruction for their diagnosed abilities and motives. They refer to the teacher's dilemma as treading the thin line between individualization and discrimination. That is, too frequently well-intended attempts to design special instruction for youngsters with special needs unintentionally becomes a source of disservice rather than of service.

Two examples may illustrate this danger. Allington (1980) has reported a study of the interruption behavior of teachers while they conduct reading recitations in elementary classrooms. He contrasts teacher behavior with high-achieving reading groups and that with low-achieving reading groups. The teachers displayed a marked tendency to treat the two groups differently. This difference in treatment is no cause for alarm because we would expect teachers to provide special help for students who demonstrate greater need. The form this help takes, however, is much higher frequencies of interruption of the reading among the low-achieving students before these students can spontaneously correct a reading error. Those same teachers tend to remain silent in the face of errors produced by high-achieving readers and thus provide them with the important opportunity to catch and correct their own errors. Moreover, when teachers intervene with low-achieving readers, their tendency is to call the attention of the reader to the phonetic features of the miscalled word. When correcting high-achieving readers, the teachers have the tendency to call attention to the semantic or syntactic context, rather than to letter-sound correspondences, as the major source of reading cues.

Allington claims that these contrasting strategies, while undoubtedly likely to be defended on the grounds that students are being provided the instruction that meets their needs, in fact has the insidiously unintentional consequence of doing more long-term damage to the reading strategies of the low achievers. It should be noted that

Allington states this criticism normatively. He has no achievement data nor observations of groups experiencing different patterns of intervention to support his claim that these interventions are miseducative.

Another observation of the same sort has been reported by Confrey and Good (1981) based on their pilot study in middle-school mathematics classrooms. They observe that one of the favorite methods for reducing the difficulty of mathematics instruction at the middle-school level is markedly to slow the pace of instruction. What might be taught in the space of a week under normal instructional conditions will be spread over two or three weeks for poor achievers. Confrey and Good observed, however, that this slowing down appears to have exactly the opposite effect from that intended. When the pace of instruction is slowed markedly, the curriculum runs the danger of becoming disintegrated. The effect is like reading a long number series so slowly that one has forgotten the beginning by the time one reaches the end. Although, here again, no outcome data are available, the authors suggest that a sincere attempt to match instruction to individual differences by slowing the pace has ultimately made learning more rather than less difficult for the participants. The similarity between this incident and the study reported earlier regarding abortive attempts to reduce the reading difficulty of basal textbooks is too clear to require commentary.

It is perhaps appropriate at this point to recall William Rohwer's (1980) warning about the frequently deleterious effects of instruction on learning. Rohwer argued that almost any sort of instructional intervention will necessarily inhibit learning more than no instruction at all. He pointed out that only groups which encounter difficulties in learning receive special instruction. Individuals who experience no problems receive initial instructions and a few prompts and are on their way. Even with the best of cognitive psychological intentions, argued Rohwer, the instructional psychologist who assists a learner to perform tasks through practice on components of the task or through direct instruction on the cognitive strategies controlling execution of the task or through both is slowing down and rendering explicit precisely those processes engaged automatically, effortlessly, and smoothly by the successful learner. Our instructional intervention simply slows the process down even further. And in that way, claimed Rohwer, "the smart get smarter."

But our attempts to modify instruction in order to match better the characteristics of the learning group are not always fated to fail. A particularly encouraging example of success in this area is a study conducted in Hawaii by Katherine Au (1980). Unlike most of the studies reporting mismatches between characteristics of learner groups and instructional interventions, this study confirms its findings through the collection of achievement outcome data.

Au reports on the efforts of a school for native Hawaiians where elementary school pupils were consistently experiencing failure in reading as measured by the standardized achievement tests. Anthropologists observed that, in the culture of the native Hawaiians, youngsters participated jointly with an adult in the telling of stories, employing a form of discourse known as the "talk story." Unlike the standard reading group in which discreet turn taking was the norm to be enforced, the talk story involved group participation through highly overlapping speech patterns in which individuals would interrupt their peers to complete sentences others had begun. But in the Hawaiian context these overlapping speech patterns were not treated as interruptions but as legitimate and helpful joint participation structures.

When the form of discourse for the reading groups was modified to fit the traditional talk story pattern, performance in reading immediately began to improve. Au reports that at the end of the second year using the new approaches, achievement had exceeded national reading achievement norms.

The examples in this section introduce a new dimension to the analyses of teaching and learning presented heretofore. Consistent with our disciplinary heritage and its emphasis on Psyche, we psychologists have studied the individual. But in the societal artifacts we call schools, individuals are taught rarely as such but most often as members of groups. Thus most work on learning has traditionally investigated *individual* learning, remembering, transferring, forgetting, erring, and trying. Only more recently have we come to witness a concern for the classroom group, the individual-difference-within-a-group, or the group-of-different (or similar)-individuals.

Teaching and learning in the classroom do not occur to the student in isolation. Indeed, the unavoidable feature of classroom life, so vividly captured by Jackson (1968), is its groupness. The classroom is a collective setting in which the rare commodities of time and space must be distributed by the teacher and competed for and shared in by all the members in an economy the complexity of which is worthy of analysis by the finest economists. Thus it is not sufficient to modify our understanding of how tasks function in classrooms in light of the distinction between a problem and an assignment because the performance-grade exchange influences the manner in which students approach the assigned task. We must further understand the modifications the task undergoes when it is assigned to a classroom full of pupils with differing abilities and predispositions. In some classroom settings, cooperative learning of various kinds is not only permitted but also encouraged. In others, because the existence of the group is seen as an impediment rather than a facilitator of learning, no intercourse among participants is allowed. As these social contexts change, the opportunities to learn and the aspects of ability to exploit undergo change as well.

As a number of the other examples show, decades of debate over some educational issues have been illuminated by process studies of a phenomenon the operation of which was an object of speculation during an era of input-output black box studies of classrooms and schools. In similar fashion, debates over optimal class size or ability composition of classrooms have continued endlessly with little hope of resolution. In recent years, however, studies of what actually happens interactively within classrooms have begun to clarify the variety of consequences that both group size and classroom ability composition can engender.

An extremely clever example of an approach to the class size problem was taken by Cahen, Filby, and their colleagues (Cahen, Filby, McCutcheon, & Kyle, in press) of the Far West Laboratory in San Francisco. After doing intensive classroom observations in urban and rural classrooms for the first half of the year in order to establish baseline data regarding teacher and student functioning in those settings, the researchers experimentally reduced class sizes by one third to one half. Classes that had averaged approximately 35 students dropped to about 27, while others that began with 26 dropped to the high teens. With that reduction of class size as the major change, the researchers continued observations for the rest of the year to detect the manner in which the reduction of class size had affected the actions of teachers and students as well as the achievement outcomes. One finding was that achievement did not change for the students although the interaction patterns between teachers and students became markedly different. The researchers speculated that, had the teachers received instruction on how to exploit the opportunities presented by smaller class sizes, even the achievement outcomes might have been changed. (It would be interesting to examine whether a class that is reduced from 35 to 27 students functions any differently than a class that begins the year at 27.)

Heretofore, perhaps the best one could say about the ideal class size is reflected in the following aphorism. If one asks any teacher what the ideal class size is, one will receive the same reply: three less than I have now—and let me name the three. There is little doubt that a great deal of truth remains in that observation. Unfortunately, no one has yet decided where to send the three.

Settings, Groups, and Tasks

The tour of the province of Educational Psychology will conclude with an examination of examples of research which emphasize the role of group context in the performance of students and teachers in classrooms. The examples are from the work of new generations of aptitude-treatment interaction researchers, such as Noreen Webb, and of ethnographic psychologists, such as Michael Cole and Sylvia Scribner. Webb has examined the interaction of instructional treatment with both the distribution of aptitudes within a learning group and the associated distribution of learner roles within groups of different aptitude composition. Cole, Scribner, and their associates have used very different perspectives to examine the relationship between the social organization of groups and the performances of individuals within these groups (e.g., Cole, Hood, & McDermott, 1978). What I find particularly significant about these bodies of work is the manner in which they draw together several of the themes discussed earlier: the meaning of ability or aptitude, the dynamics of classroom teaching, and interactive studies of classroom life.

Although Webb (1980) comes out of the aptitude-treatment interaction tradition, she approaches questions of ATI from a novel and, from a classroom perspective, particularly fruitful angle. Her research questions concern the relationship between the instructional treatments and the aptitudes of groups of individuals being taught. The key aspects of the group aptitude are the distribution of abilities

within the group and the norms which develop within the group regarding the responsibility individual group members have for one
another's learning. Webb summarizes her results:

> Group composition in terms of ability had important effects on
> the nature of the behavioral norms that developed. Groups with
> mixed ability and groups uniformly medium in ability interpreted
> the instructions for group work literally, developing norms that
> encouraged asking questions and offering explanations to fellow
> members. Groups uniformly high in ability and uniformly low in
> ability developed an alternative goal for the group session: solving
> the problem in the least possible amount of time. Behavioral
> norms corresponding to the modified goal discouraged asking
> questions and taking time to explain to group members. . . . A
> tentative recommendation for group composition can be made on
> the basis of the apparent aptitude-treatment interaction of ability
> and kind of grouping: medium ability students may learn most
> when working with others of similar ability; high ability and low
> ability students may do best when working with each other. (p. 81)

The manner in which Webb's research combines the ATI model with
the approaches for studying the properties of group interaction in a
classroom-like setting is very promising, as it may prefigure a new
level of sophistication in the joining of these traditionally disparate
research areas.

Parallel to the work of Webb but oriented far more to instructional development and experimentation is the work of the cooperative learning researchers. Slavin (1980), Sharan and Sharan (1976),
and Aronson et al. (1978) are among the growing group of scholars
who are interested in the creation of classroom settings that emphasize the advantages to be gained from planned cooperation among
students rather than competition between them. Research results in
this area are extremely encouraging, and they can only be further
informed by work on the interaction of aptitude distributions and
group activity conducted by Webb. Research has come a long way
since the early studies of leadership in groups by Lewin, Lippitt, and
White (1939).

I shall end my stories of research in educational psychology with
the study of a learning disabled child conducted by Cole and
Traupmann (1979). Cole was seeking a way to investigate the same
aptitudes or cognitive processes and the same tasks in an individual

testing setting, a formal classroom context, and an informal group situation. Cole and his group organized an after-school cooking club to provide themselves an opportunity to observe several students dealing with tasks that presented both cognitive and manipulative demands in an informal and potentially collaborative context. The cooking club gave the students an opportunity to cook and bake a variety of recipes over the course of several months.

The researchers discovered that one child whom they had been observing had been classified by the school as learning disabled. This classification surprised them because they had failed to note any particular deficits in his performance within the club setting. Indeed, the student seemed particularly effective in the cooking club. Only through a careful, microscopic review of his protocols in formal testing situations, as he worked with classroom tasks, and in the interactions of the cooking club, were the researchers able to identify behaviors which consistently demonstrated his learning disability. Most important, however, they came to understand why his deficits were not readily apparent in the informal context of the cooking club.

The child was able to compensate for and adapt to his ostensible disabilities in the social context of the cooking club because he had learned how to use peers to complement the deficits in his own abilities while he exploited those cognitive and interpersonal qualities with which he was well endowed. On one hand, he had a great deal of trouble reading and remembering details. On the other hand, he was extremely good at grasping the overall structure of a problem and at recognizing the optimal sequence or strategy for solving the problem. Therefore he took on those organizational and coordinative roles in the cooking club and assigned such tasks as recipe reading and remembering to fellow club members. One other club member, who could read and remember extremely well but had real problems grasping the overall structure and optimal strategies for a task, was almost his perfect complement. Thus the informal structure of the club afforded the learning-disabled student the opportunity to function effectively within the limits of his abilities, whereas such strategies were unavailable to him in the more structured and constrained setting of a formal ability test or a normal classroom task.

Thus two parallel, yet fairly isolated, senses of expertise are emerging. Both these conceptions of expertise share affinities with a cognitive psychological tradition. The cognitive science perspective of

Greeno, Resnick, and others uses exclusively the Simon and Newell (Newell & Simon, 1972; Simon, 1979) model of the thinker in isolation. The work of Cole, Scribner, and their colleagues reflects a perspective in the tradition of Vygotsky (1978) who looks at the organism historically in a social setting. Each perspective has significant implications for an educational psychology of school learning and teaching. Are they mutually exclusive? Or are the two conceptions fundamentally complementary? Vygotsky clearly thought not only that the two senses of ability were compatible but also that each needed the other. These two senses of ability—that revealed in individual problem-solving performance in independent work and that displayed in problem-solving performance as facilitated by an adult or a group of peers—defined for Vygotsky one of his most important concepts, "the zone of proximal development." The difference between the ability of an individual to perform in the isolation typical of psychological tests or classroom tasks and that same person's performance in a context where he or she receives the guidance or assistance of an adult or a group of peers defines the zone and constitutes a potentially powerful pedagogical concept.

In Vygotsky's own words,

> the zone of proximal development . . . is the distance between the actual development level as determined by independent problem solving and the level of potential development as determined through problem solving under adult guidance or in collaboration with more capable peers.
>
> The actual developmental level characterizes mental development retrospectively, while the zone of proximal development characterizes mental development prospectively. . . . Thus, the notion of a zone of proximal development enables us to propound a new formula, namely that the only "good learning" is that which is in advance of development. (Vygotsky, 1978, pp. 86–87)

A common theme in these types of investigation is the manner in which the learning task changes in the face of the group instructional context. When most of my generation were trained as psychologists, the learning task was like the rose of Gertrude Stein. A task was a task was a task. The way one changed a task was to modify the instructions, to shift the pace or order of presentations of stimulus material, to increase the complexity of displays, and the like. But the assumption was always that the task was an individual challenge which remained stable across presentations. Moreover, the assumption was made that individual task performance could serve as a proper basis for inferences about pupil performance within a classroom context. Indeed, several years ago when the assertion was made by statisticians that the classroom, rather than the individual, was the proper basis for calculating the degrees of freedom in a multi-classroom experimental study, a hue and cry arose from educational psychologists across the world. Such a shift would encumber what they saw as the undeniable centrality of the individual and the task as the proper foci for educational research.

There are at least four senses of the task in educational psychology: First, there is the *task-as-given,* the task of traditional experimental psychology. Second, in the work of information-processing psychologists such as Groen and Resnick, there is the *task-as-transformed,* the task that results from the transformation of a task environment into a problem space. Third, there is the *task-as-personally-defined,* as exemplified in the work of the pupil-mediation researchers, who examine the pedagogical demands in terms of which the task is understood and apprehended and who emphasize the distinction between a problem and an assignment. Fourth, from the perspective of the psychoethnographers with their emphasis on the multiplicity and fluidity of the task structure in classroom settings, there is the *task-as-socially-negotiated.* In this last sense, tasks and subtasks move from the center of group attention to the periphery, and the components of tasks are negotiable among members of the group who serve one another as colleagues, memory surrogates (thus reducing the effects of limitations of short-term memory), and sources of feedback, correctives, or alternative approaches.

Finally, one can see that, from the perspective of a new educational psychology, the relationship between individual ability and task is analogous to the relationship between stimulus and response defined so persuasively by Dewey (1896) in his classic paper on the reflex arc. Task and ability are mutually defined and defining. It is nearly impossible to speak conclusively about an individual's ability unless one speaks of the context in which the ability will be displayed. Similarly, it is difficult to speak about a task unless the intended sense of task is clarified.

Concluding Remarks

These research topics are coalescing into an educational psychology that extends beyond the limits of psychology as traditionally defined, that involves the traditional subjects of such inquiries as active participants in the research process, and that articulates with the common-sense understanding of teachers and learners while it also extends and builds upon that knowledge. One of the major characteristics of this new educational psychology grows out of the volitional, goal-directed, thinking and feeling individuals now envisioned by contemporary psychology. These individuals and their metacognition are important to us—that is, their thinking about their own thinking is a central attribute of their learning, remembering, and problem solving, and they are approached differently in instruction than their paleobehaviorist ancestors who apparently neither thought about nor sought after anything. Even the teacher is slowly being conceptualized as someone who can think, invent, and innovate, just like the students. But that is a topic for yet another lecture.

The problems of educational psychology reflect those of the general state of psychology. The cognitive revolution has been won but not without significant losses. In finding its mind, educational psychology has lost its feelings. The cold cognitions of information processing must be heated up if they are to correspond to the joys, anxieties, frustrations, and excitements of classroom life. Educational psychologists must learn to understand the "hot cognitions" (or thoughtful passions) characteristic of teachers, pupils, and other inhabitants of our schools. Psychology will certainly rediscover emotion in the next decade, and so will educational psychology.

The triumphs of contemporary educational psychology are predominantly triumphs of description and explanation. But education is essentially an enterprise of action, intervention, and planned change. Our progress in description must ultimately translate into the ability to inform and effect educative change. The insightful descriptive studies I have described must be complemented by experimental investigations directed at the purposeful improvement of teaching and learning.

Educational psychology is both the parent and the child of American psychology. Educational concerns stimulated some of the earliest work in psychology, and those same concerns currently comprise both the mainstream and applications of our contemporary discipline. Education must serve as one of the key proving grounds for social science's claim to be important for social progress. If schools and classrooms cannot be helped to function well, can psychology continue to assert with pride that it constitutes the foundational social science discipline for education? Psychology receives many of its problems from education and, in turn, uses educational settings to validate or verify its theories and applications.

The problems of educational psychology require the attention of social scientists who combine the highest levels of talent and commitment. Those who teach introductory courses in psychology have a special role to play in fulfilling this requirement. They have a major obligation to tell the stories of research in educational psychology and to portray the challenge and excitement of inquiry in this field in a manner likely to attract our finest young minds to a career engaged with research and practice in the area of education. The prevailing views, the climates of opinion psychology teachers foster regarding educational psychology, will have significant consequences for the career paths students choose. The pressures on this border province are great, the expectations are high, and the rewards are uncertain. But the opportunities to make significant contributions to social progress through educational psychology are vast.

References

Allington, R. L. Teacher interruption behaviors during primary-grade oral reading. *Journal of Educational Psychology,* 1980, *72*(3), 371–377.

Anderson, L. M. *Student responses to seatwork: Implications for the study of students' cognitive processing.* Paper presented at annual meeting of the American Educational Research Association, Los Angeles, Calif., 1981.

Anderson, L., Evertson, C., & Brophy, J. An experimental study of effective teaching in first-grade reading groups. *Elementary School Journal,* 1979, *79*(4), 193–223.

Aronson, E., et al. *The jigsaw classroom.* Beverly Hills, Calif.: Sage Publications, 1978.

Au, Katherine Hu-Pei. *The comprehension-oriented reading lesson: Relationships to proximal indices of achievement.* Paper presented at annual meeting of the American Educational Research Association, Boston, Mass., April, 1980.

Barr, R., & Dreeben, R. Instruction in classrooms. In L. S. Shulman (Ed.), *Review of Research in Education: V.* Itasca, Ill.: Peacock, 1978.

Becker, H. S., Geer, B., & Hughes, E. *Making the grade: The academic side of college life.* New York: Wiley, 1968.

Berliner, D. Tempus educare. In P. Peterson & H. Walberg (Eds.), *Research on teaching: Concepts, findings, and implications.* Berkeley, Calif.: McCutchan Publishing Corp., 1979.

Bloom, B. S. *Human characteristics and school learning.* New York: McGraw-Hill, 1976.

Brookover, W., Beady, C., Flood, P., Schweitzer, J., & Wisenbaker, J. *School social systems and student achievement: Schools can make a difference.* New York: Praeger, 1979.

Brophy, J. Teacher behavior and its effects. *Journal of Educational Psychology,* 1979, *71,* 733–750.

Brophy, J. E., & Good, T. L. *Teacher-student relationships: Causes and consequences.* New York: Holt, Rinehart & Winston, 1974.

Brown, A. L., Campione, J. C., & Barclay, C. R. Training self-checking routines for estimating test readiness: Generalization from list learning to prose recall. *Child Development,* 1979, *50,* 501–512.

Brown, J. S., & Van Lehn, K. Toward a generative theory of bugs in procedural skills. In T. Romberg, T. Carpenter, & J. Moses (Eds.), *Addition and subtraction: Developmental perspectives.* Hillsdale, N.J.: Erlbaum, 1981.

Bruner, J. S., Goodnow, J. J., & Austin, G. A. *A study of thinking.* New York: Wiley, 1956.

Cahen, L., Filby, N., McCutcheon, G., & Kyle, D. *The role of class size in teaching and learning.* Institute for Research on Teaching Monographs for the Study of Teaching. New York: Longman, in press.

Carew, J., & Lightfoot, S. L. *Beyond bias.* Cambridge, Mass.: Harvard University Press, 1979.

Carroll, J. A model for school learning. *Teachers College Record,* 1963, *64,* 723–733.

Cole, M., Hood, L., & McDermott, R. P. *Ecological niche-picking: Ecological invalidity as an axiom of cognitive psychology.* (Tech. Rep.) San Diego: University of California, Laboratory of Comparative Human Cognition, 1978.

Cole, M., & Traupmann, K. Comparative cognitive research: Learning from a learning disabled child. *Minnesota symposium on child development,* St. Paul, 1979.

Confrey, J., & Good, T. *A view from the back of the classroom.* Colloquium presentation, Institute for Research on Teaching, East Lansing, Mich., April, 1981.

Cronbach, L. J. Beyond the two disciplines of scientific psychology. *American Psychologist,* 1957, *12,* 671–684.

Davison, A. Readability: Appraising text difficulty. In R. C. Anderson, J. Osborne, & R. J. Tierney (Eds.), *Learning to read in American schools.* Urbana, Ill.: Center for the Study of Reading, University of Illinois, 1981.

Denham, C., & Lieberman, A. (Eds.). *Time to learn.* Washington, D.C.: U.S. Department of Education, 1980.

Dewey, J. The reflex arc concept in psychology. *Psychological Review,* 1896, *3,* 357–370.

Doyle, W. Paradigms for research on teacher effectiveness. In L. S. Shulman (Ed.), *Review of Research in Education V.* Itasca, Ill.: Peacock, 1977.

Doyle, W. Classroom tasks and students' abilities. In P. Peterson & H. Walberg (Eds.), *Research on teaching: Concepts, findings, and implications.* Berkeley, Calif.: McCutchan Publishing Co., 1979.

Edmonds, R. Some schools work and more can. *Social Policy,* 1979, *9,* 28–32.

Elstein, A. S., Shulman, L. S., & Sprafka, S. A. *Medical problem solving: An analysis of clinical reasoning.* Cambridge, Mass.: Harvard University Press, 1978.

Erlwanger, S. H. Case studies of children's conceptions of mathematics, Part I. *Journal of Children's Mathematical Behavior,* 1975, *1,* 157–283.

Fisher, C., Filby, N., Marliave, R., Cahen, L., Dishaw, M., Moore, J., & Berliner, D. *Teaching behaviors, academic learning time and student achievement. Final report of phase III-B, Beginning Teacher Evaluation Study.* San Francisco, Calif.: Far West Laboratory for Educational Research and Development, June, 1978.

Flanders, N. A. *Analyzing teacher behavior.* Reading, Mass.: Addison-Wesley, 1968.

Flavell, J. H. Metacognition and cognitive monitoring. *American Psychologist*, 1979, *34*, 906–911.

Gage, N. L. *The scientific basis of the art of teaching.* New York: Teachers College Press, 1978.

Gage, N. L., & Giaconia, R. *The causal connection between teaching practices and student achievement: Recent experiments based on correlational findings* (mimeo Tech. Rep.). Stanford, Calif.: Center for Educational Research, 1980.

Good, T. L. Classroom research. In L. S. Shulman (Ed.), *Teaching and educational policy,* in preparation.

Greeno, J. G. Process of understanding in problem solving. In N. J. Castellan, D. B. Pisoni, & G. R. Potts (Eds.). *Cognitive theory,* Vol. 2. Hillsdale, N.J.: Erlbaum, 1977.

Greeno, J. G. Some examples of cognitive task analysis with instructional implications. In R. E. Snow, P. A. Federico, & W. E. Montague (Eds.). *Aptitude, learning and instruction,* Vol. 2. Hillsdale, N.J.: Erlbaum, 1980.

Grinder, R. The "new" science of education: Educational psychology in search of a mission. In F. H. Farley & N. J. Gordon (Eds.), *Psychology and education: The state of the union.* Berkeley, Calif.: McCutchan, 1981.

Groen, G. J., & Parkman, J. M. A chronometric analysis of simple addition. *Psychological Review,* 1972, *79*(4), 329–343.

Groen, G. J., & Resnick, L. B. Can preschool children invent addition algorithms? *Journal of Educational Psychology,* 1977, *69,* 645–652.

Harnischfeger, A., & Wiley, D. E. The teaching-learning process in elementary schools: A synoptic view. *Curriculum Inquiry,* 1976, *6*(1), 5–43.

Jackson, P. W. *Life in classrooms.* New York: Holt, Rinehart & Winston, 1968.

James, W. *Principles of psychology.* New York: Henry Holt and Company, 1890.

Joncich, G. *The sane positivist: A biography of Edward L. Thorndike.* Middletown, Conn.: Wesleyan University Press, 1968.

Krutetskii, U. A. *The psychology of mathematical abilities of school children.* Chicago: University of Chicago Press, 1976.

Lakatos, I. Falsification and the methodology of scientific research programmes. In I. Lakatos & A. Musgrave (Eds.), *Criticism and the growth of knowledge.* Cambridge: Cambridge University Press, 1970.

Lewin, K., Lippitt, R., & White, R. K. Patterns of aggressive behavior in experimentally created social climates. *Journal of Social Psychology,* *10,* 271–299.

Merton, R. K. Priorities in scientific discovery: A chapter in the sociology of science. *American Sociological Review,* 1957, *22*(6), 635–659.

Newell, A., & Simon, H. A. *Human problem solving.* Englewood Cliffs, N.J.: Prentice-Hall, 1972.

Resnick, L. B. Instructional psychology. *Annual Review of Psychology,* 1981, *32,* 659–704.

Rohwer, W. D., Jr. How the smart get smarter. *Educational Psychologist,* 1981, *15,* 35–43.

Rosenshine, B. Content, time and direct instruction. In P. Peterson & H. Walberg (Eds.), *Research on teaching: Concepts, findings, and implications.* Berkeley, Calif.: McCutchan Publishing Corp., 1979.

Rosenthal, R., & Jacobson, L. *Pygmalion in the classroom: Teacher expectations and pupils' intellectual development.* New York: Holt, Rinehart & Winston, 1968.

Ross, D. G. *Stanley Hall: The psychologist as prophet.* Chicago: University of Chicago Press, 1972.

Rutter, M., Maughan, B., Mortimore, P., Ouston, J., & Smith, A. *Fifteen thousand hours: Secondary schools and their effects on children.* Cambridge, Mass.: Harvard University Press, 1979.

Sharan, S., & Sharan, Y. *Small-group teaching.* Englewood Cliffs, N.J.: Educational Technology Publications, 1976.

Shavelson, R. J., & Stern, P. Research on teachers' pedagogical thoughts, judgments, decisions and behavior. *Review of Educational Research,* 1981, *51* (4), 455–498.

Shulman, L. S., & Elstein, A. S. Studies of problem solving, judgment and decision making: Implications for educational research. In F. N. Kerlinger (Ed.), *Review of research in education, III.* Itasca, Ill.: Peacock, 1975.

Simon, H. A. *Models of mind.* New Haven, Conn.: Yale University Press, 1979.

Slavin, R. Cooperative learning. *Review of Educational Research,* 1980, *50,* 315–342.

Snow, R. E. Research on aptitude for learning: A progress report. In L. S. Shulman (Ed.), *Review of research in education, IV.* Itasca, Ill.: Peacock, 1976.

Stephens, J. M. *The process of schooling.* New York: Holt, Rinehart & Winston, 1967.

Sternberg, R. J. *Intelligence, information processing, and analogical reasoning.* Hillsdale, N.J.: Erlbaum, 1977.

Stoddard, J. F. *Stoddard's American intellectual arithmetic.* New York: Sheldon, 1860.

Thorndike, E. L. *Educational psychology.* New York: Lemcke and Buechner, 1903.

Vygotsky, L. S. *Mind in society: The development of higher psychological processes* (M. Cole, V. John-Steiner, S. Scribner, & E. Souberman, Eds.). Cambridge, Mass.: Harvard University Press, 1978.

Webb, N. M. A process-outcome analysis of learning in group and individual settings. *Educational Psychologist,* 1980, *15* (2), 69–83.

Whitehead, A. N. *Science and the modern world.* New York: Mentor, 1925.

ELIZABETH F. LOFTUS

MEMORY AND ITS DISTORTIONS

E lizabeth Loftus is Professor of Psychology at the University of Washington. She received her PhD from Stanford University in Experimental Psychology in 1970. Since that time she has published approximately 8 books and 100 scientific articles in the areas of human cognition. The books include *Eyewitness Testimony* (Harvard University Press), *Memory* (Addison-Wesley), *Psychology* (Random House, with Camille Wortman), and *Essence of Statistics* (Brooks/Cole, with Geoffrey Loftus). *Eyewitness Testimony* won a National Media Award from the American Psychological Foundation in 1980.

Loftus has served on numerous APA committees, including the Finance Committee and the Committee on Organization. She is currently a member of the Council of Representatives for Division 3. She serves on four editorial boards, including that for the *Journal of Experimental Psychology: Learning, Memory, and Cognition*. In 1978–1979 she was a Fellow at the Center for Advanced Study in the Behavioral Sciences. Finally, she has lectured widely to legal groups and, since 1975, has served on the faculty of the National Judicial College.

ELIZABETH F. LOFTUS

MEMORY AND ITS DISTORTIONS

S tar witness Kenneth Bianchi gave crucial testimony to prosecutors about how he and his cousin, Angelo Buono, were joint participants in the string of strangulations that terrorized much of Los Angeles between October 1977 and February 1978. The grisly killings became known as the Hillside Strangler Murders. Later Bianchi flip-flopped in his testimony, and prosecutors began to wonder whether they could win their case against Buono. The problems with Bianchi's "memory" were numerous, but the principal problem was that over the years Bianchi gave conspicuously conflicting accounts of the slayings to psychiatrists, investigators, lawyers, and others. One may consider, for example, Bianchi's recollections of the death of the first victim in the series of killings, a 19-year-old, part-time waitress and prostitute, Yolanda Washington. Yolanda was kidnapped from the Hollywood area late one evening in October, 1977. Her nude body was discovered the next morning. Bianchi gave no fewer than four versions of her murder: In March 1979 he told a psychologist that he

The writing of this chapter was facilitated by grants from the National Science Foundation and the National Bureau of Standards. The author was introduced to the importance of survey research as a source of data on memory during a workshop on the National Crime Survey sponsored by the Bureau of the Census and the Bureau of Social Science Research. Please address all correspondence to Elizabeth Loftus, Department of Psychology, University of Washington, Seattle, Washington, 98195, USA.

walked in and was surprised to find Buono in the act of killing Yolanda; in the fall of 1979 he told police that he strangled Yolanda in the back of a car while his cousin drove; in late 1980 he denied he had personally killed Yolanda or any of the victims; and finally, during a subsequent preliminary hearing, he testified he was not sure who actually strangled Yolanda Washington. Bianchi explained this last version by maintaining that "when he draws upon his memory to recreate the event, on some occasions he is able to picture himself perpetrating the strangulation and on others he is able to picture Buono doing the killing" (*Los Angeles Times,* July 26, 1981). Bianchi now maintains that he has no "independent recollection" of the murders and has gained most of his knowledge about the stranglings from police reports provided to him.

Is it really possible that people could be confused about whether an act of such magnitude as murder was committed by them or by someone else? Could the passion of the moment, the passage of time, or possibly the interference from similar acts have contributed to a massive distortion in Bianchi's memory? An examination of the literature on memory distortions reveals no study that is quite like this situation—obviously. But the research does show that memory distortions are quite easy to produce, that memory is malleable and subject to all kinds of suggestive influences. The legal notion of an "independent recollection," it seems, may actually be a psychological impossibility.

Of course, it is always possible that Kenneth Bianchi may be a devious, perhaps pathological, liar. His so-called forgetting might be willful withholding of information. The possibility of genuine forgetting, however, deserves serious consideration.

To understand how someone like Kenneth Bianchi might honestly come to forget whether it was he or his cousin who killed Yolanda Washington, one needs to know something about the operation of human memory. Most introductory psychology textbooks devote at least one chapter to this important topic. Most include something about the various types of memory tasks (recall, recognition, relearning) and speculations about what causes the loss of information from memory; and most include some information about the variety of factors that influence forgetting, such as the length of the interval between the initial learning and subsequent recall. Unfortunately, much of the material typically fed to eager and not-so-eager students comes from experiments that use relatively pallid stimulus materials, such as lists of words; and it would stretch the imagination of even the most creative researcher to apply much of this material to an understanding of the constructed memories of Kenneth Bianchi. What comes closest, perhaps, is the research on constructive and reconstructive processes in memory—processes that can be among the most fascinating aspects of the working of human memory.

The remainder of this chapter is divided into two major sections. In the first, I present some new sources of data for learning about the factors that influence memory. Specifically, these data come from large-scale surveys designed to measure people's recollections of automobile accidents, hospitalizations, and other important events in their lives. Accuracy of memory is then compared to actual records. In many cases, these data confirm the discoveries of experimental researchers in that they document the importance of certain factors associated with forgetting. The survey data permit us to see the operation of many psychological factors in real-world, interesting situations. (Such a statement does not mean that these data can ever completely replace the laboratory studies, for the laboratory provides the properly controlled settings that allow investigators to understand the mechanisms by which certain factors operate.) The survey data also serve another purpose: They provide cases showing that the memory of survey respondents can look very different from the memory of subjects in experimental studies. When this discrepancy occurs, psychologists may be forced to rethink their theories of human memory storage and retrieval.

In the second section, I discuss specific research on constructive processes in memory. This research demonstrates that, when people try to remember their past, the process of reconstruction plays an important role. New information is assimilated within the framework of existing knowledge and beliefs, making people prone to recast or dismiss facts that do not fit their expectations. At the same time, information acquired after an event has taken place can transform one's memory of that experience. One's own thoughts and inferences commonly fill in the gaps of a vague memory. The tendency to edit and embellish what people learn and recall seems to be a natural outcome of the way the human memory works.

Old Wine in New Bottles

The Forgetting Curve

Few students escape the introductory course in psychology without learning about the work of Hermann Ebbinghaus (1885). Back in the time of Ebbinghaus there was apparently no crush of college students eager to participate in psychological experiments. So Ebbinghaus used himself as his sole subject. Because he did not want his experiments tainted by any previous knowledge or emotions that he held, he exposed himself to material that could never exist in the outside world—nonsense syllables like JAT, LEM, and DAX. His general procedure was to present himself a list of these syllables under various conditions and then test his recall at various times afterward. Ebbinghaus plotted his results in what is now sometimes referred to as the "forgetting curve," shown in Figure 1. A typical comment about the curve can be found in almost any recent introductory textbook: "For

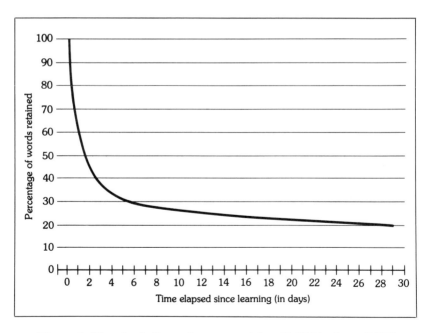

Figure 1. The classic forgetting curve. After H. Ebbinghaus (1885).

nonsense syllables forgetting is quite dramatic. Many kinds of forgetting curves drop rapidly at first and then level off, as Ebbinghaus demonstrated a century ago" (Houston, Bee, Hatfield, & Rimm, 1979).

Brilliant though he may have been, Ebbinghaus probably deserves part of the blame for today's common notion that memory is a dreary list-learning skill. Its apparent dreariness can be minimized, however, by demonstrating, rather than merely asserting, that the forgetting curve applies to many different memory situations. For example, it is possible to show that memory for important personal experiences, such as automobile accidents and hospitalizations for disease or injury, are also subject to laws of forgetting that are similar to those that Ebbinghaus demonstrated nearly a century ago.

For example, some time ago the National Center for Health Statistics conducted a study to evaluate injuries by motor vehicles. The study consisted of interviews with persons known to have been in injury-producing motor vehicle accidents during the 12-month period preceding the interview. Information obtained from each respondent during the interview was compared with data on the official report form filed at the time of the accident. Of primary interest was the relationship between the respondent's ability to report the motor vehicle injuries and the length of time between the occurrence of the accident and the date of the interview (Cash & Moss, 1972). Interviews were conducted with 590 persons who were involved in an accident in which one or more persons in the accident were injured, and, of those interviewed, approximately 14 percent did not report the accident at all.

Figure 2 presents the percentage of individuals who reported the accident as a function of the time between the accident and the interview. As can be seen, the percentage declines as the length of the retention interval increases. In other words, the nonreporting of accidents increases over the retention interval. In the words of the investigators:

> The nonreporting of accidents increases . . . from 3.4% for less than 3 months to a maximum of 27.3 percent for the interval of 9–12 months. The obvious reason for this trend is a decreased ability to recall the occurrence of a motor vehicle accident as the time between the date of the accident and the date of interview increases. (Cash & Moss, 1972, p. 5)

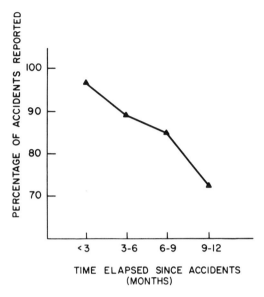

Figure 2. Percentage of accidents reported as a function of time elapsed since the accident. Adapted from Cash and Moss, 1972.

A second example of the laws of forgetting comes from the U.S. National Health Survey, one of the major data collection programs in this country designed to secure health statistics. One part of the project concentrated on people's ability to report their own hospitalizations (Reporting of Hospitalization, 1965). The respondents in this survey were approximately 1500 persons who had been discharged from a hospital during the one-year period beginning April 1, 1958. Individuals were interviewed shortly after April 1, 1959. Figure 3 demonstrates the decrease in reporting of hospitalization that occured as the interval increased between the date of the event and the date of the interview. The data have been characterized in the following way: "This appears to be a typical 'forgetting' curve in which failure to report an event grows as time passes" (Cannell, Marquis, & Laurent, 1977). Actually, while the graph shows a decline in reporting as time passes, the shape of the curve is rather different from the forgetting curve produced by Ebbinghaus. An important characteristic of the hospitalization data is the sudden drop in reporting during the final period, that is, at approximately one year. Since there are explanations for this drop-off that have little to do with actual memory loss (but rather with interviewer strategies for recording responses),

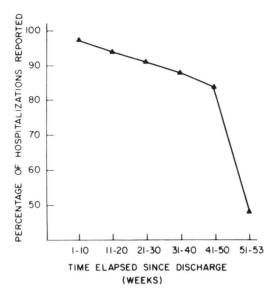

Figure 3. Percentage of hospitalizations reported as a function of time elapsed since discharge. Adapted from Reporting of Hospitalization, 1965.

it is useful to examine the curve with the last point excluded, in which case one sees a more gradual loss of memory over the course of the year.

Although the forgetting curves of Ebbinghaus and those obtained from survey respondents are all monotonically decreasing, for Ebbinghaus severe losses developed quickly; but for other researchers losses have not been as severe and quick. Psychologist Marigold Linton (1979) studied her own memory every day for a six-year period from 1972 until 1977. She wrote on cards individual memories such as "I have dinner at the Canton Kitchen; delicious lobster dish" or "I land at Orly Airport in Paris." By 1977 she had written down descriptions of more than 5,000 items. Every month she tested her memory, and her results revealed a forgetting curve that was shaped a bit differently from Ebbinghaus's. In general, she seemed to forget things at a low, fairly steady rate, with the numbers of forgotten items usually increasing slightly from year to year. From this example, one learns that it is important to remember that not all forgetting curves look exactly like the one obtained by Ebbinghaus; their precise shape will depend upon the type of material to be remembered as well as upon many other factors.

Measures of Retention

Another important aspect of memory typically discussed in introductory treatments concerns the various measures of retention. It is generally pointed out that not all tests of memory are equally effective (e.g., Wingfield & Byrnes, 1981, and most introductory psychology textbooks). When different measures of retention are used to chart the time course of forgetting, typically recognition memory is found to produce the highest retention scores and free recall to produce the lowest (although there are exceptions; see Watkins & Tulving, 1975). Cued recall, which occasionally resembles recognition, is also typically superior to free recall in its capacity to pull recalcitrant items from memory. The effect of these various measures of retention is easily shown with meaningless to-be-remembered information, but it can also be shown in a more meaningful way.

For example, the survey conducted by Neuman (1976) was designed to measure patterns of recall among television news viewers. For this purpose, a sample of San Francisco Bay area telephone listings was drawn, and households were called in the early evening over a two-week period in the spring of 1971. Only adults (232 individuals) who had watched the network newscast that evening were interviewed. They were asked the following: "We are interested in what TV viewers can recall from watching the dinner-hour news. Often people can only remember a few stories. Can you recall any of the news stories on the network news this evening? Do any details come to mind?" (p. 115). These initial data were thus obtained using the method of free recall. After the respondent gave all the information he or she could, a "cued recall" procedure was used. Skipping stories already mentioned, the interviewer read down a list of "headlines" from the particular newscast watched. The form of the questions was "Do you recall the story about the Secretary of State's speech on the Middle East situation?" Whenever the respondent indicated that a story was remembered, he or she was asked for any details that came to mind.

The results showed that, even though people were interviewed relatively soon after watching the news (from several minutes to three hours after), they could recall very little. Of an average of 19.8 news stories per network broadcast, respondents reported recalling an average of only 1.2 stories; however, memory proved to be better when headlines were provided. On the average, respondents reported re-calling 4.4 stories with supporting details and an additional 4.3 stories without details. The averages add up to 9.9 out of 19.8 stories for a total recall rate of 50 percent. Clearly, then, the various measures of retention produced different results, in the direction expected from the results of classic experimental studies of memory.

Exposure Time

Other memory phenomena demonstrated by experimental psycholo-gists with rather pallid materials can be seen in the data from their surveys. For example, it is well known that the amount of time that a person has to look at whatever is going to be later remembered—exposure time—affects the likelihood of accurate memory. In this vein, researchers have shown that words presented at a nine-second rate are recalled better than words presented at a three-second rate (Glanzer & Cunitz, 1966) and faces presented for thirty-two seconds are remembered better than those same faces presented for only ten seconds (Laughery, Alexander, & Lane, 1971).

As one might expect, a similar result occurs when people try to remember their own hospitalizations. As can be seen in Figure 4, as the duration of hospital stay increases, the chances of the hospitaliza-tion being remembered also increases. Less than 75 percent of all hospitalizations lasting one day are reported whereas approximately 98 percent of hospitalizations lasting more than three weeks are re-ported.

In all fairness, it must be noted the hospitalization data do not demonstrate the "pure" exposure-time effect that is shown in the lab-oratory studies. For one thing, the type of illness that would require a short stay in the hospital is different from the type of illness that would require a longer stay, and thus the length of stay is confounded with the severity of the illness. To some extent, the severity of the illness is related to the likelihood that the hospitalization will be re-ported. For example, nonsurgical cases (presumably less serious) are more seriously underreported than surgical cases (19 percent under-reporting versus 12 percent underreporting, when deliveries are ex-cluded from the surgical count). But an important additional factor in underreporting is how embarrassing or threatening the hospitaliza-tion is. In the study by Glanzer and Cunitz, respondents failed to

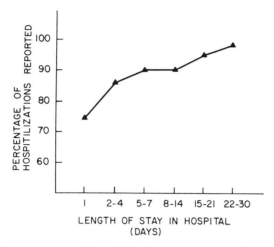

Figure 4. Percentage of hospitalizations reported as a function of length of stay in the hospital. Adapted from Reporting of Hospitalization, 1965.

report nonembarrassing hospitalizations such as pneumonia and appendicitis 10 percent of the time, whereas for embarrassing hospitalizations such as those involving syphilis, diseases of the genital organs, or psychoneurotic disorders, respondents failed to report 21 percent of the time.

Hypermnesia

Data collected from individuals regarding their own personal experiences also provide documentation for some of the more recently researched phenomena such as hypermnesia. The results of Erdelyi and his colleagues (Erdelyi, 1970; Erdelyi & Goldberg, 1979; Erdelyi & Kleinbard, 1978) have been said to corroborate Freud's clinically based observation that what appears to be hopelessly forgotten can be recovered into consciousness. This phenomenon is called hypermnesia. Hypermnesia research has shown that subjects who are tested on, for example, their memory for pictures can often improve their recall by close to 100 percent over initial recall levels (Erdelyi, 1981).

As it happens, survey respondents also recover unreported incidents when questioned about them at a later time. This phenomenon can be seen most clearly in the hospitalization survey. In that study, a special follow-up interview was conducted with respondents who failed to report their hospitalization, in part to discover the reasons for the nonreporting. This interview occurred a week or two after the first interview, and the results were dramatic. In 170 follow-up interviews, the respondents now reported the hospitalization on 106 occasions (or 62 percent). The researchers called this percentage "a particularly high proportion" (Reporting of Hospitalization, p. 39). Most of these hospitalizations were reported in response to the same question that had been asked during the earlier interview: "During the past 12 months has anyone in the family been a patient in a hospital overnight or longer?" Some, however, were picked up by subsequent questions such as "Have you ever been a patient in a hospital?" followed by probing for the date, or "Were you in a hospital for any accidents or injuries during the past 12 months?"

Several hypotheses for the good reporting observed in the follow-up interviews are suggested. One hypothesis is that the additional questions may have helped to stimulate the respondent to think about episodes he or she may have overlooked. The subsequent questions may have encouraged the respondent to think more deeply and try harder to recall hospitalizations. The mere fact of a second interview tells respondents that the agency conducting the survey considers the information important. If the survey is so important to this agency, the respondent thinks that working harder at the task must be worthwhile. Whatever the actual explanation, the data of the hospitalization survey and those of Erdelyi demonstrate that additional recall attempts are likely to yield additional information from memory.

Time-Coding

Even more esoteric memory phenomena found in the literature can be seen in the memory of survey respondents. I refer to the research concerning how memory keeps track of when an event happened, sometimes called "time-coding" (Morton, 1971). A number of laboratory studies have been conducted in which a subject is exposed to a long series of items such as words or nonsense syllables and then memory for the times the items appeared is tested. In some cases, each item appears twice, the two presentations being separated by a controlled number of intervening items; and, when the second presentation occurs, the subjects must indicate how far back in the series the first presentation was (Hinrichs, 1970). In other studies, subjects are shown two items that have been presented earlier and must decide which of the two occurred more recently (Yntema & Trask, 1963). In the first case, the subject is making absolute judgments of recency whereas, in the second case, the subject is making relative judgments. In both cases, the memory strength of items seems to affect judgments of recency in a positive direction; that is, stronger items are judged to be more recent (see also Bower, 1972; Morton, 1968). A related finding is that the recency judgments of inaccurately recalled items is worse than the recency judgments of accurately recalled (and presumably stronger) items (Brelsford, Freund, & Rundus, 1967).

A similar time-coding distortion occurs when people try to recall the instances in their past in which they were victims of crimes. The National Crime Survey (NCS) is a major statistical series instituted by the Law Enforcement Assistance Administration (LEAA) in 1972 to develop new information on the incidence of crime and its impact on society. Data are collected via personal interviews at six-month intervals in thousands of households (Surveying Crime, 1976). Several questions on the 1980 survey ask about victimizations that may have occurred in the last six months, for example, "Did anyone try to rob you by using force or threatening to harm you?" or "Did anyone beat you up, attack you, or hit you with something, such as a rock or bottle?" In general, information is collected on the circumstances under which the event occurred, on the effects on the victim, and on the reporting of the incident to the police.

A major concern of the designers of the National Crime Survey is the extent to which the respondents accurately remember, and accurately report to the interviewers, incidents that happened to them. One problem for the interviewers is that victims forget victimizations have occurred or else deliberately fail to mention a victimization. But an equally serious problem is "forward telescoping," or a memory distortion in which victimizations that occurred prior to the beginning of the reference period are telescoped forward into the reference period. In one study, a check of known victimizations revealed that about 20 percent of those shown in police records as having occurred prior to the beginning of the reference period were reported by victims as having occurred within the reference period (Garofalo & Hindelang, 1977). Such forward telescoping obviously inflates the estimated number of victimizations reported as occurring in the reference period. The opposite error, "backward telescoping," or movement of events into the more distant past, is not common (Sudman & Bradburn, 1973).

The analogy between the forward telescoping of crime experiences that can be assumed to be quite salient to people with the forward movement of stronger items in the word-list experiments is straightforward. The theoretically oriented studies may help us understand the forward telescoping problem and devise solutions to minimize it (for example, see Loftus & Marburger, 1981). And the observations from the crime studies certainly provide an interesting example of distortions in time-coding at work in a real-world setting.

Aging and Memory

There are instances, however, in which data derived from laboratory studies do not match what is observed in these surveys. An example is in the research on long-term memory in older people. Aging is a process typically accompanied by a perceived decline in the ability to store and retrieve information from memory. And, in fact, it has been said that one of the clearest findings from the laboratory research in the field of aging and memory is that, once the amount of material to be remembered exceeds the span of primary memory, older people are unable to recall as much of the material as their younger counterparts (Hartley, Harker, & Walsh, 1980). This result has been found when older people try to recall recently presented word lists (Schonfield & Robertson, 1966) and when other procedures such as recognition (Botwinick & Storandt, 1974) and cued recall (Drachman & Leavitt, 1972; Smith, 1977) are used. Since this finding is so "clear," many researchers have concentrated their efforts on understanding the nature and causes of age-related deficits in long-term memory.

Although the universal conclusion to be reached from the laboratory studies is that older individuals have more difficulty storing and retrieving information from long-term memory, a different conclusion could be reached from an examination of age effects in the memory of survey respondents about their own past experiences. In an auto accident study conducted in Michigan (Henson, Cannell, & Lawson, 1973), age effects were examined. The respondents were drivers of automobiles involved in accidents in a single county in Michigan during the years 1968–1971 and had records on file. For analysis purposes, age was grouped into three categories: 16–19 years, 20–49 years, and 50–70 years. An overall index of accuracy was constructed for all items for which reliable validity information could be obtained. The index covered 39 items about the accident including the environment, the car, the time, the personal injuries, and the damage to the vehicle. Contrary to the predictions of the investigators, there were no age effects. The mean accuracy rates for the three age groups were .72, .75, and .75 respectively.

A strong aging effect does exist, however, in the data from a large national household survey taken in the fall months of 1974 (Schuman, 1980). About one third of the way through the hour-long interview the following question was asked: "The Arab nations are trying to work for real peace with Israel. . . . Do you agree or disagree?" There were no other questions in the survey that were similar and that might easily have been confused with this one.

About four months later, respondents were reinterviewed by telephone. They were asked the "Arab-Israel" question again and were also asked whether they recalled being asked it before. In addition, other respondents who had not earlier been asked the Arab-Israel question were asked whether they recalled the question. The results were striking: Of those who had been asked the question before, 24 percent said they remembered it. Of those who had not been asked the question, however, 8 percent said they "remembered" it. When the recollections of the Arab-Israel question were examined for age effects, two results emerged. Older respondents (more than 65 years old) who had been asked the item were significantly less likely to recall it, while older respondents who had not been asked the question before were marginally more likely to recall (incorrectly) having heard it. The full data are shown in Table 1.

What have we gained by using survey data as a source of information about the operation of human memory? First, we have discovered

Table 1
Percentages of Subjects Who Said "Yes" to Arab-Israel Question

Answer	Age Group					
	18–24	25–34	35–44	45–54	54–65	>65
Correct	23.2	33.3	27.6	21.3	16.4	11.2
Incorrect	7.3	2.8	7.3	10.0	7.3	14.0

Note. Data from Schuman, Personal Communication, December 1980.

some regularities in the survey data that are consistent with our laboratory observations: for example, the observations that memory declines with the passage of time and that more memory can be retrieved with additional retrieval attempts. The survey data allow us to see various phenomena at work outside the laboratory, and they nicely supplement the controlled laboratory findings. These results are especially interesting since they reflect memory for real-life episodes and are thus less vulnerable to attacks on their ecological validity.

But there is more. Occasionally we discover in the survey data a result that runs counter to those results produced in laboratory studies, for example, that long-term memory functioning declines with advancing age. Such findings must be interpreted cautiously since, as any memory researcher knows, the results of any particular experiment depend to a great extent on the methods being used. And yet a survey study that shows that some variable operates differently than in a laboratory study may tell us something. Perhaps we have learned a bit about the boundary conditions for that variable. Perhaps we are forced to modify, even slightly, our theoretical interpretations on the nature of human memory functioning.

Constructive Processes in Memory

The distortions in memory that arise when people try to reconstruct their past constitute one of the most fascinating aspects of the way humans remember. People commonly confuse what happened one time with what happened another. When memories are vague, people fill in the gaps with what they believe to be true or what they infer to be true. In short, the process of piecing together the past can often be highly prone to distortion. Two types of distortions can be distinguished: schema-based reconstructions and induced reconstructions.

Schema-Based Reconstructions

The study of constructive processes in memory has a long and interesting history. An important early figure was Sir Fredrick C. Bartlett (1932) who was motivated by an interest in how people transmitted and recalled simple stories. Bartlett had subjects play a version of the "telephone game" popular among children. He gave one subject a story to read—his favorite story was a North American Indian tribal legend. The first subject read the story and then told it to another subject who in turn told it to another and so on. After many subjects and many renditions, the story became substantially changed. But the changes were not random aberrations; rather several important patterns emerged. First, items that were not easily assimilated into the subject's existing concepts of life, warfare, and death—the themes of the story—were simply dropped. Other themes were sharpened, for example, the theme of family responsibility. The original version told of concerned relatives, and this theme was occasionally mentally transformed into an elderly mother's dependence upon her son. Many subjects introduced distortions into the story that conformed to their expectations based upon past experience. Less familiar items such as "canoe" and "hunting seals" became the more familiar items "boat" and "fishing." At other times, elements that never appeared in the original story, such as "dark forests," were added. Often subjects added a "moral" to the story because this kind of ending is typical for this type of folktale.

The constructive side of memory has since been demonstrated many times. In a classic study from the 1940s, two psychologists showed subjects the scene from a subway car reproduced in Figure 5 (Allport & Postman, 1947). Among other things, the drawing shows a black man apparently arguing with a white man who is carrying a razor. In the typical procedure, one subject looked at the drawing and described it to another, who described it to another, and so on until the description had passed through many people. When the last person was asked "What did the picture show?" it was common for the razor to mentally migrate from the white hand to the black hand. The common stereotype that blacks are more likely than whites to be violent influenced what subjects perceived and remembered.

Distortions such as these provide important clues as to how human memory works. Apparently people try to assimilate new information within the framework of existing knowledge and beliefs. Bartlett used the term "schemata" to describe the organization of information into conceptual frameworks or meaningful units. New information to which we are exposed gets organized into existing schemata. For example, if we learn about an Indian going to battle, we try to fit this fact into our preexisting notions about what Indian battle

Figure 5. Drawing shown to subjects in the study of G. W. Allport and L. J. Postman, *The Psychology of Rumor* (New York: Holt, 1947), p. 71. Reprinted by permission of L. J. Postman.

is like. Information that does not conform to our expectations we may drop or modify in some way. Thus the process of storing information into memory has a strong constructive component to it. Similarly, the process of retrieving information involves constructive processes. Our retrieval is guided by our existing concepts about the world. If we know that a black man, a white man, and a razor appear in a certain picture, and if we believe that blacks are generally more violent than whites, then we construct an image of the razor within the black man's grasp. This construction then becomes our memory. This view of memory emphasizes its creative aspects, and, indeed, remembering appears to involve more of a reconstructive than of a simple reproductive process.

These classic studies of distortion involve the method of serial reproduction in which the recollection of one person is fed to another and so on. It is natural to ask whether similar distortions occur when a single individual is given information that must be remembered later. As it happens, there are numerous demonstrations of the fact that our general knowledge, or what we know about the world, will introduce distortions into our recollections. For example, in one study (Bransford, Barclay, & Franks, 1972) subjects studied sentences like this one: "Three turtles sat on a log, and a fish swam beneath it." Naturally, if the fish swam beneath the log, it must have swum beneath the turtles.

This inference would be natural, and, if made, would be likely to become part of the memory for the sentence. In fact, in the study many subjects later thought they had seen this sentence: "Three turtles sat on a log, and a fish swam beneath them." The second sentence is such a natural inference from the first one that subjects typically had difficulty telling which of the two they actually had seen. Here again we have an example of the constructive nature of memory.

People add to the original input thoughts and inferences that are likely to follow. Occasionally this behavior will lead to erroneous recall. For example, if we hear the statement "While Harvey was drinking in his favorite bar, he got in a fight and broke a bottle over Frank's head," we are likely to infer that it was a beer bottle or a whiskey bottle rather than a bottle of Perrier water. We might very well add this inference to our memory for the statement and then come to believe we actually heard about a specific kind of bottle. Our final memory would consist of more information than the original told to us.

A modern-day way of discussing these constructive phenomena is in terms of scripts. A script is a hypothesized cognitive structure that, when activated, organizes comprehension of new information (Abelson, 1981). Thus the "restaurant script" involves a bundle of expectations about food being prepared by a cook, served by a waiter, and eaten by a customer. In its weakest sense, a script is simply a bundle of expectations about the potential occurrence of a set of events; in its strongest sense, it involves an expectation about the order of these events as well as about their mere occurrence. A major demonstration of the predictive power of scripts is the "gap-filling" phenomenon. Subjects who are given stories to remember very often falsely recognize information as though it had been presented when it had not. Subjects do not falsely recognize just anything, however; rather they tend falsely to recall nonmentioned script events. Thus it would be likely for a subject incorrectly to remember reading about a waiter bringing a customer a menu but not falsely to think the waiter took off his shoe (Bower, Black, & Turner, 1979; Graesser, Woll, Kowalski, & Smith, 1980). The tendency to fill in the gaps in memory with script-related information has been used to support the notion that a person's long-term memory for many events consists of a generic script modified by explicit memories of unusual aspects.

In these examples, the shifts in memory are brought about by an individual's prior knowledge, schema, scripts, and expectations based upon past experience with the world. Whatever the exact construct, clearly rich packages of information in memory guide the storage and retrieval of new information. Other forces that produce serious distortions in memory are at work, however. These distortions are brought about by the interjection of new information or suggestive influences from the outside. I refer to this influence using the term "induced reconstruction" to indicate that it is induced from external rather than internal forces.

Induced Reconstruction

To study the process of distortion, researchers have been deliberately distorting people's memories rather than waiting for distortions to occur on their own. (See Loftus, 1979, for a review of this research.) Briefly, an experiment in which subjects are presented with a film of a complex event and immediately afterward are asked a series of questions is representative of the paradigm that has been used to study the incorporation of new information into memory. Typically, some of the questions are designed to suggest the existence of an object that did not exist. Thus, in one study, some subjects who had watched a film of an automobile accident were asked, "How fast was the white sports car going when it passed the barn while traveling along the country road?" whereas no barn existed. Other subjects were asked a control question, such as "How fast was the white sports car going while traveling along the country road?" All subjects were later asked whether they had seen a barn.

The misleading questions were found to increase by a factor of six the likelihood that subjects would later report having seen the non-existent barn. The researchers advanced the argument that the questions were effective because they contained information—in this case false information—that became integrated into the person's recollection of the event, thereby supplementing that memory.

In other studies, new information was shown to do more than simply supplement a recollection: It could occasionally alter, or transform, a recollection. Thus, in one study, subjects saw a series of color slides depicting successive stages in an accident involving a car and a pedestrian. In the midst of the series, the car, a red Datsun, was seen traveling along a side street toward an intersection at which there was a stop sign for half of the subjects and a yield sign for the remaining subjects. Some subjects then received a question containing a piece of misinformation. For example, the question "Did another car pass the red Datsun while it was stopped at the stop sign?" contains a piece of misinformation when it is asked of subjects who actually saw the yield sign. And, finally, subjects were tested for their recollection of the sign. Depending on the time intervals that occurred between the slides, the intervening questions, and the final recollection, as many as 80 percent of the subjects indicated that their recollections were influenced by the misinformation.

In other experiments, new information presented as another witness's description or as an overheard conversation similarly caused changes in memory for details. For example, Loftus & Greene (1980) showed subjects photographs of individuals such as the person depicted in Figure 6a. Afterward, some subjects read a description attributed to another person that either did or did not contain an erro-

Figure 6a. Target face seen by subjects in the study by E. F. Loftus and E. Greene, "Warning: Even Memory for Faces May Be Contagious," *Law and Human Behavior*, 1980, *4* (4), p. 326. Reprinted by permission of Plenum Publishing Corporation.

neous detail—in this case that the fellow had curly rather than straight hair. When later tested, 22 percent of the subjects included the misleading detail in their own verbal descriptions of the target face; 33 percent included the detail in their reconstructions of the face. The erroneous details rarely occurred when they had not been mentioned by the other witness. Figure 6b shows a reconstruction of one of the target faces made by a subject who had not been exposed to misleading information and a reconstruction made by a subject who had been exposed to misinformation of curly hair.

These experiments, along with many others using similar procedures, indicate that false information can be introduced into a person's recollection, whether that recollection is measured by a recall or a recognition procedure. Further, the information can supplement the previously acquired memory (as in the case of the barn) or it can actually transform it (as in the case of the stop sign/yield sign or that of the curly/straight hair). Even though the researchers have taken great pains to use rich and complex events, the ecological validity of such experiments has still been questioned (for example, see Ellis, 1980).

Figure 6b. Subject reconstruction of target face in the absence of misleading information about curly hair, and a reconstruction of face after exposure to that misinformation. Reprinted from Loftus and Greene, 1980, by permission of Plenum Publishing Corporation.

The criticism, often in question form, goes something like the following: To what extent do the studies tell us something about constructive processes in real people remembering real experiences? As it happens, constructive processes are rampant in the memories of people for their own past experiences. Thus, once again, the respondents in surveys provide data that dovetail nicely with those obtained in the laboratory.

Memory for Personal Experiences

Natural shifts in memory can be seen to occur when people remember their own past experiences. The author Thomas Hinde expressed it well in his novel "The Day the Call Came" (discovered by Morton, Hammersley, & Berkerian, 1981):

> I was able to invent incidents in my past and elaborate them and after a few weeks become genuinely unsure whether I was remembering what had happened or what I had thought about so carefully that I now believed. And even when something seemed to obtrude as a real memory, by remembering it and rethinking it I could make it not more but less real because any real memory there might have been was obscured by the process of remembering it. (p. 1)

Anecdotal observations aside, again a comparison of memory with actual records reveals some interesting facts about the constructive nature of human memory. Research shows that people often remember themselves as having held more responsible, better-paying jobs than they actually had. People also recall donating more to charity, voting more frequently, and raising more intelligent children than object records indicate (Cannell & Kahn, 1968). I shall examine one of the studies in more detail.

One enormous research effort investigated mothers' recollection of their child's early behavior and also the child's recollection of his or her own early behavior (Yarrow, Campbell, & Burton, 1970). The mothers who furnished retrospective reports had at least one child enrolled in a particular nursery school sometime between 1928 and 1958; the mothers were interviewed anywhere from 3 to 30 years later. The "child" was also interviewed at this time. The memories of these respondents revealed sizable and systematic departures from the original information. Thus mothers recalled that their children walked at an earlier age than they had; were taller than they actually were; ate, slept, and toilet trained better than they actually did; and had a higher IQ than objective measures revealed. Similarly, the children themselves remembered that they walked at an earlier age than they had; ate, slept, and toilet trained better than they actually did; and also had a higher IQ. The memories of both mother and child had shifted so as to cast the child in a more favorable light.

Some of the case histories provided in the research monograph illustrate dramatic discrepancies in memory. For example, the child Jimmy is described by his teacher as "timid, sensitive . . . likes nonaggressive children because he cannot defend himself against stronger ones." Six months later a psychologist described him as "more introverted and tense rather than overt and relaxed." Yet Jimmy's mother's recollection, given when Jimmy was 32 years old, was entirely different: "I think he was quite extroverted. He was an effervescent child, gay, happy, outgoing. He liked other children very much and played well with them" (pp. 78–79). With the passage of 28 years, the mother's recollection contained some serious distortions of the past.

Of course, positive shifts in memory occur far more quickly than this. The case of Mary provides a nice example. Mary's school psychologist reported on comments made by her mother at a conference:

> [A]t home she is a demanding, domineering child. . . . She dominates the home too much. . . . [T]his dependency on me depresses me. I don't like it . . . she has cost me a tremendous amount of vitality to break away from her hold on adults. She has drained everything out of me some days. . . . I have been unbearably tired because of Mary. . . . I had a miserable time at the Cape, where I went for a month for a rest. I couldn't leave her even to go for a swim and leave her with a friend. . . . It is a constant tension she keeps me under. (pp. 79–80)

When Mary was eight years old, her mother was interviewed and recalled Mary's early childhood in these words:

> I had no particular behavior problems. . . . At three to five years she was very manageable. . . . She was a very amenable child. There were no stresses or strains at home, we were a very contented threesome and when her brother would come home from school she was very, very thrilled, she adored him. . . . She rarely showed any anger as a young child, she would seem to be very well-adjusted. (pp. 79–80)

Even though only four years separated the two sets of data, there were dramatic contrasts in the information.

What causes these distortions in memory? One possibility is that memory naturally shifts in a positive or prestige-enhancing direction, perhaps for the purpose of allowing us to have a more comfortable recollection of the past. Other possibilities exist, however. For example, the investigators in the mother/child memory study suggest that one's present situation wields an influence in reconstructions of the past. (A similar suggestion was made by Haggard, Brekstad, & Skard, 1960, who said that the mothers' recollections did not reflect earlier experiences and attitudes so much as their "current picture of the past" p. 317.) If the grownup child is now smart and happy, the mother has a tendency to recall that the child always was that way.

A similar example of alteration in personal memories brought about by the intrusion of the present into one's memory for the past comes from a study of the memories of adolescents regarding past drug use (Single, Kandel, & Johnson, 1975). Students from 18 public secondary schools in New York were questioned about their drug use in the fall of 1971 and again 5 to 6 months later in the spring of 1972. Usable questionnaires from both occasions were returned from over 7000 students. Several questions asked about the use of various legal and illegal substances; the exact wording of the questions varied slightly for different drugs. For hard liquor, marijuana, and hashish, students were asked "How often have you ever used?" and "How often have you used during the past 30 days?"

Although occasionally students reported the use of a nonexistent drug ("adrenochromes or wagon wheels"), the underreporting problem was much more serious. Of interest to the present analysis are those instances in which students reported at Time 2 never to have used the drug although they did report use at Time 1. For example, 21 percent of students who claimed to be nonusers of hard liquor at Time 2 had earlier claimed to have used hard liquor. The figures for cocaine, marijuana, or hashish were on the order of 1 percent to 4 percent. Based upon the totality of data, the investigators concluded that these errors were not due to random fluctuation or to willful misrepresentation but rather to errors in recall. Specifically, these errors of recall occurred in cases in which students only infrequently used a particular drug in the past and were not currently using the drug and thus viewed themselves as non-drug users. This current image caused the students to forget they had ever had any experience with the substance at all.

Mechanisms of Memory Change

One question that arises is whether there are differences between memories derived through one's own perceptual processes and memories generated by suggestions from the outside or by internal processes such as imagination or thought. It has been recently suggested that "real" memories differ from created memories along several dimensions: Real memories are thought to be more semantically detailed and to contain more information, whereas created memories are thought to be more schematic (Johnson & Raye, 1981). The experiments on which these ideas are based involved memory for individual words and pictures that were presented, so whether the theory would apply to the more complex memories with which this chapter has been concerned still remains to be shown. The very act of thinking about an event has recently been shown to make the image of that event clearer and more vivid (Loftus, 1981). This finding suggests that even if "real" memories begin with some advantage over generated ones, that advantage may disappear if the generated memory is refreshed a number of times.

When a recollection has altered, whether a stop sign becomes a yield sign or a sad and difficult child becomes a happy, easy-going one, it is natural to ask about the fate of the underlying memory traces. Have the traces truly been altered by the postevent suggestions so that they could not be recovered in the future? Or have they merely been made less accessible but potentially recoverable at some future time? While I have taken the position that some memories may undergo destructive transformations (Loftus & Loftus, 1980), other investigators have preferred to believe that, as a general rule, all memories are potentially recoverable and that faulty recall is a problem of accessibility (Morton, Hammersley, & Berkerian, 1981).

Whether or not the true memory trace exists under layers of other memories, one can still wonder why we humans might have been constructed with malleable memories. An emerging area of research suggests that there may be clinical reasons for such memories. In a study comparing depressed and nondepressed individuals, nondepressed people's recollections were found to be characterized with a halo or glow that involved an illusory self-enhancement in which they saw themselves more positively than others saw them (Lewinsohn, Mischel, Chaplin, & Barton, 1980). This glow appears to lead to greater attention to and memory for one's own positive personal attributes (Mischel, Ebbesen, & Zeiss, 1976) and poorer recall of negative feedback or punishment received in the past (Nelson & Craighead, 1977). In other words, the depressed individuals were "sadder but wiser" (Alloy & Abramson, 1979). During the course of treatment, the perceptions of depressed persons can be seen to change, in the sense that they begin to see themselves more positively but also more unrealistically. Lewinsohn et al. tentatively conjecture that a key to avoiding depression may involve recalling oneself more favorably than is perhaps warranted.

Not long ago I suggested that one way to answer the question of why people might have been constructed with malleable memories was to assume hypothetically that we have the potential for total mind malleability (Loftus, 1980). One can imagine a world in which people could go to a special kind of psychologist—a memory doctor—and have their memories modified or in which a person could regularly attend clinics that specialize in memory modification treatment to have some particularly difficult memory altered. What therapeutic uses would this treatment have? How would our world be different?

One could be treated for depression or feelings of worthlessness; the memory doctor would simply modify the memories leading to these negative feelings. One could have treatments to eliminate social prejudices; to the extent that these are based upon a few incidents involving a unique group of people, the memory doctor could wipe out or alter memory of these incidents. One might also have treatments to increase happiness. If people feel bad because they are worse off than they once were, the memory doctor could eliminate the basis for comparison. And so on.

The idea may seem far-fetched since memory obviously cannot now be modified on command; but memory can be modified partially. People's memories of past events change in helpful ways, leading them to be happier than they might otherwise be. Memories also change in harmful ways and can occasionally cause people serious trouble.

Since suggesting the idea of a memory clinic with memory doctors busily working on the minds of eager clients, I have come across the writings of practicing therapists who suggest that the idea is not all that far-fetched. For example, in a recent article in *Contemporary Psychoanalysis* (Issacharoff & Hunt, 1978), the authors argue that "by creating a new truth in the present, the truth of the past is necessarily changed" (p. 296). In fact, the authors subtitled their article "The 'New Truth' in the Psychoanalytic Process." Apparently, the psychiatrist-hypnotist Milton Erickson tried to use memory restructuring for therapeutic purposes. One of his patients was a woman who had had a very unhappy childhood and was now plagued with low self-esteem. Dr. Erickson ignored her present life but, through hypnotic suggestion, inserted into her mind memories of happy experiences with a loving father. The treatment is reported to have been successful in so far as it increased her feelings of self-worth by giving her a personal "memory" of a happy, loving childhood.

Further details about these techniques can be found in a book aptly entitled *Frogs into Princes* (Bandler & Grinder, 1979). Drawing from the techniques of Erickson, these therapists began creating entire personal histories in people. In this way, they enabled their clients to have experiences that would serve as the resources for the kinds of behaviors the clients wanted now to have. For example, in helping people to lose weight, the therapists encountered the major obstacle that many people who had been fat all their lives could not adjust to being thin. "If you've always been fat, you were never chosen first to be on a sports team. You were never asked to dance in high school. You never ran fast. You have no experience of certain kinds of athletic and physical movements" (p. 99). Instead of trying to get the clients to adjust to this dramatic change in their lives, the therapists created "new childhoods" in which the clients grew up as thin people. Similarly, the therapists created a new childhood for a woman who had grown up being asthmatic. Now her children desperately wanted to have pets, but the woman had severe allergic reactions in the presence of pets. Oddly, skin tests did not reveal this allergy. When the "memory doctors" gave the woman a childhood of growing up without being asthmatic, she lost her response to animals. In the words of the creators of *Frogs into Princes:*

> [we] could very easily install memories in you that related to real world experiences that never occurred and could not be documented in any way—that were just bizarre hallucinations out of [our] fantasy. Made-up memories can change you just as well as the arbitrary perceptions that you made up at the time about "real world events." That happens a lot in therapy. (p. 96)

Modification of Memory for Actions

No one knows just how much of our memory for the past is built up from things that never happened in the past but were real or imagined items drawn from other sources. In the case of the Hillside Strangler discussed at the beginning of this lecture, Kenneth Bianchi explained his alterations in memory by saying that "when he draws upon his memory to re-create the event, on some occasions he is able to picture himself perpetrating the strangulation and on others he is able to picture Buono doing the killing" (*Los Angeles Times,* July 26, 1981). Does this phenomenon make sense in terms of what we know about the operation of human memory? The laboratory studies have involved modification of recollection for details. Stop signs can become yield signs, and straight hair can become curly. But can similar modifications occur in memory for actions rather than details?

Some preliminary results suggest that memory for actions is modifiable. These preliminary results have arisen out of a college homework assignment given regularly in my course, "Cognitive Psychology," taught at the University of Washington. In that course, as part of the section on memory distortion, I have assigned students the task of trying to create in someone's mind a "memory" for something that did not exist. My hope has been that the students will discover how relatively easy this task can be and, further, that they would see that a memory so acquired can be as real to a person as a memory that is the result of one's own ordinary perceptual sensations. The students typically attempt the memory change on one or more family members, roommates, or colleagues at work. Over the years, several students have reported successful alteration in the memory for actions. For example, one student successfully convinced sorority sisters that a fellow sister was drinking alcohol to excess at a party when actually she did not take a single drink. Another student convinced friends who had attended a party that her husband and her close friend had been holding hands at the party when they had not.

More rigorous studies of memory for actions have recently been attempted. In one study, Lehnert, Robertson, & Black (in press) tried to modify subjects' memories for the actions of individuals by post-event questions. Specifically, subjects read a series of narratives and then answered two sets of questions about the narratives. The first set contained some questions that were misleading, and the second set tested whether these misleading questions altered memory for the narratives. The initial questions tried to mislead about the actions people engaged in or about the states people were in. For example, the experimenters tried to convince the subjects that a man had closed a window when he had actually opened it or that a man had let a dog out of the house when he actually had let it in (action modification). In other instances, the experimenters tried to convince the subjects that some lamps in a room had been too high rather than too low (a state change).

One goal of the research was to determine whether modifications are remote as well as local. A local modification is an immediate change: The subject remembers that the man closed the window, and this is the only alteration in memory. A remote change is one with additional "ripple effects": The subject remembers that the man closed the window and also recalls that the people inside had been cold rather than warm.

Overall results of the study showed that the misleading postevent questions modified subjects' memory for 20 percent of the items directly related to the questions and for 10.5 percent of the items remotely related. Thus both local and remote effects were shown. As to the question of whether both states and actions could be modified, a complex result occurred. States directly related to the misleading questions could be modified, and subsequent remote actions were also vulnerable to modification. Actions directly related to misleading questions were not easily modifiable, however. In other words, the investigators showed that "memory for states can be directly modified by misleading questions and that the modification will 'ripple' through the memory representation to also change related actions. On the other hand, our misleading questions did not directly modify actions to a significant extent" (p. 17). They go on to note that their finding of relative stability of events over states is consistent with related evidence suggesting that events are represented "more strongly" in memory than states (Graesser, Robertson, Lovelace, & Swinehart, 1980). These preliminary results do suggest, however, that despite their stronger representation, there are conditions under which memory for actions can be modified.

Although studies have thus shown that the memory of the behavior of others can be changed, as yet no one has empirically demonstrated the alteration in memory for one's own behavior. Yet the

memories of individuals in large-scale surveys suggest that this alteration is quite feasible. If people can reconstruct the past to remember
that they voted more often than they did, that they gave more to
charity, that they walked at an earlier age, that they never used a
particular drug when they actually had—if Thomas Hinde can have
trouble distinguishing what he actually did from what he merely
thought about doing—then why can't the Hillside Strangler?

References

Abelson, R. P. Psychological status of the script concept. *American Psychologist,* 1981, *36,*
715–729.

Alloy, L. B., & Abramson, L. Y. Judgment of contingency in depressed and nondepressed students: Sadder but wiser? *Journal of Experimental Psychology,* 1979, *108,*
441–485.

Allport, G. W., & Postman, L. J. *The psychology of rumor.* New York: Holt, 1947.

Bandler, R., & Grinder, J. *Frogs into princes: Neurolinguistic programming.* Moab, Utah:
Real People Press, 1979.

Bartlett, F. C. *Remembering: A study in experimental and social psychology.* New York: Cambridge University Press, 1932.

Botwinick, J., & Storandt, M. *Memory, related functions, and age.* Springfield, Ill.: Charles
C. Thomas, 1974.

Bower, G. H. Stimulus-sampling theory of encoding variability. In A. W. Melton &
E. Martin (Eds.), *Coding processes in human memory.* Washington, D.C.: Winston,
1972.

Bower, G. H., Black, J., & Turner, T. Scripts in text comprehension and memory.
Cognitive Psychology, 1979, *11,* 177–220.

Bransford, J. D., Barclay, J. R., & Franks, J. J. Sentence memory: A constructive versus
interpretive approach. *Cognitive Psychology,* 1972, *3,* 193–209.

Brelsford, J., Freund, R., & Rundus, D. Recency judgments in a short-term memory
task. *Psychonomic Science,* 1967, *8,* 247–248.

Cannell, C. F., & Kahn, R. L. Interviewing. In G. Lindzey and E. Aronson (Eds.), *The
handbook of social psychology* (2nd Ed.), *Vol. 2: Research Methods.* Reading, Mass.: Addison-Wesley, 1968.

Cannell, C. F., Marquis, K. H., & Laurent, A. *A summary of studies of interviewing methodology.* (U.S. Public Health Service, DHEW–HRA Publication No. 77–1343). Washington, D.C.: U.S. Government Printing Office, March 1977.

Cash, W. S., & Moss, A. J. *Optimum recall period for reporting persons injured in motor vehicle
accidents.* (U.S. Public Health Service, DHEW–HSM Publication No. 72–1050).
Washington, D.C.: U.S. Government Printing Office, April 1972.

Drachman, D., & Leavitt, J. Memory impairment in the aged: Storage versus retrieval
deficit. *Journal of Experimental Psychology,* 1972, *93,* 302–308.

Ebbinghaus, H. [Memory: A contribution to experimental psychology] (H. A. Ruger &
C. E. Bussenius, Trans.). New York: Teacher's College, 1913. (Originally published, 1885.)

Ellis, H. D. Psychology and the law. *Science,* 1980, *208,* 712–713.

Erdelyi, M. H. Recovery of unavailable perceptual input. *Cognitive Psychology,* 1970, *1,*
99–113.

Erdelyi, M. H. Not now: Comment on Loftus and Loftus. *American Psychologist*, 1981, *36*, 527–528.

Erdelyi, M. H., & Goldberg, B. Let's not sweep repression under the rug: Toward a cognitive psychology of repression. In J. F. Kihlstrom & F. J. Evans (Eds.), *Functional disorders of memory*. Hillsdale, N.J.: Erlbaum, 1979.

Erdelyi, M. H., & Kleinbard, J. Has Ebbinghaus decayed with time? The growth of recall (hypermnesia) over days. *Journal of Experimental Psychology: Human Learning and Memory*, 1978, *4*, 275–289.

Garofalo, J., & Hindelang, M. J. *An introduction to the National Crime Survey*. Washington, D.C.: U.S. Department of Justice, 1977.

Glanzer, M., & Cunitz, A. R. Two storage mechanisms in free recall. *Journal of Verbal Learning and Verbal Behavior*, 1966, *5*, 351–360.

Graesser, A. C., Robertson, S., Lovelace, E. R., & Swinehart, D. M. Answers to why questions expose the organization of story plot and predict recall of actions. *Journal of Verbal Learning and Verbal Behavior*, 1980, *19*, 110–119.

Graesser, A. C., Woll, S. B., Kowalski, D. J., & Smith, D. A. Memory for typical and atypical actions in scripted activities. *Journal of Experimental Psychology: Human Learning and Memory*, 1980, *6*, 503–515.

Haggard, E. A., Brekstad, A., & Skard, A. G. On the reliability of the anamnestic interview. *Journal of Abnormal and Social Psychology*, 1960, *61*, 311–318.

Hartley, J. T., Harker, J. O., & Walsh, D. A. Contemporary issues and new directions in adult development of learning and memory. In L. W. Poon (Ed.), *Aging in the 1980's*. Washington, D.C.: American Psychological Association, 1980.

Henson, R., Cannell, C. F., & Lawson, S. *Effects of interviewer style and question form on reporting of automobile accidents*. Ann Arbor: Institute for Social Research, Dec. 1972.

Hinrichs, J. B. A two-process memory strength theory for judgment of recency. *Psychological Review*, 1970, *77*, 223–233.

Houston, J. P., Bee, H., Hatfield, E., & Rimm, D. C. *Invitation to psychology*, New York: Academic Press, 1979.

Issacharoff, A., & Hunt, W. Beyond countertransference: The "new truth" in the psychoanalytic process. *Contemporary Psychoanalysis*, 1978, *14*, 291–310.

Johnson, M. K., & Raye, C. L. Reality monitoring. *Psychological Review*, 1981, *88*, 67–85.

Laughery, K. R., Alexander, J. E., & Lane, A. B. Recognition of human faces: Effects of target exposure time, target position, pose position, and type of photograph. *Journal of Applied Psychology*, 1971, *55*, 477–483.

Lehnert, W. G., Robertson, S., & Black, J. B. Memory interactions during question answering. In H. Mandel, N. L. Stein, & T. Trabasso (Eds.), *Learning and comprehension of text*. Hillsdale, N.J.: Ablex, in press.

Lewinsohn, P. M., Mischel, W., Chaplin, W., & Barton, R. Social competence and depression: The role of illusory self-perceptions. *Journal of Abnormal Psychology*, 1980, *89*, 203–212.

Linton, M. I remember it well. *Psychology Today*, July 1979, 81–86.

Loftus, E. F. *Eyewitness testimony*. Cambridge, Mass.: Harvard University Press, 1979.

Loftus, E. F. *Memory*. Reading, Mass.: Addison-Wesley, 1980.

Loftus, E. F. Remembering recent experiences. In L. Cermak (Ed.), *Amnesia and Memory*. Hillsdale, N.J.: Erlbaum, 1981.

Loftus, E. F., & Greene, E. Warning: Even memory for faces may be contagious. *Law and Human Behavior*, 1980, *4*, 323–334.

Loftus, E. F., & Loftus, G. R. On the permanence of stored information in the human brain. *American Psychologist*, 1980, *35*, 409–420.

Loftus, E. F., & Marburger, W. *Since the eruption of Mt. St. Helens, did anyone beat you up? Improving the accuracy of retrospective reports with landmark events.* Unpublished manuscript, University of Washington, 1981.

Mischel, W., Ebbesen, E. B., & Zeiss, A. R. Determinants of selective memory about the self. *Journal of Consulting and Clinical Psychology,* 1976, *44,* 92–103.

Morton, J. Repeated items and decay in memory. *Psychonomic Science,* 1968, *10,* 219–220.

Morton, J. What could possibly be innate? In J. Morton (Ed.), *Biological and social aspects of psycholinguistics.* London: Logo Press, 1971.

Morton, J., Hammersley, R., & Berkerian, D. A. *Headed records: A framework for remembering and its failures.* Unpublished manuscript, MRC Applied Psychology Unit, Cambridge, England, 1981.

Nelson, R. E., & Craighead, W. E. Selective recall of positive and negative feedback, self-control behaviors, and depression. *Journal of Abnormal Psychology,* 1977, *86,* 379–388.

Neuman, W. R. Patterns of recall among television news viewers. *Public Opinion Quarterly,* 1976, *40,* 115–123.

Reporting of hospitalization in the health interview survey. (Public Health Service, DHEW–HSM Publication No. 73–1261). Washington, D.C.: U.S. Government Printing Office, July 1965.

Schonfield, D., & Robertson, E. A. Memory storage and aging. *Canadian Journal of Psychology,* 1966, *20,* 228–236.

Schuman, H. Personal Communication, December 1980.

Single, E., Kandel, D., & Johnson, B. D. The reliability and validity of drug use responses in a large scale longitudinal survey. *Journal of Drug Issues,* 1975, *5,* 426–443.

Smith, A. D. Adult age differences in cued recall. *Developmental Psychology,* 1977, *13,* 326–331.

Sudman, S., & Bradburn, N. M. Effects of time and memory factors on response in surveys. *Journal of American Statistical Association,* 1973, *68,* 805–815.

Surveying Crime. Report of the panel for the evaluation of crime surveys. Washington, D.C.: National Academy of Sciences, 1976.

Watkins, M. J., & Tulving, E. Episodic memory: When recognition fails. *Journal of Experimental Psychology: General,* 1975, 5–29.

Wingfield, A., & Byrnes, D. L. *The psychology of human memory.* New York: Academic Press, 1981.

Yarrow, M. R., Campbell, J. D., & Burton, R. V. *Recollections of childhood: A study of the retrospective method* (Monograph 5). Society for Research in Child Development, 1970.

Yntema, D. B., & Trask, F. P. Recall as a search process. *Journal of Verbal Learning and Verbal Behavior,* 1963, *2,* 65–74.

DANIEL STOKOLS

ENVIRONMENTAL PSYCHOLOGY: A COMING OF AGE

D aniel Stokols, who received his doctorate from the University of North Carolina at Chapel Hill, is Associate Professor and Associate Director for Graduate Studies in the Social Ecology Program at the University of California, Irvine. His research and teaching interests are in the areas of environmental, social, and health psychology. His current research focuses on the health and behavioral costs of exposure to environmental stressors, including traffic congestion, residential relocation, noise, and overcrowding in the home and the workplace.

He is active in the publishing of studies in psychology. He has edited a research monograph on environmental psychology, entitled *Perspectives on Environment and Behavior: Theory, Research, and Applications,* and is currently co-editing the *Handbook of Environmental Psychology.* He is an associate editor of *Environment and Behavior* and the Book Review editor of the *Journal of Environmental Psychology,* and he serves on the editorial boards of *Population and Environment, Basic and Applied Social Psychology,* and the *Review of Personality and Social Psychology.*

Dr. Stokols is President of Division 34 (Population and Environmental Psychology) of the American Psychological Association and serves on the Board of Directors of the Environmental Design Research Association and on the Executive Council of the Society for the Psychological Study of Social Issues (Divison 9 of the American Psychological Association). He is currently Director of the NIMH-sponsored Training Program in Environmental Demands, Human Development, and Health at the University of California, Irvine.

DANIEL STOKOLS

ENVIRONMENTAL PSYCHOLOGY: A COMING OF AGE

Introduction

E nvironmental psychology, or the study of human behavior in relation to the built and natural environment, emerged during the late 1960s as the result of both societal and intellectual concerns. At the societal level, the frightening dilemmas of the "population bomb" (Ehrlich, 1968), "future shock" (Toffler, 1970), and the "tragedy of the commons" (Hardin, 1968) prompted widespread concern about the constraints of the ecological environment. Yet, as psychologists turned their attention to the study of the relationships between the physical environment and behavior, they encountered several conceptual and methodological issues that had been left unresolved by the mainstream of behavioral science. Most importantly, traditional psychological theories had neglected the molar physical environment and had focused more narrowly on the links between microlevel stimuli and intrapersonal processes such as perception, cognition, learning, and development. Theoretical and methodological guidelines for

I thank Kevin Brechner, E. Scott Geller, Maryann Jacobi, Gerhard Kaminski, Sally Shumaker, M. Brewster Smith, and Ralph Taylor for their comments on an earlier version of this manuscript.

charting the ecological context of behavior remained to be established. Thus the environmental dilemmas of the 1960s and 1970s and the scientific agenda posed by these problems facilitated the coalescence and rapid growth of environmental psychology.

The rapid expansion of environmental psychology during the past decade is reflected in the appearance of numerous textbooks (e.g., Bell, Fisher, & Loomis, 1978; Holahan, 1981; Ittelson, Proshansky, Rivlin, & Winkel, 1974; Kaplan & Kaplan, 1978), the establishment of new journals (*Environment and Behavior*, 1969; *Population and Environment*, 1978; *Architecture and Behavior*, 1981; the *Journal of Environmental Psychology*, 1981), the publication of two monograph series focusing on theoretical and empirical advances (e.g., Altman, Rapoport, & Wohlwill, 1980; Baum & Singer, 1981), and the development of several professional organizations (e.g., the Environmental Design Research Association and the environmental sections of the American Psychological Association, the American Sociological Association, and the International Association of Applied Psychology). The *Annual Review of Psychology* now incorporates chapters on environmental psychology at regular intervals. Three such chapters have appeared to date (Craik, 1973; Russell & Ward, 1982; Stokols, 1978a). Moreover, the increasingly international scope of the field is evident from the recent professional meetings that have been held in Japan, Australia, Great Britain, France, Germany, Scandinavia, Turkey, and the Soviet Union and from the establishment of graduate training programs in environmental psychology at universities within many of these countries.[1]

Judging from these developments, environmental psychology appears to have established itself as a viable branch of both psychology and the broader, multidisciplinary field of human-environment studies. Yet the sheer quantity of publication and the international scope of professional activity tell us little about the scientific quality and accomplishments of a field. In what respects, then, has environmental psychology "come of age"?

I have chosen to organize my discussion of recent developments in environmental psychology around two opposite, yet complementary meanings of the "coming-of-age" metaphor. On the one hand,

---

[1] Some of these developments are reviewed in Canter and Craik (1981), Gurkaynak and LeCompte (1979); Hagino (Note 1); Kaminski (1978); Korosec-Serfaty (1976); Levy-Leboyer (1980); and Niit, Kruusvall, and Heidmets (1981).

coming of age connotes a sense of accomplishment stemming from the attainment of a developmental milestone—a celebration of past achievements. On the other hand, coming of age implies a recognition of what has not yet been accomplished and an appreciation of the challenges that lie ahead. Because the field of environmental psychology formally emerged about 12 or 13 years ago, permit me to invoke the "bar mitzvah analogy." The bar mitzvah ceremony in Judaism, like similar rituals in other religions, is not so much a celebration of having reached the age of thirteen as it is an affirmation of one's commitment to pursue the realization of certain social and cultural values. The latter meaning of "coming of age"—the recognition of current limitations and future challenges—is what I want to emphasize here.

To be sure, environmental psychology already has recorded some impressive scientific achievements, in conceptual and methodological innovations and in the establishment of an increasingly solid empirical base within certain areas of the field. Moreover, the accumulation and the consolidation of scientific knowledge have been accompanied by several effective applications of environmental-behavioral research to issues of community planning and environmental design. The first portion of my discussion will highlight these scientific and applied contributions.

The second part of my discussion focuses on certain blind spots or gaps in our understanding of environment and behavior and on some of the scientific issues that pose difficult challenges for the future. Like the bar or bat mitzvah candidate, environmental psychologists face decisions about what agenda are worth pursuing in the coming years. Our research commitments for the future may well determine whether environmental psychology comes to be defined primarily as the ad hoc application of existing theory and methods to the analysis of community-environmental problems (see Singer & Baum, Note 2) or as a conceptually distinct and innovative field having both scientific and applied utility.

Environmental Psychology: Past Accomplishments

In 1977, Kenneth Craik characterized environmental psychology as an array of multiple scientific paradigms, each of which emphasized a particular facet of person-environment relations. Following Kuhn's (1962) discussion of scientific paradigms, areas such as environmental cognition, environmental assessment, and ecological psychology were viewed as highly coherent domains by virtue of either their firm grounding in the traditional paradigms of psychology (e.g., cognitive, developmental, and personality theory) or their more novel contributions (e.g., Barker's, 1968, conceptualization of behavior settings).

In a subsequent review (Stokols, 1978a), I examined research developments within eight sub-areas of the field, including environmental cognition, attitudes, and assessment; personality and environment; spatial behavior; operant analyses of environmentally-supportive behavior; ecological psychology; and environmental stress. These areas were grouped according to their respective emphases on (1) cognitive (informational and affective) or behavioral (physical) forms of environmental experience and (2) the individual's active or reactive phases of transaction with the environment (see Table 1). The combination of these dimensions suggested four basic modes of human-environment transaction: (1) *interpretive* (active-cognitive),

Table 1
Modes of Human-Environment Transaction
and Related Areas of Research

Phase of transaction	Form of transaction	
	Cognitive[a]	Behavioral
Active	Interpretive	Operative
	Cognitive representation of the spatial environment	Experimental analysis of ecologically relevant behavior
	Personality and the environment	Human spatial behavior (proxemics)
Reactive	Evaluative	Responsive
	Environmental attitudes	Impact of the physical environment
	Environmental assessment	Ecological psychology

Note. Adapted, with permission, from D. Stokols, Environmental psychology, *Annual Review of Psychology*, 1978, *29*, p. 259. © 1978 by Annual Reviews Inc.

[a]In the present schema, the term "cognitive" refers to both informational and affective processes.

(2) *evaluative* (reactive-cognitive), (3) *operative* (active-behavioral), and (4) *responsive* (reactive-behavioral). The first mode involved the individual's cognitive representation of the environment; the second, one's evaluation of the situation against predefined standards of quality; the third, one's movement through or direct impact on the environment; and fourth, the environment's effects on one's behavior and well-being.

The categorization of research areas according to their relative emphases on the four transactional modes yielded an oversimplified view of the field. For instance, the grouping of paradigms shown in Table 1 divides environmental experience into separable categories. Yet the processes by which people relate to the environment are highly interdependent, and the boundaries between the various transactional modes are by no means clear and distinct. Also, not all investigations of environment and behavior fit neatly into a particular cell of the matrix. Nonetheless, the proposed categorization of research areas did provide a basis for identifying certain emphases and directions of the field. Specifically, it revealed that most research in environmental psychology (as of 1978) was paradigm-specific and that very few studies had addressed the potential linkages among different modes of environmental experience.[2] Thus analyses of behavior settings from the perspective of ecological psychology emphasized people's responses to environmental forces while research on cognitive mapping gave considerably more attention to people's interpretive capacities. Given the somewhat disjointed and piecemeal approach to the study of environment and behavior reflected in the literature at that time, several of the most exciting and promising directions for future research appeared to be found at the interface of the various paradigms in the field.

If the modes-of-transaction framework offered a simplified view of the field in 1978, it provides an even less adequate representation of environmental psychology today. During the past four or five years, noticeable shifts in research interests have occurred. While the literature on environmental cognition, environmental stress, operant analyses of pro-ecological behavior, and environmental assessment has grown steadily, the pace of research on topics such as personal

[2] Exceptions to this trend include Willems' (1974) discussion of the relationship between operant and ecological psychology and Altman's (1975) analysis of the links between privacy needs, spatial behavior, and stress.

space, crowding, and environmental dispositions has markedly declined since 1978. Moreover, recent research in environmental psychology reflects a greater tendency toward paradigm merging— i.e., the integration of concepts and methods from two or more subareas of the field—than was evident in 1978. I believe that this trend toward increased conceptual and methodological eclecticism is quite significant, and I will return to it later in the discussion. There are, of course, numerous developments in environmental psychology that I will not be able to cover in this presentation. For more detailed coverage of the literature, I recommend Russell and Ward's (1982) *Annual Review* chapter as well as the many other review articles and volumes that have appeared during the past few years.[3]

Despite its limitations, the organizational framework depicted in Table 1 does highlight certain important contributions of environmental psychology during its first decade (circa the late 1960s through the late 1970s). One major accomplishment of the field was the reincorporation of the physical environment into psychological theory and research. The behavioral significance of the ecological environment was recognized several decades ago by psychologists such as Koffka (1935), Brunswik (1943), Tolman (1948), and Chein (1954). Yet the so-called cognitive revolution (Dember, 1974) of the 1950s and 1960s pushed ecological issues to the sidelines of psychological science. With the increasing awareness of urban problems during the 1960s and the publication of books such as Barker's *Ecological Psychology* (1968) and Sommer's *Personal Space* (1969), however, psychologists

---

[3] For additional reviews of recent developments in environmental psychology, see the following articles and books: *environmental cognition:* Evans (1980), Feimer (in press), Moore (1979), Saarinen & Sell (1980); *personality and environment:* F. Cohen (1979), Kobasa (1979), Krantz, Glass, Schaeffer, & Davia (in press), Little (in press), Zuckerman (1979); *environment and human development:* Bronfenbrenner (1979), Lawton (1980), Wohlwill (1980); *environmental attitudes and assessment:* Craik & Appleyard (1980), Lipsey (1977), Moos (1980), Russell & Pratt (1980); *operant analyses of environmentally protective behavior:* Baum & Singer (1981), Cone & Hayes (1980), Geller (in press), Geller, Winett, & Everett (1982), Seligman & Becker (1981), Stern & Gardner (1981); *spatial behavior:* Aiello & Thompson (1980), Baldassare (1979), Baron & Needel (1980), Epstein (1981), Knowles (1980), Schmidt & Keating (1979); *environmental stress:* Baum, Singer, & Baum (1981), Cohen (1980), Garber & Seligman (1980), Sarason & Spielberger (1979, 1980); *behavior in the built environment:* Aiello & Baum (1979), Archea (1977), Krupat (1980), Zeisel (1981); *behavior in the natural environment:* Burton, Kates, & White (1978), Kaplan & Kaplan (1978); *ecological psychology:* Barker & Associates (1978), Wicker (1979a, b); *general reviews of the field:* Proshansky & Altman (1979), Ross & Campbell (1979), Stokols (1982).

"rediscovered" the molar physical environment and became increasingly involved in studying its impact on behavior.

The 1970s witnessed several conceptual and methodological advances in the understanding of environment and behavior. At a theoretical level, important distinctions were drawn between environmental and object perception (Ittelson, 1973) and between fundamental and macrospatial cognition (Downs & Stea, 1973; Moore & Golledge, 1976). Environmental dispositions (Craik, 1976) took their place alongside the more traditional trait constructs of personality psychology. The concepts of social climate (Moos, 1976) and defensible space (Newman, 1973) provided a theoretical basis for assessing the psychosocial impacts of community settings. Ecological psychologists extended Barker's (1968) conceptualization of behavior settings by analyzing conditions of overstaffing as well as understaffing (Wicker, McGrath, & Armstrong, 1972). And within the areas of proxemics and environmental stress, detailed models of spatial behavior (cf. Altman, 1975; Baum & Epstein, 1978) and the "aftereffects" of exposure to environmental demands (see Glass & Singer, 1972) were developed.

At a methodological level, several new strategies were devised for examining the links between environment and behavior. In research on environmental cognition, sketch maps, wayfinding, and photograph-recognition tasks were combined to assess the imageability of urban environments (e.g., Milgram & Jodelet, 1976; Moore & Golledge, 1976). Indices of perceived environmental quality (Craik & Zube, 1976) and strategies of environmental simulation were refined (Appleyard & Craik, 1978). Techniques of behavioral mapping (Ittelson, Rivlin, & Proshansky, 1976) and behavior setting surveys (Barker & Schoggen, 1973) were used to assess activity patterns within buildings, public parks, and communities, and researchers in the areas of proxemics and environmental stress employed a diversity of observational, self-report, and physiological probes to assess people's reactions to environmental demands (cf. Altman, 1975; Glass & Singer, 1972).

The scientific developments outlined above facilitated a second major accomplishment of environmental psychology: namely, the application of concepts, methods, and findings from the various research paradigms to the analysis and, in many instances, the amelioration of community problems. The practical significance of environmental-behavioral research has been demonstrated in several applied areas including transportation planning, environmental protection, architectural design, management of environmental hazards, and family planning. For example, Stern and Gardner (1981) estimated that 47 percent of the energy consumed by American households is related to transportation (primarily to the widespread use of private automobiles). The remaining 53 percent of household energy consumption is associated with in-home uses such as air conditioning and water heating. These figures suggest that the modification of transportation behavior (e.g., increasing the use of public transit or the purchase of energy-efficient automobiles) could have a substantial impact on household energy consumption. Along these lines, Everett and his colleagues at the Pennsylvania State University have developed token-reinforcement strategies for the modification of travel behavior (see Everett, 1981). In several field experiments, these procedures have been proven effective as means of increasing community levels of bus ridership. Travel modification programs combining token-reinforcement procedures with informational strategies (such as advertising campaigns and the development of legible route maps) are currently being evaluated through a multiple-community intervention study.

Other community programs involving the provision of cash rebates, social praise, and feedback concerning the favorable consequences of environmentally supportive behavior have proven effective in modifying patterns of in-home energy consumption, waste disposal, and recycling (cf. Cone & Hayes, 1980; Geller, in press; Geller, Winett, & Everett, 1982). For instance, environmentally protective behavior has been enhanced in several settings through anti-litter prompts (e.g., printed messages on disposable materials; see Geller, Witmer, & Orebaugh, 1976) and design modifications of waste receptacles (cf. Geller, Brasted, & Mann, 1979).

In the areas of architectural assessment and design, methods for estimating people's reactions to potential environmental changes have been developed. Indices of perceived environmental quality have been applied in the development of environmental impact reports (cf. Craik & Zube, 1976). Also, techniques of dynamic, environmental simulation have been devised for potential use by urban planners. One of the most ambitious studies undertaken to date is being conducted at the University of California, Berkeley. The Berkeley Environmental Simulation Laboratory, developed by Appleyard and Craik (1978), features a computer-guided camera which provides simulated tours (via television monitor and videotape) through a scale model representing a 1¹/₂-square-mile section of Marin County. An important advantage of this research is that it permits a comparison of observers' reactions to both simulated video displays and actual automobile tours of the same environment. The preliminary data from this project indicate a high degree of correspondence between observers' evaluations of the simulated and actual tours.

The potential applications of simulation methods to the realm of urban planning are numerous. Scale models of proposed buildings are currently used by many architects to assess the preferences of their clients prior to the construction process. At the community level, simulation procedures have been used less widely, but they are potentially applicable to a diversity of planning problems. Because scale models can be altered to provide previews of alternative, future environments, they can be used to forecast residents' reactions to urban settings before the plans are carried out. Such procedures might enable planners to avoid costly design mistakes such as the infamous Pruitt Igoe Housing Project in St. Louis, which was constructed in 1954 only to be demolished in 1972 because of high rates of crime, vandalism, and vacancy.

Assessments of social conditions within existing settings offer an additional basis for evaluating and improving environments. For example, Wilcox and Holahan (1976), using the Social Climate Scales developed by Moos and his colleagues (see Moos, 1976, 1980), found that, among students living in high rise dormitories (10 to 13 stories) at the University of Texas, the residents of the higher floors placed less emphasis on social relationships and group cohesion than those living on the lower floors. Also, Holahan and Saegert (1973) observed that the remodeling of a psychiatric ward (i.e., repainting the walls in bright colors, adding new furniture, and increasing opportunities for privacy) led to greater social involvement among the patients and increased levels of interaction among the patients and the staff. More recently, Baum and Davis (1980) experimentally demonstrated the effectiveness of an architectural intervention (i.e., dividing a dormitory corridor into two sections by incorporating an interior lounge area) designed to reduce the perception of crowding and interpersonal problems in a college dormitory. All of these studies suggest the potential utility of environmental assessment methodology as a community-planning tool.

Research on the perception and prediction of environmental hazards also highlights the relevance of psychological research to environmental-decisionmaking processes. Several personal factors have been found to enhance individuals' comprehension of future environmental risks, including the amount of their prior experience with similar hazards, the accuracy of their beliefs about the likelihood of such events, and their anxiety about environmental uncertainties (Slovic, Fischhoff, & Lichtenstein, 1981; Weinstein, 1978). The personality dimensions of future time perspective and internality of control also have been found to be associated with increased effectiveness in coping with environmental risks (Burton, Kates, & White, 1978). Moreover, the dimension of future time perspective has been identified as a determinant of successful contraceptive behavior and family planning. In a prospective study of Planned Parenthood participants, individuals exhibiting future time perspective were better able to avoid unwanted pregnancies than those whose time perspective was more restricted (cf. Oskamp, Mindick, Berger, & Motta, 1978). Thus the tendency to think about future events is directly relevant to the individual's environmental decisionmaking and well-being.

The practical implications of environmental stress research have been vividly revealed in studies of residential relocation conducted by Pastalan (Note 3). Over a period of several years, Pastalan has experimentally evaluated intervention programs to reduce the negative impact of relocation on the elderly. For instance, on-site visits to one's future residence and participation in group discussions, prior to moving, about the relocation process have been shown to lower the risk of postrelocation mortality among individuals with certain demographic, attitudinal, and health profiles.

These examples illustrate some of the potential applications of environmental psychology to community problem-solving. The practical significance of environmental research is, of course, tempered by the political, legal, and economic realities of environmental decisionmaking. The perspectives of researchers and practitioners are characteristically dissimilar and often opposed (cf. Altman, 1973; DiMento, 1981; Sommer, 1980). And the reconciliation of opposing viewpoints concerning environmental issues is largely a political and economic matter. Nonetheless, the research applications cited above suggest that environmental psychologists *can* play a vital role in certain community planning situations—particularly those in which (1) relevant research strategies (e.g., environmental simulation, survey research, and behavioral mapping) have been validated; (2) the existing data from similar situations are extensive and convergent in their policy implications; and (3) the target environment is of circumscribed size and complexity, such that the potential for attitudinal and value conflicts among participant groups (e.g., residents and users, practitioners and researchers) is reduced.

In summary, the first decade of research in environmental psychology convincingly documented the behavioral significance of the built and natural environment and yielded a wealth of conceptual and methodological tools for expanding our knowledge of environment and behavior. During the same period, several effective applications of psychological concepts and methodology were achieved within various community problem-solving arenas. Although research on environment and behavior over the past four to five years has continued to bolster these scientific and applied contributions, it also reflects some new directions and challenges for the field. I turn now to a discussion of these developments.

Environmental Psychology: Current Challenges

The scientific and applied accomplishments of environmental psychology during its first decade suggest two different characterizations of the field. The first is that environmental psychology basically involves the incorporation of physical-environmental variables into traditional theories of learning, cognition, personality, social behavior, and development. A classic example of this approach is Festinger, Schachter, and Back's (1950) investigation of the effects of physical and functional distance on processes of social comparison, friendship formation, and attitude change. In such research (as in many of the more recent studies cited earlier), environmental conditions are examined as they mediate between or directly impinge on psychological and behavioral outcomes. From this first perspective, the scientific contributions of environmental psychology have involved primarily extending existing theories to include physical-environmental variables rather than creating entirely new theories.

A second view of the field is suggested by the community oriented studies of travel behavior, energy conservation, environmental assessment, and stress mentioned above. According to that view, environmental psychology is essentially an area of applied research involving the application of existing psychological theory and methodology to the analysis and treatment of community problems (such as resource shortages and environmental degradation).

A fundamental question posed by these alternative views of the field concerns the theoretical uniqueness and viability of environmental psychology vis-à-vis other areas of behavioral research. Specifically, are the theoretical underpinnings and directions of the field distinguishable from those of other substantive areas within psychology? A related question is whether the future research emphases of environmental psychology will be determined solely by the immediate demands of community problem-solving or, alternatively, through a more balanced interplay between applied concerns and enduring scientific agenda?

My own opinion is that each of the characterizations of environmental psychology outlined above offer an inadequate representation of the field. On the one hand, the research agenda of environmental psychology during its first decade were largely influenced by prevailing theories of cognition, learning, development, personality, and social behavior and by a growing awareness of global environmental problems. On the other hand, several innovative departures from existing theory and methodology occurred, as exemplified by the concepts of behavior setting (Barker, 1968), boundary regulation processes (Altman, 1975), and social climate (Moos, 1976) and by the newly developed techniques of environmental simulation (cf. Appleyard & Craik, 1978; Craik & Zube, 1976), behavioral mapping (Ittelson et al., 1976), and behavior setting analysis (Barker & Schoggen, 1973; Wicker, 1979a, b). Although these theoretical and methodological contributions did not coalesce into an integrated, over-arching theory of environment and behavior, they did serve to awaken researchers and practitioners to the environmental context of human behavior.

The more recent literature in environmental psychology (from the late 1970s to the present) reveals some fundamental shifts in our conceptualization of environment and behavior. These shifts, I believe, reflect the increasingly contextual orientation of contemporary research and suggest a potentially novel theoretical trajectory for environmental psychology during the coming years: namely, the elucidation of the spatial and temporal context of individual and collective behavior. The remainder of my discussion elaborates upon this third characterization of the field.

The "Contextualization" of Environment

The distinguishing feature of environmental psychology, as compared to other domains of behavioral research, has been its explicit emphasis on the physical environment. In earlier research, the environment was construed primarily as a determinant or a product of behavior—i.e., as an independent or dependent variable. The predominant methodological approach associated with this orientation was the systematic isolation of environmental conditions, such as noise, temperature, density, architectural design, litter, and pollution, for experimental analysis. More recently, this experimentalist and decontextualized view of the environment has been balanced or qualified by an increasing concern with the complex structure of environmental units. A basic goal of this contextual orientation is to identify, through descriptive (or taxonomic) as well as experimental research, those relatively enduring properties of situations and settings that mediate the relationships between behavior and more transient environmental conditions. The contemporary emphasis on contextual analyses of behavior is suggested by three recent shifts in our conceptualization of the environment: (1) increasing concern with the intrasetting and intersetting contexts of environmental experience; (2) the integration of objectivist and subjectivist views of the environment; and (3) greater emphasis on the temporal context of environmental experience.

An emphasis on the intrasetting and intersetting contexts of environmental experience. Environmental units can be described in terms of their scale or complexity. The scale of an environment ranges from the specific stimuli and situations that occur within a given setting (e.g., a professor's response to a student's question during class) to the life domains that are comprised of multiple situations and settings—a college campus, for example, in which students attend classes, reside in dorms or apartments, and socialize with friends on various occasions (cf. Magnusson, 1981; Pervin, 1978; Stokols & Novaco, 1981). The more complex the environmental context of behavior, the greater the range of factors—psychological, social, cultural, architectural—that affect people's relationships with their surroundings.

Psychologists such as Barker (1968), Bronfenbrenner (1979), and Magnusson (1981) have emphasized the nested or hierarchical structure of environmental units. The assumption of environmental hierarchy implies that the behavioral effects of particular stimuli and events are mediated by the situational or intrasetting context in which they occur. And the psychological significance of molar situations and settings, in turn, depends on their relationships to the individual's overall life situation and plans.

Research in areas such as spatial behavior and stress reflects the widespread attention now being given to contextual mediators of environmental experience. The concepts of privacy, personal space, and territoriality—targets of extensive laboratory investigation during the mid-1970s—are increasingly being studied within the context of naturalistic settings. Early and recent work on proxemics indicates that the psychological and behavioral consequences of interpersonal proximity depend on a host of situational factors including cultural norms (cf. Aiello & Thompson, 1980; Altman & Chemers, 1979), the degree of interaction among people in the setting (Knowles, 1980), and the levels of acoustic and visual separation among proximal individuals (Sundstrom, Burt, & Kamp, 1980). Also, recent conceptualizations of territoriality suggest that the functions and consequences of territorial behavior depend on the type of setting (e.g., dormitory room, urban neighborhood) in which it occurs (cf. Taylor, 1978; Vinsel, Brown, Altman, & Foss, 1980).

In research on density, noise, and other environmental demands, earlier work focused on the negative consequences of specific uncontrollable stimuli and events, while neglecting to consider the broader context in which these events are embedded. This overemphasis on the impact of isolated stressors precluded an analysis of issues such as the ratio of uncontrollable/controllable events within a situation, the relative importance of personal and group goals with which a stressor interferes, and the extent to which the impact of a stressor is ameliorated by the availability of concurrent, compensatory rewards. More recent studies, however, highlight the contextual moderators of stress reactions (see Stokols, 1979). Research on residential density, for example, has examined the specificity of crowding stress in relation to a variety of situational factors including family structure and composition (Baldassare, 1981), lifestyle (Gillis, 1979), opportunities for privacy regulation (Schmidt, Goldman, & Feimer, 1979; Verbrugge & Taylor, 1980), building height and other aspects of architectural design (Aiello & Baum, 1979; Saegert, Note 4). Similarly, studies of people's response to chronic noise exposure, travel constraints, and acute life events have underlined the importance of situational variables (e.g., the kinds of activities disrupted by the stressor) as moderators of stress reactions (cf. Cohen & Weinstein, 1981; Novaco & Vaux, in press; Stokols & Novaco, 1981).

Evidence for the situational specificity of spatial behavior and stress is consistent with the concept of person-environment fit or "congruence"—the extent to which personal goals and needs are supported by a particular environment (see Harrison, 1978). The congruence notion suggests that environmental conditions such as high density and noise will adversely affect the individual to the extent that they disrupt personally important goals and activities. Where such disruption is minimal, the negative impact of environmental demands should be reduced.

Recent analyses have extended the concept of fit in at least two important respects. First, whereas earlier formulations focused on the degree of fit between single dimensions of the environment and corresponding personal needs (e.g., the extent of one's job responsibilities in relation to his or her desire for responsibility at work), the revised models emphasize the ways in which multiple personal goals interact with environmental supports and constraints to determine the overall level of fit experienced within a given setting. Second, the overall level of fit within a setting is considered to be a function not only of the controllability of environmental conditions but also of the perceived, relative importance of those needs that are supported or constrained by the environment (cf. Michelson, 1980a; Stokols, 1979). In recent investigations using setting-specific measures of need facilitation and importance, the experience of poor levels of fit within particular life domains (e.g., home, work, or peer relationships) was found to be significantly associated with health and behavioral disorders among adolescents (Greenberger, Steinberg, & Vaux, in press) and with violent behavior among adult psychiatric patients (Klassen, Note 5).

In Klassen's study of violence prediction, discriminant analyses incorporating multi-environment measures of social support differentiated psychiatric cases from outpatient controls more reliably than did those based on single-domain scores. This finding highlights the importance of considering the intersetting as well as the intrasetting context of behavior and well-being. There is increasing evidence to suggest that people's reactions to specific environmental demands are jointly mediated by the levels of congruence existing within their multiple life domains. For example, research on commuters' attempts to cope with travel constraints indicates the important role of residential and work environments in moderating the effects of traffic congestion on health and behavior, with high-distance, low-congruence travelers exhibiting highest levels of stress (see Stokols & Novaco, 1981). Similarly, a longitudinal study of children's reactions to chronic noise exposure revealed the interactive effects of classroom and home noise levels on systolic and diastolic blood pressure (Cohen, Krantz, Evans, & Stokols, 1981). Among those students attending noisy schools, the implementation of noise abatement procedures in the classroom was associated with lower blood pressure in students from quieter as opposed to noisier residential areas. Also, in a study of the effects of residential density on elementary school children, students from high-density apartments obtained lower scores on vocabulary tests and exhibited higher levels of behavioral disturbance at school than those of their low-density counterparts (Saegert, Note 4).

The preceding studies illustrate the interdependence of events and experiences that occur within the multiple domains of one's life situation. Environmental demands experienced in one setting are apparently exacerbated or buffered by the availability of coping resources in other domains (e.g., Bronfenbrenner, 1979; Stokols & Novaco, 1981; Klassen, Note 5). Furthermore, the aftereffects of environmental stressors are not always confined to the settings in which the demands occur and sometimes "spill over" into seemingly unrelated life domains (cf. Becker, 1981; Cohen, 1980; Saegert, Note 4). These findings suggest at least two important directions for contextually oriented research: (1) to establish a more complete understanding of the diverse ways in which separate behavior settings and life domains are linked (cf. Wicker, 1979a); and (2) to develop criteria for identifying which dimensions of what settings are most relevant to the analysis of particular psychological phenomena.

Toward an integration of objectivist and subjectivist views of the environ-

ment. The scale or complexity of environments, discussed earlier, reflects a continuum of spatial hierarchy or inclusiveness.[4] For instance, life domains contain settings which, in turn, contain objects and events which, themselves, consist of multiple stimuli. Yet environmental units also can be arrayed along a continuum of psychological hierarchy reflecting their relative importance to individuals and groups. The psychological significance of environments may be closely related to their degree of symbolic transformation. That is, environments which have been transformed from a melange of purely physical elements into symbolically meaningful settings may be of greater personal and social significance than relatively nontransformed areas. Although certain environments (such as many uninhabited or infrequently occupied areas) may have little symbolic significance, other places (and the objects within them) are experienced as a composite of both physical affordances (Gibson, 1977) and social meanings. Thus the dimensions of psychological hierarchy and symbolic transformation offer potentially useful criteria for describing and comparing diverse environments.

For several decades, psychologists construed the environment either in terms of its objective, material features (cf. Brunswik, 1943; Gibson, 1977) or in terms of the individual's subjective impressions of those features (cf. Lewin, 1936; Neisser, 1976). Rarely were the objective and subjective elements of environments considered within the same analysis. The recent literature in environmental psychology, however, reflects some progress toward the integration of these two perspectives. For example, Lynch's (1960) seminal research on the physical imageability of places has been extended through recent analyses of environmental symbolism (cf. Appleyard, 1979; Groat, 1981). The symbolic qualities of objects and places have been studied in relation to both their psychological and social functions. The concepts of place identity (Proshansky, 1978), place dependence (Stokols & Shumaker, 1981), and environmental personalization (e.g., Vinsel, Brown, Altman, & Foss, 1980) emphasize the strong affective ties that often develop between individuals and places. Also, the notion of social imageability—i.e., the capacity of physical environments to evoke vivid and widely-held social meanings among their users—implies that groups become closely identified with (and sometimes dependent

[4] See Russell and Ward's (1982) discussion regarding the geographical hierarchy of environmental units.

on) places, just as individuals do (cf. Altman & Chemers, 1979; Jacobi & Stokols, in press; Rapoport, 1979; Stokols, 1981). The recent work on environmental symbolism, then, suggests that a crucial function of objects and places is to provide a material reflection of personal and collective identity.

The study of environmental symbolism has stimulated some important conceptual and methodological innovations. First, the previously separate paradigms of environmental cognition, attitudes, and assessment have been more closely linked in recent studies of cognitive mapping (see Wofsey, Rierdan, & Wapner, 1979) and perceived environmental quality (cf. Levi, Ittelson, & Black, 1981; Russell & Pratt, 1980). By combining the conceptual and methodological approaches of multiple paradigms (e.g., using hand-drawn maps in conjunction with verbal reports of environmental meaning), these studies more effectively revealed the interdependence of interpretive and evaluative modes of environmental experience than did earlier, "single-paradigm" studies.

Second, the current emphasis on social meanings of environments has prompted an assessment of collective, as well as individual, perceptions of place meanings. Whereas most research on environmental cognition has emphasized the individual's perception of the environment (cf. Evans, 1980; Moore & Golledge, 1976), the study of consensually defined place meanings encompasses the phenomena of social perception—i.e., the processes by which setting members collectively perceive and ascribe meaning to their sociophysical milieu (see Stokols, 1981). By focusing on the common or widely recognized meanings that become associated with the molar environment, these analyses offer a "middle ground" between subjectivist perspectives, which construe environmental perception as essentially a personal, idiosyncratic phenomenon, and objectivist views of the environment, which avoid reference to perceptual processes altogether.[5]

Techniques for measuring aggregate perceptions of places were developed by Milgram & Jodelet (1976) in their study of Parisians' cognitive maps of Paris. Specifically, the maps sketched by 218 Pari-

---

[5] Psychologists such as Allport (1955) and Jackson (1966) suggested that group cohesion (or "interstructurance") and the clarity of social norms ("norm crystallization") could be assessed by analyzing the aggregate perceptions of group members. Also, Katona (1979) developed procedures for predicting national economic trends from aggregate measures of consumer attitudes. But, for the most part, psychological research has focused on processes of individual rather than collective perception.

sians were examined individually and in conjunction with several aggregate measures derived from the responses of all participants. For instance, the frequency with which various elements of Paris (e.g., the Eiffel Tower) appeared in residents' sketch maps, the order in which they were drawn, and the percentage of participants who did or did not recognize specific elements in a photograph-recognition task, were among the group measures used in this study. Based upon their multimethod analyses, Milgram and Jodelet concluded that the imageability of cities depends as much on social factors as on physical attributes. In their words, "The perception of a city is a social fact and, as such, needs to be studied in its collective as well as its individual aspect. It is not only what *exists* but also what is *highlighted* by the community that acquires salience in the mind of the person" (p. 108).

The increased use and refinement of methods for measuring collective perceptions of environments remain as important priorities for future research. Aggregate indices of the content, intensity, and prevalence of environmental meanings might offset the individualistic bias that has characterized many areas of psychological research (cf. Gergen, 1973; Sampson, 1981).

Analyzing the temporal context of environmental experience. A third important trend in the literature of environmental psychology is the increasing emphasis on temporal dimensions of environment and behavior. Barker's research during the 1960s gave explicit attention to the temporal regularities of behavior within small-scale settings (Barker, 1968). In 1972, Kevin Lynch published an insightful volume on the role of time and history in mediating people's experiences within urban environments (Lynch, 1972). Yet only recently has the importance of temporal factors in person-environment relations been widely recognized among psychologists (see Schoggen & Schoggen, Note 6).

Research on the temporal context of environment and behavior reflects both objectivist and subjectivist conceptions of time. At an objective level, the flow of time as measured by recurring cycles of natural and human events exerts direct (but often unrecognized or imperceptible) effects on emotional and physical well-being. The duration of exposure to physical stressors and negative life events, for example, is an important determinant of their behavioral impact (cf. Cohen et al., 1981; Novaco & Vaux, in press). Similarly, objectively measured levels of the temporal and spatial constraints on people's daily routines have been found to be associated with increased irritability and social strain among family members (cf. Cullen, 1978; Hall & Hall, 1980; Michelson, 1980b).

At a subjective level, people's perceptions and symbolic constructions of time may be strongly related to personal and collective well-being. For instance, immediate or imagined proximity to "auto-biographically significant" places may enable elderly individuals to maintain a sense of self-continuity, thereby enhancing emotional stability (see Rowles, 1981). And traditional rituals and holidays may provide a basis for maintaining family and cultural cohesion over extended periods (cf. Doob, 1971; Jacobi & Stokols, in press; Lynch, 1972; Shils, 1981).

An explicit emphasis on temporal concerns is presently reflected in several areas of environmental-behavioral research. Studies of environmental cognition suggest a shift of focus from people's perception of isolated, physical elements to their comprehension and recall of place-activity composites, or "scripts" (Abelson, 1981). The temporal context of environmental perception also is reflected in a recent study of cognitive mapping by Wofsey et al. (1979). This research found a significant relationship between people's plans to move from an environment and the size and detail of their cognitive maps. Specifically, those individuals having articulated plans for moving provided less detailed and more abstract sketches of their current environment than did those without such plans. In another study, the temporal and affective significance of environments was examined in relation to the memories of people and places evoked by the cherished objects within families' homes (cf. Csikszentmihalyi & Rochberg-Halton, 1981).

Although recent research on environmental dispositions has not been extensive, the work that has been done reflects a strong temporal orientation. For instance, Little (in press; Palys & Little, 1980) introduced the concept of personal projects, or extended sequences of behavior organized around one's current goals and plans. The analysis of personal projects emphasizes the dynamic role of goals, plans, and activities as organizers of environmental experience while deemphasizing static trait conceptualizations of environment and behavior.

In those studies where environmental dispositions have been assessed, a concern with the individual's temporal orientation is evident. As a case in point, Taylor and Konrad (1980) developed scales for measuring people's dispositions toward the past, particularly with respect to environmental symbols such as historically significant buildings and places. Also, in an investigation linking the personality and environmental stress paradigms, Kobasa (1979) documented the importance of people's commitment to current and future plans in mediating their reactions to stressful life events. Further, Stokols, Shumaker, and Martinez (Note 7; see also Stokols & Shumaker, in press) found that, among residentially mobile individuals (those who had moved several times during their lives), persons scoring high on an index of environmental exploratory tendency reported more favorable health status than their less exploratory counterparts. These studies, in conjunction with Pastalan's (Note 3) research on residential relocation and mortality among the elderly, suggest a strong positive association between favorable attitudes toward future events and personal resistance to stress. The current literature on environmental stress, in general, reflects a transactional and longitudinal perspective, whereby sequential processes of appraisal and coping are thought to play a crucial role in mediating people's reactions to environmental demands (cf. Garber & Seligman, 1980; Lazarus & Launier, 1978).

In the area of ecological psychology as well, a concern with temporal issues is reflected in analyses of the "life cycles" of behavior settings—i.e., the processes by which settings are established, maintained, modified, or terminated (cf. Stokols & Shumaker, 1981; Wicker, 1979a, b). The current emphasis on environmental transformation processes (cf. Saegert, Note 4; Stokols, 1981) is exemplified by Leff and Gordon's (1979) research on environmental cognitive sets—i.e., plans to focus on selected attributes of immediate or imagined environments. In Leff's studies, the inducement of cognitive sets focusing on current problems and possible solutions significantly enhanced the creativity of participants' proposals for remedial environmental change. This research suggests a potential link between cognitive analyses of creativity and ecological perspectives on environmental change.

The current emphasis on temporal dimensions of environment and behavior is closely related to the two research trends mentioned earlier, namely, the recognition of environmental scale and complexity and the analysis of behavior at multiple contextual levels, and the increased linkage between objectivist and subjectivist views of the environment. In the research cited above, the temporal meanings (e.g., historical significance) of the material environment have been assessed in relation to multiple environmental units ranging from cherished objects in the home (Csikszentmihalyi & Rochberg-Halton, 1981) to whole geographical areas (Proshansky, 1978; Rowles, 1981). Moreover, the conceptualization of time as an objective phenomenon (i.e., one measured with reference to observable cycles of natural events) has been broadened to include analyses of people's subjective representation of time—their perceptions of the autobiographical or sociobiographical significance of objects and places, for example.

Thus the three research trends I have discussed appear to be closely intertwined. Taken together, they suggest that environmental psychologists' conceptualization of the environment has expanded both spatially and temporally. The analytical focus has shifted from isolated units of the physical environment experienced by individuals during the short-run toward an analysis of hierarchically related settings experienced in terms of their sociocultural and temporal significance as well as through their more immediate, physical affordances. And, as the conceptualization of the environment has broadened in scope and complexity, the research orientation has become increasingly eclectic, evidenced by the diverse connections that have been established between previously separate theoretical paradigms.

Contextualized Views of the Environment as a Basis for Contextually Oriented Research

The research developments I have summarized are part of a broader movement in psychology as a whole to develop a contextual analysis of human behavior. Psychologists within every major area of the discipline have noted the deficiencies of decontextualized research and the importance of establishing a more holistic or contextual orientation.[6] And, among sociologists, considerable attention has been given to the conceptual and methodological complexities posed by contextual

---

[6] The widespread interest in contextualism is reflected in recent research on cognition (e.g., Jenkins, 1974; Neisser, 1976; Sampson, 1981), development (e.g., Bronfenbrenner, 1979), learning (e.g., Rogers-Warren & Warren, 1977), mental health (e.g., Kelly, 1966; Peele, 1981), personality (e.g., Cronbach, 1975; Magnusson, 1981; Sarbin, 1976), and social psychology (e.g., Cartwright, 1979; Gergen, 1973; Israel & Tajfel, 1972; McGuire, 1973; Pepitone, 1981; Sherif, 1982; Smith, 1973; Triandis, 1975). For a more general discussion of the philosophical roots of contextualism as a world view, see Jessor (1958) and Pepper (1961).

analyses of social phenomena (cf. Boyd & Iversen, 1979; Farkas, 1974; Hannan, 1971; Hauser, 1974). Yet the arguments for developing a contextual perspective in psychology have been more philosophical and ideological than programmatic and operational. What appears to be missing from earlier psychological analyses of contextualism is a specification of the conceptual and procedural assumptions underlying this research orientation and the development of guidelines for translating these core assumptions into programmatic research. Lest contextualism become an empty buzzword, several difficult questions, including the following, must be addressed: (1) What are the distinguishing features of contextual research? That is, what differentiates a contextual analysis from a noncontextual one? (2) Are psychological research questions differentially amenable to a contextual approach? That is, for which psychological phenomena is a contextual analysis warranted and for which is it not? (3) In those instances where a contextual perspective is adopted, what criteria determine the scope and specificity of the variables included in the analysis? I do not pretend to have easy answers to these questions. I do suggest, however, that the analysis of these issues could provide a distinctive and valuable theoretical thrust for the field of environmental psychology over the next several years.

Before addressing the preceding questions, I should emphasize that I do not view these contextural concerns as the special province of any particular subarea of psychology. Obviously, they are relevant to a broad array of research areas both within psychology and, more generally, in the social sciences. But, because much behavioral research is narrowly circumscribed in relation to highly specific substantive questions, it is not clear that a systematic framework for contextual research will emerge without explicit consideration of the general issues implied by such a perspective. Thus the analysis of these general concerns ("general" in the sense that they span a large number of research areas) could provide a useful direction for environmental psychology. Although the development of a framework for contextual research is not the only potentially valuable direction for the field, it does appear to be one that has been relatively neglected because of our paradigm-specific research orientation.

I turn now to a discussion of the research questions I have raised regarding the nature and objectives of contextual research.

What distinguishes contextual research from noncontextual research?

Virtually any psychological phenomenon can be described in terms of four basic analytical components. These components are (1) the identifying and structural attributes of the *people* participating in a particular situation (for example, their ages, their learning histories, the degree of cohesion among the participants); (2) the *physical environment* in which participants are situated (ranging in scale and complexity from momentary situations and established behavior settings to larger-scale units such as neighborhoods and geographical regions); (3) the *activities and experiences* that occur among participants in the situation (for example, the various modes of people-environment transaction depicted in Table 1); and (4) the *temporal context* of the situation viewed in terms of both its objective and its subjective properties. These components of situations are summarized in Table 2.

The contextual analysis of a psychological phenomenon involves a set of assumptions about the relationships that exist among variables located within the People, Environment, Activity, and Time compo-

Table 2
Basic Components of the Human-Environment Transaction

	Contextual Components			
	People	Environment	Activity	Time
Dimensions of Contextual Components	*Composition and organization* • Individuals • Aggregates • Groups *Identifying attributes* • Genetic and biobehavioral • Learning history • Dispositional • Developmental • Subjective life stage • Group cohesion	*Physical and locational* • Geographic • Architectural *Scale and complexity* • Stimulus • Object • Event • Situation • Life domain • Life situation *Meaning* • Material • Symbolic quality intensity	*Mode* • Interpretive • Evaluative • Operative • Responsive *Structure and focus* • Simple, complex tasks • Active, passive orientation	*Segments* • Cycles • Stages *Perspective* • Natural • Personal • Sociocultural

nents. These interdependencies can exist both among the variables within a particular component as well as between those located within different components. On one hand, the concept of social norm has been invoked in the behavioral sciences to describe the kinds of relationships that can exist among participants within social situations (see Sherif, 1982). As such, social norms exemplify intracomponent relationships (i.e., interdependencies among those individuals comprising the People component of a situation). On the other hand, the concept of place identity (Proshansky, 1978) refers to a type of relationship that involves multiple components of the same situation, namely, the degree to which personal or social identity (People variables) reflects one's earlier experiences with and current attachment to a particular place (Environmental component).

The task of contextual research is to identify which relationships within one set of variables provide the most explanatory leverage for understanding the relationships within a different set of variables. In other words, the first set of variables provides a frame of reference from which a second set of variables can be better understood. I refer to the first set as the "contextual cluster" of variables and the second set as the "target cluster."

In the research literature on crowding, for example, the target variables typically include some measure of population density and various criteria of emotional and behavioral well-being. A general conclusion that can be drawn from the crowding literature is that the effects of high density on people depend largely on situational or contextual factors (see Baron & Needel, 1980). Thus we might hypothesize that the existence of social norms which enhance cooperation among participants in a situation would mitigate the potentially negative consequences of social density. Similarly, the concept of place identity, mentioned earlier, suggests that the effects of neighborhood density on residents may be mediated by the degree to which the residents identify with the area and feel attached to it. In both of these examples, the hypotheses suggest an explanatory link between the target variables of density and behavior and the contextual variables of interpersonal cohesion and place identity, respectively.

The designation of "contextual" and "target" clusters of variables implies certain assumptions about the relationships among those categories. First, it is assumed that a hierarchy of influence exists among the two clusters. That is, within a given temporal frame, relationships among the contextual variables are more likely to influence or change the target variables than to be changed by them. A second and closely related assumption is that the relationships among contextual variables are temporally more durable than those existing among the target variables. This is not to say that the variables which have been designated as contextual are unchanging or unresponsive to the target variables, since all of the interrelations among people, their environments, and their activities are ultimately changeable over time. Rather, I am suggesting that within a particular time frame, a hierarchy of influence and relative degree of temporal stability are assumed to exist among the two sets of variables.

These assumptions suggest a distinction between "strong" and "weak" forms of contextual research. The strong form of contextual research is that in which the key explanatory variables are specified prior to data collection and the presumed directionality of influence and relative stability of the contextual variables can be posited on theoretical or empirical grounds or on both. The weak version of contextual research involves a set of hunches about the possible links between the target variables and a number of situational factors, but neither the relative importance of these contextual factors nor the nature of their relationships to the target variables can be specified in advance of the proposed research. In such instances, the empirical assessment of nontarget variables is initially an exploratory strategy that may subsequently prompt a more explicit and coherent formulation of the links between relevant contextual dimensions and the target phenomenon. In contrast to both the strong and weak versions of contextual research, noncontextual analyses focus entirely on the proposed target variables and exclude contextual factors from theoretical and empirical consideration.

To illustrate the above categories of research, I will now consider the phenomena of automobile commuting, job performance, and emotional well-being. From a noncontextual perspective, one could simply measure the direct relationships between commuting distance and various criteria of performance and well-being. Alternatively, one might adopt a broader, contextual orientation by considering the links between travel distance, performance, and well-being and the commuter's perception of his or her origin and destination—namely, the residential and work environments. In one such investigation of automobile commuters, preliminary analyses of the links between travel distance, residential satisfaction, job involvement, and mental and physical well-being suggested that the perceived level of person-environment fit (see Harrison, 1978) existing within the home, work, and transportation domains is an important mediator of commuters' reactions to travel constraints (Stokols & Novaco, 1981). In this instance, then, the research progressed from a relatively weak version of contextual analysis (i.e., one suggesting a number of potential mediating variables) toward a stronger version in which concepts linking the individual's life domains were derived and the relationships between these contextual dimensions and the target variables (commuting distance, performance, and well-being) were specified. Had the research focused only on the target variables, it would have remained at a noncontextual level.

It should be emphasized that the mere inclusion of mediating variables in the analysis of a target phenomenon is not synonymous with contextual research. Contextual analyses incorporate a specialized subset of mediating variables having the following features: (1) Contextual mediating variables summarize some aspect of the interdependence among multiple elements of a situation; and (2) they highlight the situational specificity of the target variable relationships. In contrast, noncontextual mediating variables refer to single, isolated attributes of persons or environments whose influence on the target variables is assumed to be independent of the immediate situation.

In the research on density and behavior mentioned earlier, the mediating variables of social cohesion and place identity are contextual in that both summarize the interdependencies among multiple elements of the situation (i.e., person-person and person-place dependencies) and both suggest a range of situations over which the density-behavior relationship would vary (e.g., within competitive as opposed to cooperative situations or in neighborhoods characterized by high or low levels of place identity among residents). The personality dimension of introversion-extroversion, however, would exemplify a noncontextual mediating variable insofar as it refers to an isolated personal trait the influence of which on the target variables is assumed to be uniform across all crowded situations. Similarly, the duration of the individual's exposure to high density would be viewed as a noncontextual mediator if its influence on the density-behavior relationship were studied as independent of situational factors (e.g., whether exposure to high density occurs within "primary" or "secondary" environments; see Stokols, 1978b).

By emphasizing the interdependence among selected situational elements and the situational relativity of target phenomena, contextual variables serve an important theoretical function. That is, they offer potential criteria for describing and categorizing diverse situations and, thereby, provide a basis for assessing the generalizability of research findings from one context to another. In the behavioral and social sciences, any attempt to assess the ecological validity of research (cf. Bronfenbrenner, 1979; Brunswik, 1956; Winkel, Note 8) depends, first and foremost, on the availability of criteria for specifying the crucial (i.e., phenomenon-relevant) similarities and dissimilarities of diverse situations. By identifying those situational dimensions essential to the understanding of a phenomenon, contextual variables provide just such criteria for gauging the ecological validity of empirical research, assessing the range of applicability of theories pertaining to person-environment relations, and predicting the differential effects of environental change strategies on people occupying similar and dissimilar kinds of settings.

Which psychological phenomena are amenable to contextual research? Psychologists, like most people, often exhibit a proclivity for viewing the world in terms of rigid polarities. We are fond of dividing ourselves into opposing camps and taking extreme positions on such issues as the relative virtues of objectivist versus subjectivist definitions of the environment, the usefulness of experimental versus nonexperimental methodologies, the applicability of transactional versus nontransactional theories, and the utility of contextual versus noncontextual research (to name just a few such polarities). Often we forget the possibility that these reified polarities might be better viewed as continua encompassing several different mixtures of the two extremes. Karl Weick (1979), for example, has suggested that systems theorists too often treat the assumption of interdependence among situational elements as a constant (or a given) rather than as a variable. Many situations, he contends, are "loosely coupled" (cf. Glassman, 1973), which is to say that their elements exhibit a low degree of interdependence. This variability in the coupling of events suggests that scientific perspectives such as transactionalism (which assumes a reciprocal "give and take" between people and their environment) and contextualism (emphasizing the situational specificity of events) ought to be applied selectively on a phenomenon-by-phenomenon basis. Not all psychological research questions need to be framed in relation to broad contextual concerns since, as Weick has cogently argued, the degree of interdependence among target variables and ambient situational conditions varies from phenomenon to phenomenon.

One can consider, for example, a research program examining the biochemical processes associated with the accumulation of arterial plaque following prolonged exposure to emotional distress. If the researcher subscribes to a physiological model of stress (see Selye, 1956) in which different experiences of arousal are thought to evoke identical, non-specifically induced stress reactions, then the structure of those situations that induce physiological arousal becomes theoretically less important than the fact that a state of arousal exists. If, however, one subscribes to a specificity model of stress (e.g., Frankenhaeuser, 1979; Lazarus & Launier, 1978) whereby the emotional quality of the arousal presumably influences the resulting pattern of physiological responses, then a theoretical approach incorporating situational antecedents of emotion becomes essential for understanding the psychophysiology of stress. Regardless of the researcher's theoretical predilections, the relative utility of the two models ultimately depends on their capacity to explain the phenomenon under investigation—in this case, the extent to which physiological stress reactions are in fact moderated by the situational context of arousal.

Generally speaking, the adoption of a contextualist perspective is most strategic for examining phenomena that are susceptible to situational mediation. In such cases, the ecological validity of the research (i.e., the extent to which it is representative of, and can be generalized to, particular settings) depends on the precise specification of situational parameters. Alternatively, certain behavioral phenomena are relatively stable across a wide range of settings and circumstances. In those instances, where the validity of the research is less bound by situational constraints, analyses of the target phenomena may not be appreciably enhanced by the inclusion of contextual variables.

What criteria determine the scope and specificity of contextual research? Assuming that the contextualist perspective offers an advantageous approach for analyzing situationally dependent phenomena and that such phenomena have been identified for investigation, then several procedural questions concerning the appropriate scope and specificity of the analysis arise. First, how broadly should the spatial and temporal context of the target variables be construed? Second, considering that the target phenomenon can be assessed in relation to any number of alternative situational dimensions, which contextual variables are to be selected as providing the most explanatory leverage?

Before discussing criteria for determining the scope and specificity of contextual research, the meaning of these terms should be clarified. The scope of research refers to the spatial and temporal depth of the contextual variables included in a particular analysis. The term "depth" essentially denotes the relative proximity, in time and space, of the contextual and target variables. Spatial depth increases to the extent that the contextual boundaries of an analysis encompass places, processes, and events that are geographically distant from the site at which the target variables are assessed. For instance, the physiological effects of exposure to traffic congestion while driving to work can be assessed in relation to the immediate conditions of the journey or within the broader context of the commuter's residential and employment domains. Similarly, the temporal depth of an analysis increases to the extent that its contextual boundaries encompass places, processes, and events that are temporally remote from the period during which the target variables are assessed. Thus an analysis of the links between travel constraints and physiology could be restricted to conditions of the commuter's current situation or could be broadened in temporal scope to incorporate factors such as the duration of the individual's cumulative exposure to the present route and the existence of plans to modify the commute by changing one's job or residence in the near future.

The spatial and temporal depth of contextual variables can be measured in both objective and subjective terms. Accordingly, the target variables can be examined in relation to the individual's actual or perceived experiences with settings and events that are either proximal or remote from the immediate situation. While the spatial and temporal dimensions of contextual depth are often positively correlated (e.g., as when spatially distant portions of the individual's life situation are correspondingly remote in time), they are not entirely overlapping. For example, by reminiscing about earlier experiences, an elderly person may remain psychologically involved with these events though, objectively, they are temporally remote from his or her current situation. Similarly, one's anticipation of an upcoming trip to visit relatives in a distant city renders the places to be visited psychologically proximal despite their geographical distance.

The dimensions of spatial and temporal depth suggest a continuum of research ranging from narrow to broad contextual scope. Located at the narrow end of the continuum are those analyses which are conceptually and methodologically reductionistic. That is, the conceptualization and measurement of the phenomena under study are limited to target events that occur within a spatially and temporally restricted situation. At the broad end of the continuum are those analyses in which the target variables are examined within a broadly defined spatial and temporal context.

The specificity of contextual research refers to the particular concepts and variables that are chosen to represent the spatial and temporal boundaries of a target phenomenon. Clearly, any phenomenon can be analyzed in relation to alternative contextual frames of varying scope. Moreover, analyses of similar scope can incorporate very different variables to represent the spatial and temporal context of the same phenomenon. Thus, for any program of research, the investigator must decide how broadly to construe the context of the target phenomenon and which variables best represent the relevant contextual dimensions.

Decisions regarding the contextual breadth and specificity of research are typically based on two kinds of criteria: (1) existing evidence (both theoretical and empirical) concerning the situational parameters of the target phenomenon; and (2) more general considerations about the appropriate strategies and goals of theory development in the behavioral sciences. The relative importance of these criteria depends on the extent and quality of information about a phenomenon that exists prior to the proposed research. The literature on human crowding, for example, reflects a progression over the past ten years from highly reductionistic toward contextually oriented research (see Stokols, 1978b). More specifically, this work has identified several situational parameters of human response to crowding. Therefore, the contextual scope and specificity of future research on crowding should reflect and extend the earlier findings.

Of course, for certain phenomena the available evidence may suggest the utility of a contextually narrow perspective. If the investigator is interested in the physiological impact of high intensity noise, then the existing literature would suggest that situational mediators become less relevant as the intensity and duration of the stimulus increases beyond certain tolerance levels. In such instances, physiological arousal and hearing loss reliably occur irrespective of contextual factors. Therefore, the latter variables could be reasonably excluded from the proposed research.

The second criterion, involving the researcher's general assumption about the goals of behavioral science, is more likely to influence the conceptualization of phenomena that have received little theoretical and empirical attention. In the absence of clear guidelines about the appropriate scope and specificity of the intended research, a tension between two different theoretical orientations becomes quite evident. One perspective emphasizes parsimony and testability as the critical attributes of "good" theory (see Platt, 1964). This orientation is often associated with theories and methodologies that are of narrow contextual scope. According to the other perspective, the key functions of theorizing are to sensitize researchers to previously unrecognized dimensions of a phenomenon (Cronbach, 1975; Merton, 1968) and to restructure prevailing scientific and social structures (Gergen, 1973, 1978). By emphasizing the sensitization, taxonomic, and generativity functions of theory, the latter perspective encourages research that is relatively broader in its contextual scope.

The tension between these two perspectives on theory and research is reflected in the tradeoffs that occur at either end of the continuum. That is, highly reductionist research, with its emphasis on theoretical parsimony, severely limits opportunities for discovering the contextual dimensions of a phenomenon. Alternatively, theories of broad contextual scope sacrifice parsimony and testability for comprehensiveness. Faced with these tradeoffs, and lacking clear information about the critical dimensions of the target phenomenon, the researcher might find adopting a broad contextualist orientation during the initial stages of investigation most strategic. This approach reduces the potential for premature narrowing of contextual scope and permits the gradual deletion of irrelevant situational dimensions as additional evidence about the phenomenon is acquired. The strategy of maximizing theoretical and contextual parsimony at the outset may unduly limit the possibilities for discovering situation-specific moderators of the target phenomenon as the research proceeds.

*Subjective Life Stage: Developing Taxonomic Terms for
Describing the Contextual Units of Environmental Experience*

A basic prerequisite for applying the contextual perspective to programmatic research is the development of descriptive terms for representing the spatial and temporal boundaries of psychological
phenomena. In general, such terms will need to be phenomenon-
specific—that is, tailored to the unique dimensions of the research
topic. Yet it may be possible to delineate contextual units of analysis
that are applicable to several closely related phenomena.

In the ensuing discussion, the concept of subjective life stage is
developed to illustrate a contextual unit of analysis that appears relevant to a variety of research topics in environmental psychology and,
in particular, to the study of human stress. Subjective life stages are
spatially and temporally bounded phases of a person's life that are
associated with particular goals and plans. The spatial depth of a life
stage is reflected in the diversity and geographical spread of those
settings and domains comprising the individual's "overall life situation" (Magnusson, 1981) during a given period. The temporal depth
of a life stage is reflected in the duration (and continued salience) of
activity patterns and plans that are construed by the individual as
being associated with a particular phase of his or her life. Thus each
life stage encompasses a unique constellation of personal projects (Little, in press), settings, and routines that remain psychologically salient
for a given period. Moreover, the individual's perceived lifespan can
be viewed as a sequence of subjectively differentiated and motivationally significant life stages (see Figures 1 and 2).

Although life stages can be conceptualized in terms of objective,
spatial, and temporal markers (e.g., place-specific periods such as college attendance and military service), the subjective representation of
life stage is emphasized here to differentiate the concept from related
theoretical terms. The constructs of developmental stage and life
cycle, for example, are defined primarily in terms of age-specific and
biological events. The concept of subjective life stage, however, places
relatively greater emphasis on idiosyncratic and psychologically salient
events. Thus two individuals of comparable developmental stage may
construe the various phases of their lives quite differently as a result
of their dissimilar backgrounds and plans (e.g., two working mothers,

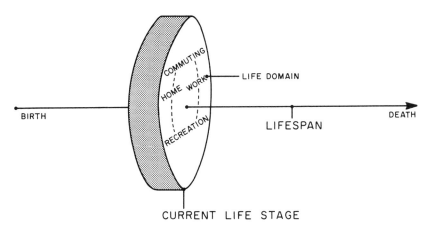

Figure 1. Intrastage context of environmental experience

one of whom has chosen to pursue her career while the other has been forced to work by economic constraints).

The concept of subjective life stage is also distinguishable from Lewin's (1936) notion of the life space, or "the totality of (psychological) facts which determine the behavior of an individual at a certain moment" (p. 12). Subjective life stage differs from the life space in the following respects. (1) Subjective life stage emphasizes the temporal and spatial organization of personal experience and the tendency of individuals to construe their experiences as occurring within behaviorally and motivationally organized life phases. (2) Unlike the psychological facts that comprise the momentary life space, the spatial and temporal boundaries of life stages (as well as the cyclical, organized quality of the experiences occurring within them) are not salient to the individual at all moments of a particular period. Rather, the spatial, temporal, and motivational coordinates of the life stage establish a psychological frame of reference of which the individual becomes cognizant at appropriate times (e.g., when one contemplates or experiences a shift from one life stage to another or periodically evaluates personal progress toward the accomplishment of stage-specific goals). (3) Finally, subjective life stage, unlike the life-space concept, explicitly emphasizes the relevance of interstage comparison processes (e.g., recollection, anticipation) for understanding the individual's response to immediate environmental conditions. Closely related functions of

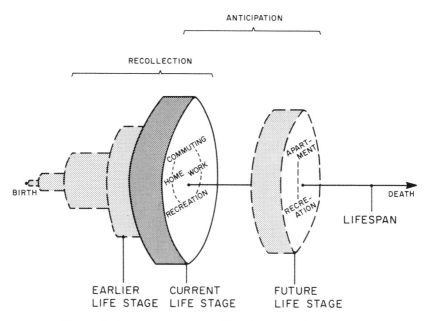

Figure 2. Interstage context of environmental experience

temporal comparison processes include the establishment of subjective comparison levels (Thibaut & Kelley, 1959) for judging the quality of one's interpersonal relationships, and the maintenance of personal identity and sense of self through reminiscence about one's earlier experiences (Albert, 1977).

An important reason for emphasizing the subjective dimensions of life stage in this discussion is that the research literature in environmental psychology clearly indicates the crucial role of perceptual and motivational processes in mediating people's transactions with their sociophysical milieu. The literature on environmental stress, for instance, highlights the importance of personal goals, expectations, satisfactions, and coping resources in moderating individuals' reactions to environmental demands over a given period (cf. Baum, Singer, & Baum, 1981; Glass & Singer, 1972; Stokols, 1979).

The influence of subjective environmental dimensions on people's response to life stressors can be illustrated in terms of the intrastage and interstage contexts of environmental experience (see Figures 1 and 2). The intrastage context of experience refers to those settings, goals, and activities that are most relevant during a particular phase of one's life (e.g., during the current life stage). The interstage context of experience refers to those settings, goals, and activities that are associated with multiple phases of one's life (e.g., recollected or anticipated events from earlier or future life stages).

The intrastage and interstage units of analysis reflect the assumptions that (1) environmental experience can be "chunked" according to psychologically meaningful temporal and spatial coordinates, and (2) the experiences occurring within each chunk are highly integrated and interdependent. These assumptions suggest that, in order to understand the effects of environmental demands occurring in a single life domain, one must consider these effects in relation to the supports and constraints available in other life domains during a given temporal frame. Furthermore, the events that have occurred during previous life stages and those that are anticipated for the future may significantly influence the individual's response to more immediate environmental demands (for example, when the quality of earlier experiences affects one's evaluation of current events, or when the anticipation of an improved future enables one to cope with undesirable aspects of the current life stage).

The intrastage and interstage concepts provide a general framework in which the relevant spatial and temporal boundaries of a target phenomenon can be established. Yet a further prerequisite for implementing contextual research on psychological issues is the development of more specific terms for representing, in a theoretically strategic manner (i.e., in a way that enhances the understanding of a particular phenomenon), the interdependencies among events and experiences within various life stages.

The development of stage-specific terms for representing the relationships between contextual and target variables can be illustrated through examples drawn from the literature on human stress. In Figure 1, an individual's current life stage is depicted in terms of the events within and of the links between four major life domains: home, work, commuting, and recreation. Within each of these domains, any number of environmental supports (i.e., conditions facilitating goal attainment) or constraints (i.e., conditions hampering goal attainment) can exist—for example, residential overcrowding, excessive work demands, daily exposure to rush-hour commuting, and either the presence or absence of supportive relationships within home, work, and recreational settings. The individual's pattern of exposure to these conditions is assumed to be relatively stable throughout the duration of the life stage.

The previously mentioned conditions suggest certain basic categories of interdependence that can exist among stage-specific events and experiences. First, the conditions existing in one life domain can directly determine those associated with other domains. For example, the relative proximity of the home and workplace may preclude the necessity of automobile commuting and routine exposure to rush-hour traffic; or one's activities at work may promote the development of social contacts and recreational opportunities outside of the work-place. Second, circumstances within one or more life domains can mediate the individual's experiences in another domain. Thus chronic exposure to residential crowding and excessive work demands can exacerbate the individual's sensitivity to commuting constraints. Alternatively, highly desirable conditions at home and work can ameliorate or compensate for the inconveniences of commuting.

A third type of interdependence between different life domains is exemplified by events which originate in one domain and abruptly transform the individual's overall life situation. Events such as unemployment and residential change not only modify one's work and home situations but also restructure conditions within the commuting and recreation domains. Often, these transformational events mark a progression from one life stage to another. The degree to which such events are voluntary or involuntary may determine their impact on emotional and physical well-being. Unemployment and residential relocation can have markedly different consequences depending on whether these experiences are construed as part of a smooth and voluntary progression from one life stage to another (as when the individual looks forward to the benefits of retirement) or as an undesirable and uncontrollable sequence of events (e.g., when a person is laid off from work and forced to find more affordable housing). Thus, as illustrated in Figure 2, the processes of anticipation and recollection link one's current situation with earlier and future life stages and thereby establish a psychologically salient, temporal context that is relevant to the analysis of certain acute environmental demands.

The relationship between reminiscence and personal well-being has been discussed by Albert (1977), Merriam (1980), and Rowles (1981). Also, the role of future time perspective in the maintenance of health is examined by Kobasa (1979). Earlier analyses, however, have not considered the interplay among recollection and anticipation processes and their joint role in establishing a subjective frame of reference from which the individual can interpret and respond to immediate environmental demands.

The categories of deterministic, mediational, and transformational interdependence among intrastage and interstage events offer a taxonomic scheme for deriving hypotheses about the relationships between contextual and target variables. If the target variables include measures of commuting conditions and personal stress, then a researcher could examine alternative contextual dimensions that are thought to (1) preclude or require one's exposure to commuting constraints, (2) exacerbate or ameliorate the demands arising from those constraints, or (3) provide a basis for eliminating or otherwise restructuring those constraints. These same categories of interdependence could be used as a basis for developing hypotheses about the contextual parameters of several other target phenomena, including human response to noise, overcrowding, residential change, and employment demands.

Clearly, the selection of specific contextual variables for inclusion in a research program is a matter of scientific judgment, informed by prevailing knowledge of the target phenomenon. The preceding discussion suggests, however, that the availability of general taxonomic terms for describing the spatial and temporal units of environmental experience could facilitate a more systematic and thorough analysis of contextual factors than has been evident in prior psychological research.

The proposed conceptualization of subjective life stage raises several important questions for future research, including the following: (1) What personal and situational factors affect the psychological salience of past, present, and future life stages? (2) Through what cognitive and motivational processes do individuals establish the spatial and temporal boundaries of their life stages, and by what procedures can these stage-specific coordinates be most adequately assessed? (3) How might collectively perceived, group life stages be conceptualized and measured, and what relationship do they bear to the personal life stages of group members? It seems reasonable to assume, for example, that group goals and activities, like those of individuals, are organized within certain widely recognized spatial and temporal boundaries and that these coordinates of group experience reflect a progression of collectively perceived phases in the development and organization of the group.[7] The preceding questions illustrate the kinds of theoretical and procedural issues that must be systematically addressed before the principles of contextual research, outlined earlier, can be made operational.

Conclusions

For those who identify with the field of environmental psychology or are interested in its concerns, there appear to be several reasons for optimism about the future of the field. In response to the question, "Of what age has environmental psychology come?" I would suggest that the field has matured to the point where we environmental psychologists can be proud of its basic and applied contributions, yet we are beginning to temper our earlier enthusiasm about how much we know with a greater appreciation of how much we have to learn. The last four or five years have seen the development of an increasingly contextualized view of environment and behavior. Moving beyond the mere advocacy of contextualism toward the development of a systematic approach to contextual research poses several theoretical and procedural challenges. How effectively these challenges are met may well determine the viability of environmental psychology as a scientific enterprise.

Reference Notes

1. Hagino, G. Trends in studies of environmental psychology in Japan. In G. Hagino & W. H. Ittelson (Eds.), *Japan–U.S. seminar on interactive processes between behavior and the environment, September, 1980.* Proceedings available from the Psychology Department, University of Arizona, Tucson.
2. Singer, J. E., & Baum, A. Environmental psychology is applied social psychology. Paper presented at the Colloquium Toward a Social Psychology of the Environment, Maison des Sciences de l'Homme, Paris, 1981.
3. Pastalan, L. A. *Relocation, mortality, and intervention.* Paper presented at the Annual Convention of the American Psychological Association, Montreal, Canada, September, 1980.

[7] The analyses of group-environment transactions and the life cycles of behavior settings, presented by Stokols & Shumaker (1981) and Wicker (1979a, b), are closely related to these issues.

4. Saegert, S. The effect of residential density on low income children. Paper presented at the Annual Convention of the American Psychological Association, Montreal, Canada, September, 1980.
5. Klassen, D. *Family, peer, and work environment correlates of violent behavior.* Doctoral dissertation, Program in Social Ecology, University of California, Irvine, 1981.
6. Schoggen, P., & Schoggen, M. Some emerging common themes in behavior-environment research. Paper presented at Annual Convention of American Psychological Association, Montreal, Canada, September, 1980.
7. Stokols, D., Shumaker, S. A., & Martinez, J. *Residential mobility and personal well-being.* Unpublished manuscript available from the Program in Social Ecology, University of California, Irvine.
8. Winkel, G. The role of ecological validity in environmental research. *Proceedings of the Wisconsin Conference on Behavior-Environment Research Methods.* University of Wisconsin, Madison, October, 1977.

References

Abelson, R. P. Psychological status of the script concept. *American Psychologist,* 1981, *36,* 715–729.

Aiello, J. R., & Baum, A. (Eds.). *Residential crowding and design.* New York: Plenum, 1979.

Aiello, J. R., & Thompson, D. E. Personal space, crowding, and spatial behavior in a cultural context. In I. Altman, A. Rapoport, & J. F. Wohwill (Eds.), *Human behavior and environment: Advances in theory and research,* Vol. 4. New York: Plenum, 1980.

Albert, S. Temporal comparison theory. *Psychological Review,* 1977, *84,* 485–503.

Allport, F. H. *Theories of perception and the concept of structure.* New York: Wiley, 1955.

Altman, I. Some perspectives on the study of man-environment phenomena. *Representative Research in Social Psychology,* 1973, *4,* 109–126.

Altman, I. *The environment and social behavior.* Monterey, Calif.: Brooks/Cole, 1975.

Altman, I., & Chemers, M. M. *Culture and environment.* Monterey, Calif.: Brooks/Cole, 1979.

Altman, I., Rapoport, A., & Wohlwill, J. F. (Eds.). *Human behavior and environment— advances in theory and research: Vol. 4 Environment and culture.* New York: Plenum, 1980.

Appleyard, D. The environment as a social symbol: Within a theory of environmental action and perception. *American Planning Association Journal,* April 1979, 143–153.

Appleyard, D., & Craik, K. H. The Berkeley Environmental Simulation Laboratory and its research programme. *International Review of Applied Psychology,* 1978, *27,* 53–55.

Archea, J. The place of architectural factors in behavioral theories of privacy. *Journal of Social Issues,* 1977, *33,* 116–137.

Baldassare, M. *Residential crowding in urban America.* Berkeley: University of California Press, 1979.

Baldassare, M. The effects of household density on subgroups. *American Sociological Review,* 1981, *46,* 110–118.

Barker, R. G. *Ecological psychology: Concepts and methods for studying the environment of human behavior.* Stanford, Calif.: Stanford University Press, 1968.

Barker, R. G., & Associates. *Habitats, environments and human behavior.* San Francisco: Jossey-Bass, 1978.

Barker, R. G., & Schoggen, P. *Qualities of community life.* San Francisco: Jossey-Bass, 1973.

Baron, R. M., & Needel, S. P. Toward an understanding of the differences in the responses of humans and other animals to density. *Psychological Review,* 1980, *87,* 320–326.

Baum, A., & Davis, G. E. Reducing the stress of high-density living: An architectural intervention. *Journal of Personality and Social Psychology*, 1980, *38*, 471–481.

Baum, A., & Epstein, Y. (Eds.). *Human response to crowding*. Hillsdale, N.J.: Erlbaum, 1978.

Baum, A., & Singer, J. E. (Eds.). *Advances in environmental psychology, volume 3: Energy: Psychological perspectives*. Hillsdale, N.J.: Erlbaum, 1981.

Baum, A., Singer, J. E., & Baum, C. S. Stress and the environment. *Journal of Social Issues*, 1981, *37*, 1, 4–35.

Becker, F. D. *Workspace: Creating environments in organizations*. New York: Praeger, 1981.

Bell, P. A., Fisher, J. D., & Loomis, R. J. *Environmental psychology*. Philadelphia: Saunders, 1978.

Boyd, R., & Iversen, J. *Contextual analysis*. Belmont, Calif.: Wadsworth, 1979.

Bronfenbrenner, U. *The ecology of human development*. Cambridge, Mass.: Harvard University Press, 1979.

Brunswik, E. Organismic achievement and environmental probability. *Psychological Review*, 1943, *50*, 255–72.

Brunswik, E. *Perception and the representative design of experiments*. Berkeley, Calif.: University of California Press, 1956.

Burton, I., Kates, R. W., & White, G. F. *The environment as hazard*. New York: Oxford University Press, 1978.

Canter, D. V., & Craik, K. H. Environmental psychology. *Journal of Environmental Psychology*, 1981, *1*, 1–11.

Cartwright, D. Contemporary social psychology in historical perspective. *Social Psychology Quarterly*, 1979, *42*, 82–93.

Chein, I. The environment as a determinant of behavior. *Journal of Social Psychology*, 1954, *39*, 115–127.

Cohen, F. Personality, stress, and the development of physical illness. In G. C. Stone, F. Cohen, & N. E. Adler (Eds.), *Health psychology: A handbook*. San Francisco, Calif.: Jossey-Bass, 1979.

Cohen, S. Aftereffects of stress on human performance and social behavior: A review of research and theory. *Psychological Bulletin*, 1980, *88*, 82–108.

Cohen, S., Krantz, D., Evans, E., & Stokols, D. Cardiovascular and behavioral effects of community noise. *American Scientist*, 1981, *69*, 528–535.

Cohen, S., & Weinstein, N. Nonauditory effects of noise on behavior and health. *Journal of Social Issues*, 1981, *37*, 36–70.

Cone, J., & Hayes, S. *Environmental problems/behavioral solutions*. Monterey, Calif.: Brooks/Cole, 1980.

Craik, K. H. Environmental psychology. *Annual Review of Psychology*, 1973, *24*, 403–422.

Craik, K. H. The personality research paradigm in environmental psychology. In S. Wagner, S. B. Cohen, & B. Kaplan (Eds.), *Experiencing the environment*. New York: Plenum, 1976.

Craik, K. H. Multiple scientific paradigms in environmental psychology. *International Journal of Psychology*, 1977, *12*, 147–157.

Craik, K. H., & Appleyard, D. Streets of San Francisco: Brunswik's lens model applied to urban inference and assessment. *Journal of Social Issues*, 1980, *36*(3), 72–85.

Craik, K. H., & Zube, E. H. *Perceiving environmental quality: Research and applications*. New York: Plenum, 1976.

Cronbach, L. J. Beyond the two disciplines of scientific psychology. *American Psychologist*, 1975, 116–127.

Csikszentmihalyi, M., & Rochberg-Halton, E. *The meaning of things: A study of domestic symbols and the self*. New York: Cambridge University Press, 1981.

Cullen, I.G. The treatment of time in the explanations of spatial behavior. In T. Carlstein, D. Parkes, & V. Thrift (Eds.), *Human activity and time geography.* London: Edward Arnold, 1978.

Dember, W. N. Motivation and the cognitive revolution. *American Psychologist,* 1974, 161–168.

DiMento, J. F. Making usable information on environmental stressors: Opportunities for the research and policy communities. *Journal of Social Issues,* 1981, *37*(1), 172–204.

Doob, L. W. *Patterning of time.* New Haven, Conn.: Yale University Press, 1971.

Downs, R. M., & Stea, D. (Eds.). *Image and environment.* Chicago: Aldine, 1973.

Ehrlich, P. *The population bomb.* New York: Ballantine Books, 1968.

Epstein, Y. M. Crowding stress and human behavior. *Journal of Social Issues,* 1981, *37*(1), 126–144.

Evans, G. W. Environmental cognition. *Psychological Bulletin,* 1980, *88,* 259–287.

Everett, P. B. Reinforcement theory strategies for modifying transit ridership. In I. Altman, J. F. Wohlwill, & P. B. Everett (Eds.), *Human behavior and environment— advances in theory and research: Vol. 5. Transportation environments.* New York: Plenum, 1981.

Farkas, G. Specification, residuals, and contextual effects. *Sociological Methods and Research,* 1974, *2,* 333–364.

Feimer, N. R. Environmental perception and cognition in rural contexts. In A. W. Childs & G. B. Melton (Eds.), *Rural Psychology.* New York: Plenum, in press.

Festinger, L., Schachter, S., & Back, K. *Social pressures in informal groups.* New York: Harper, 1950.

Frankenhaeuser, M. Psychoneuroendocrine approaches to the study of emotion as related to stress and coping. In H. E. Howe & R. A. Dienstbier (Eds.), *Nebraska Symposium on Motivation.* Lincoln, Nebr.: University of Nebraska Press, 1979.

Garber, J., & Seligman, M. E. P. (Eds.). *Human helplessness: Theory and applications.* New York: Academic Press, 1980.

Geller, E. S. The energy crisis and behavioral science: A conceptual framework for large scale intervention. In A. W. Childs & G. B. Melton (Eds.), *Rural Psychology,* New York: Plenum, in press.

Geller, E. S., Brasted, W. S., & Mann, M. F. Waste receptacle designs as interventions for litter control. *Journal of Environmental Systems,* 1979, *9,* 145–160.

Geller, E. S., Winett, R. A., & Everett, P. B. *Preserving the environment: New strategies for behavior change.* New York: Pergamon, 1982.

Geller, E. S., Witmer, J. F., & Orebaugh, A. L. Instructions as a determinant of paper disposal. *Environment and Behavior,* 1976, *8,* 417–439.

Gergen, K. J. Social psychology as history. *Journal of Personality and Social Psychology,* 1973, *26,* 309–320.

Gergen, K. J. Toward generative theory. *Journal of Personality and Social Psychology,* 1978, *36,* 1344–1360.

Gibson, J. J. The theory of affordances: Toward an ecological psychology. In R. Shaw & J. Bransford (Eds.), *Perceiving, acting, and knowing.* Hillsdale, N.J.: Erlbaum, 1977.

Gillis, A. R. Coping with crowding: Television, patterns of activity, and adaptation to high density environments. *The Sociological Quarterly,* 1979, *20,* 267–277.

Glass, D. C., & Singer, J. E. *Urban stress.* New York: Academic Press, 1972.

Glassman, R. B. Persistence and loose coupling in living systems. *Behavioral Science,* 1973, *18,* 83–98.

Greenberger, E., Steinberg, L. D., & Vaux, A. Person-environment congruence as a predictor of adolescent health and behavioral problems. *American Journal of Community Psychology,* in press.

Groat, L. Meaning in architecture: New directions and sources. *Journal of Environmental Psychology*, 1981, *1*, 73–85.

Gurkaynak, M. R., & LeCompte, W. A. *Human consequences of crowding*. New York: Plenum, 1979.

Hall, D. T., & Hall, F. S. Stress and the two career couple. In C. L. Cooper and R. Payne (Eds.), *Current concerns in occupational stress*. New York: Wiley, 1980.

Hannan, M. T. Problems of aggregation. In H. M. Blalock, Jr. (Ed.), *Causal models in the social sciences*. Chicago: Aldine, 1971.

Hardin, G. The tragedy of the commons. *Science*, 1968, *162*, 1243–1248.

Harrison, R. V. Person-environment fit and job stress. In C. L. Cooper and R. Payne (Eds.), *Stress at work*. New York: Wiley, 1978.

Hauser, R. M. Contextual analysis revisited. *Sociological Methods and Research*, 1974, *2*, 365–375.

Holahan, C. J. *Environmental psychology*. New York: Random House, 1981.

Holahan, C. J., & Saegert, S. Behavioral and attitudinal effects of large-scale variation in the physical environment of psychiatric wards. *Journal of Abnormal Psychology*, 1973, *82*, 454–462.

Israel, J., & Tajfel, H. (Eds.). *The context of social psychology*. New York: Academic Press, 1972.

Ittelson, W. H. (Ed.). *Environment and cognition*. New York: Seminar Press, 1973.

Ittelson, W. H., Proshansky, H. M., Rivlin, L. G., & Winkel, G. *An introduction to environmental psychology*. New York: Holt, Rinehart, & Winston, 1974.

Ittelson, W. H., Rivlin, L. G., & Proshansky, H. M. The use of behavioral maps in environmental psychology. In H. M. Proshansky, W. H. Ittelson & L. G. Rivlin (Eds.), *Environmental psychology: People and their physical settings*. New York: Holt, Rinehart, & Winston, 1976.

Jackson, J. A conceptual and measurement model for norms and roles. *Pacific Sociological Review*, Spring, 1966, 35–47.

Jacobi, M., & Stokols, D. The role of tradition in person-environment transactions. In N. R. Feimer & E. S. Geller (Eds.), *Environmental psychology: Directions and perspectives*. New York: Praeger, in press.

Jenkins, J. J. Remember that old theory of memory? Well, forget it! *American Psychologist*, 1974, *29*, 785–795.

Jessor, R. The problem of reductionism in psychology. *Psychological Review*, 1958, *65*, 170–178.

Kaminski, G. Environmental psychology. *German Journal of Psychology*, 1978, *2*, 22–239.

Kaplan, S., & Kaplan, R. *Humanscape: Environments for people*. North Scituate, Mass.: Duxbury Press, 1978.

Katona, G. Toward a macropsychology. *American Psychologist*, 1979, *34*, 118–126.

Kelly, J. G. Ecological constraints on mental health services. *American Psychologist*, 1966, *21*, 535–539.

Knowles, E. S. An affiliative conflict theory of personal and group spatial behavior. In P. B. Paulus (Ed.), *The psychology of group influence*. Hillsdale, N.J.: Erlbaum, 1980.

Kobasa, S. C. Stressful life events, personality, and health: An inquiry into hardiness. *Journal of Personality and Social Psychology*, 1979, *37*, 1–11.

Koffka, J. *Principles of gestalt psychology*. New York: Harcourt, Brace, & World, 1935.

Korosec-Serfaty, P. (Ed.). *The appropriation of space: Proceedings of the Third International Architectural Psychology Conference*. Strasbourg: Strasbourg University Press, 1976.

Krantz, D. S., Glass, D. C., Schaeffer, M. A., & Davia, J. E. Behavior patterns and coronary disease: A critical evaluation. In J. T. Cacioppo & R. E. Petty (Eds.), *Focus on cardiovascular psychophysiology*. New York: Guilford Press, in press.

Krupat, E. (Ed.). Urban life: Applying a social psychological perspective. *Journal of Social Issues, 36,* 1980, 1–152.

Kuhn, T. *The structure of scientific revolutions.* Chicago: University of Chicago Press, 1962.

Lawton, M. P. *Environment and aging.* Monterey, Calif.: Brooks/Cole, 1980.

Lazarus, R. S., & Launier, R. Stress-related transactions between person and environment. In L. A. Pervin and M. Lewis (Eds.), *Perspectives in international psychology.* New York: Plenum, 1978.

Leff, H. L., & Gordon, L. R. Environmental cognitive sets: A longitudinal study. *Environment and Behavior,* 1979, *11,* 291–327.

Levi, D., Ittelson, W., & Black, E. The experience of environmental quality: A journey into remembrances. In A. E. Osterberg, C. P. Tiernan, & R. A. Findlay (Eds.), *Design research interactions. Proceedings of the Twelfth International Conference of the Environmental Design Research Association.* Washington, D.C.: Environmental Design Research Association, 1981.

Levy-Leboyer, C. *Psychologie et environment.* Paris: Presses Universitaires de France, 1980.

Lewin, K. *Principles of topological psychology.* New York: McGraw-Hill, 1936.

Lipsey, M. W. Attitudes toward the environment and pollution. In S. Oskamp (Ed.), *Attitudes and Opinions.* Englewood Cliffs, N.J.: Prentice Hall, 1977.

Little, B. Personal projects: A rationale and method for investigation. *Environment and Behavior,* in press.

Lynch, K. *The image of the city.* Cambridge, Mass.: M.I.T. Press, 1960.

Lynch, K. *What time is this place?* Cambridge, Mass.: M.I.T. Press, 1972.

Magnusson, D. Wanted: A psychology of situations. In D. Magnusson (Ed.), *Toward a psychology of situations: An interactional perspective.* Hillsdale, N.J.: Erlbaum, 1981.

McGuire, W. J. The yin and yang of progress in social psychology: Seven koan. *Journal of Personality and Social Psychology,* 1973, *26,* 446–456.

Merriam, S. The concept and function of reminiscence: A review of the research. *The Gerontologist,* 1980, *20,* 604–608.

Merton, R. K. Manifest and latent functions. *Social theory and social structure.* New York: Free Press, 1968.

Michelson, W. Long and short range criteria for housing choice and environmental behavior. *Journal of Social Issues,* 1980, *36*(3), 135–149. (a)

Michelson, W. Spatial and temporal dimensions of child care. *Journal of Women in Culture and Society,* 1980, *5,* 242–247. (b)

Milgram, S., & Jodelet, D. Psychological maps of Paris. In H. M. Proshansky, W. H. Ittelson, & L. G. Rivlin (Eds.), *Environmental psychology* (2nd ed.). New York: Holt, Rinehart, & Winston, 1976.

Moore, G. T. Knowing about environmental knowing: The current state of theory and research on environmental cognition. *Environment and Behavior,* 1979, *11,* 33–70.

Moore, G. T., & Golledge, R. G. (Eds.). *Environmental knowing.* Stroudsburg, Pa.: Dowden, Hutchinson, & Ross, 1976.

Moos, R. H. *The human context.* New York: Wiley, 1976.

Moos, R. H. Specialized living environments for older people: A conceptual framework for evaluation. *Journal of Social Issues,* 1980, *36*(2), 75–84.

Neisser, U. *Cognition and reality: Principles and implications of cognitive psychology.* San Francisco: W. H. Freeman, 1976.

Newman, O. *Defensible space.* New York: MacMillan, 1973.

Niit, T., Kruusvall, J., & Heidmets, M. Environmental psychology in the Soviet Union. *Journal of Environmental Psychology,* 1981, *1,* 157–177.

Novaco, R. W., & Vaux, A. Human stress: A theoretical model for the community-oriented investigator. In E. Susskind & D. Klein (Eds.), *Research in community psychology.* New York: Holt, Rinehart, & Winston, in press.

Oskamp, S., Mindick, B., Berger, D., & Motta, E. A longitudinal study of success versus failure in contraceptive planning. *Journal of Population,* 1978, *1,* 69–83.

Palys, T. S., & Little, B. R. A project-based analysis of community dynamics and satisfactions. In R. R. Stough, & A. Wanderman (Eds.), *Optimizing environments: Research, practice, and policy. Proceedings of the Eleventh Annual Conference of the Environmental Design Research Association.* Washington, D.C.: Environmental Design Research Association, 1980.

Peele, S. Reductionism in the psychology of the eighties: Can biochemistry eliminate addiction, mental illness, and pain? *American Psychologist,* 1981, *36,* 807–818.

Pepitone, A. Lessons from the history of social psychology. *American Psychologist,* 1981, *36,* 972–985.

Pepper, S. C. *World hypotheses: A study in evidence.* Berkeley, Calif.: University of California Press, 1961.

Pervin, L. A. Definitions, measurements, and classifications of stimuli, situations, and environments. *Human Ecology,* 1978, *6,* 71–105.

Platt, J. R. Strong inference. *Science,* 1964, *146,* 347–353.

Proshansky, H. M. The city and self identity. *Environment and Behavior,* 1978, *10,* 147–169.

Proshansky, H. M., & Altman, I. Overview of the field. In W. P. White (Ed.), *Resources in environment and behavior.* Washington, D.C.: American Psychological Association, 1979.

Rapoport, A. Cultural origins of architecture. In J. C. Snyder, & A. J. Catanese (Eds.), *Introduction to architecture.* New York: McGraw-Hill, 1979.

Rogers-Warren, A., & Warren, S. F. (Eds.). *Ecological perspectives in behavior analysis.* Baltimore, Md.: University Park Press, 1977.

Ross, R. P., & Campbell, D. E. A review of the *EDRA Proceedings:* Where have we been? Where are we going? In A. D. Seidel & S. Danford (Eds.), *Environmental design: Research, theory, and application. Proceedings of the Tenth Annual Conference of the Environmental Design Research Association.* Washington, D.C.: Environmental Design Research Association, 1979.

Rowles, G. D. Geographical perspectives on human development. *Human Development,* 1981, *24,* 67–76.

Russell, J. A., & Pratt, G. A description of the affective quality attributed to environments. *Journal of Personality and Social Psychology,* 1980, *38,* 311–322.

Russell, J. A., & Ward, L. M. Environmental psychology. *Annual Review of Psychology,* 1982, *33,* 651–688.

Saarinen, T. F., & Sell, J. L. Environmental perception. *Progress in Human Geography,* 1980, *4,* 525–548.

Sampson, E. E. Cognitive psychology as ideology. *American Psychologist,* 1981, *36,* 730–743.

Sarason, I. G., & Spielberger, C. D. (Eds.). *Stress and anxiety* (Vols. 6 & 7). New York: Wiley, 1979, 1980.

Sarbin, T. R. Contextualism: A world view for modern psychology. In A. W. Landfield (Ed.), *Nebraska Symposium on Motivation.* Lincoln, Nebr.: University of Nebraska Press, 1976.

Schmidt, D. E., Goldman, R. D., & Feimer, N. R. Perceptions of crowding: Predicting at the residence, neighborhood, and city levels. *Environment and Behavior,* 1979, *11,* 105–130.

Schmidt, D. E., & Keating, J. P. Human crowding and personal control: An integration of the research. *Psychological Bulletin,* 1979, *86,* 680–700.

Seligman, C., & Becker, L. J. (Eds.). Energy conservation. *Journal of Social Issues,* 1981, *37*(2).

Selye, H. *The stress of life.* New York: McGraw-Hill, 1956.

Sherif, C. Social and psychological bases of social psychology. In A. Kraut (Ed.), *G. Stanley Hall Lectures, Volume 2.* Washington, D.C.: American Psychological Association, 1982.

Shils, E. *Tradition.* Chicago, Ill.: University of Chicago Press, 1981.

Slovic, P., Fischhoff, R. & Lichtenstein, S. Perception and acceptability of risk from energy systems. In A. Baum and J. E. Singer (Eds.), *Advances in environmental psychology, Volume 3: Energy: Psychological perspectives.* Hillsdale, N.J.: Erlbaum, 1981.

Smith, M. B. Is experimental social psychology advancing? *Journal of Experimental Social Psychology,* 1973, *8,* 86–96.

Sommer, R. *Personal space.* Englewood Cliffs, N.J.: Prentice Hall, 1969.

Sommer, R. Architecture, psychology: The passion has passed. *American Institute of Architects Journal,* April, 1980.

Stern, P. C., & Gardner, G. T. Psychological research and energy policy. *American Psychologist,* 1981, *36,* 329–342.

Stokols, D. Environmental psychology. *Annual Review of Psychology,* 1978, *29,* 253–295. (a)

Stokols, D. A typology of crowding experiences. In A. Baum and Y. Epstein (Eds.), *Human response to crowding.* Hillsdale, N.J.: Erlbaum, 1978. (b)

Stokols, D. A congruence analysis of human stress. In I. G. Sarason & C. D. Spielberger (Eds.), *Stress and anxiety* (Vol. 6). New York: Wiley, 1979.

Stokols, D. Group x place transactions: Some neglected issues in psychological research on settings. In D. Magnusson (Ed.), *Toward a psychology of situations: An interactional perspective.* Hillsdale, N.J.: Erlbaum, 1981.

Stokols, D. The environmental context of behavior and well-being. In D. Perlman and P. Cozby (Eds.), *Social Psychology: A Social Issues Perspective.* New York: Holt, Rinehart, & Winston, 1982.

Stokols, D., & Novaco, R. W. Transportation and well-being: An ecological perspective. In J. F. Wohlwill, P. B. Everett, & I. Altman (Eds.), *Human behavior and environment— advances in theory and research: Vol. 5. Transportation environments.* New York: Plenum, 1981.

Stokols, D., & Shumaker, S. A. People in places: A transactional view of settings. In J. Harvey (Ed.), *Cognition, social behavior and the environment.* Hillsdale, N.J.: Erlbaum, 1981.

Stokols, D., & Shumaker, S. A. The psychological context of residential mobility and well-being. *Journal of Social Issues, 38,* in press.

Sundstrom, E., Burt, R. E., & Kamp, D. Privacy at work: Architectural correlates of job satisfaction and job performance. *Academy of Management Journal,* 1980, *23,* 101–117.

Taylor, R. B. Human territoriality: A review and a model for future research. *Cornell Journal of Social Relations,* 1978, *13,* 125–151.

Taylor, S. M., & Konrad, V. A. Scaling dispositions toward the past. *Environment and Behavior,* 1980, *12,* 283–307.

Thibaut, J., & Kelley, H. *The social psychology of groups.* New York: Wiley, 1959.

Toffler, A. *Future shock.* New York: Random House, 1970.

Tolman, E. C. Cognitive maps in rats and men. *Psychological Review,* 1948, *55,* 189–208.

Triandis, H. C. Social psychology and cultural analysis. *Journal for the Theory of Social Behavior*, 1975, *5*, 81–106.

Verbrugge, L. M., & Taylor, R. B. Consequences of population density and size. *Urban Affairs Quarterly*, 1980, *16*, 135–160.

Vinsel, A., Brown, B. B., Altman, I., & Foss, C. Privacy regulation, territorial displays, and effectiveness of individual functioning. *Journal of Personality and Social Psychology*, 1980, *39*, 1104–1115.

Weick, K. E. *The social psychology of organizing* (2nd ed.). Reading, Mass.: Addison-Wesley, 1979.

Weinstein, N. D. Cognitive processes and information seeking concerning an environmental health threat. *Journal of Human Stress*, 1978, *4*, 32–41.

Wicker, A. W. Ecological psychology: Some recent and prospective developments. *American Psychologist*, 1979, *34*, 755–765. (a)

Wicker, A. W. *An introduction to ecological psychology*. Monterey, Calif.: Brooks/Cole, 1979. (b)

Wicker, A. W., McGrath, J. E., & Armstrong, G. E. Organization size and behavior setting capacity as determinants of member participation. *Behavioral Science*, 1972, *17*, 499–513.

Wilcox, B. L., & Holahan, C. J. Social ecology of the megadorm in university housing. *Journal of Educational Psychology*, 1976, *68*, 453–458.

Willems, E. P. Behavioral technology and behavioral ecology. *Journal of Applied Behavior Analysis*, 1974, *7*, 151–164.

Wofsey, E., Rierdan, J., & Wapner, S. Planning to move: Effects on representing the currently inhabited environment. *Environment and Behavior*, 1979, *11*, 3–32.

Wohlwill, J. F. The confluence of environmental and developmental psychology: Signpost to an ecology of development? *Human Development*, 1980, *23*, 354–358.

Zeisel, J. *Inquiry by design: Tools for environment-behavior research*. Monterey, Calif.: Brooks/Cole, 1981.

Zuckerman, M. *Sensation seeking: Beyond the optimal level of arousal*. Hillsdale, N.J.: Erlbaum, 1979.

DONN BYRNE

PREDICTING HUMAN SEXUAL BEHAVIOR

Dr. Byrne, who received the Ph.D. degree from Stanford University in 1958, has had academic positions at the California State University at San Francisco, the University of Texas, and Purdue University. He has also had visiting positions at Stanford University and at the University of Hawaii. Since 1979, he has been in the Department of Psychology at the State University of New York at Albany.

Dr. Byrne and his wife (Kathyrn Kelley) are currently editing a series of books on sexual behavior for the State University of New York Press. In addition to being the author or co-author of numerous articles, chapters, and books, Dr. Byrne has served as President of the Midwestern Psychological Association and is listed in *Who's Who in America*.

PREDICTING HUMAN SEXUAL BEHAVIOR

A bout ten years ago, I spent an evening with some nonpsychologist friends from my undergraduate days who asked in passing about my current research activities. I described my project sponsored by the President's Commission on Obscenity and Pornography and my growing interest in adolescent contraceptive (or noncontraceptive) behavior. In an off-hand way, I also threw out the comment that psychologists had really not become terribly involved in the study of sexual behavior until about 1970.

That remark led to a moment of puzzled silence and then sceptical questions as my friends recalled what they retained from psychology classes about Freud, Havelock Ellis, Kinsey, and even some of the revealed mysteries of the Rorschach and the TAT. Once they questioned my expertise, I attempted to dazzle them with fancy footwork. I pointed out that the people they named were not psychologists by profession and that our two most popular projective tests were developed by individuals trained in other fields. Later, with more time to reflect, I remembered that a number of psychologists over the years *had* been interested in various aspects of sexual behavior, from Lewis Terman and John B. Watson to Harry Harlow, and thus my initial statement was incorrect. The difference between the pre- and post-

1970 investigations was not a matter of academic field but, more importantly, a change in methodological interests. The shift of emphasis was from observational-correlational studies to experimental-predictive ones and from descriptive empiricism to hypothesis testing. Some of the implications of these shifts will now be described.

Descriptive Studies of Sexual Behavior

At the risk of stating the obvious, I should emphasize that psychologists do not hold a proprietary interest in the study of sex. On the basis neither of historical precedent nor of pedantic definition is sex an exclusively psychological domain, so psychologists must take a place in line along with anthropologists, sociologists, ethologists, physiologists, various medical researchers, and others. With respect to application, the acquired knowledge is of potential use to physicians, therapists, nurses, social workers, sex educators, parents, ministers, and each of us as individuals. It is perhaps best, then, to lay aside the disciplines involved and concentrate instead on what has been studied, how it has been studied, and what has been learned.

As has been discussed previously (Byrne, 1977a), much of the early interest in sexuality was provisionally acceptable in the scientific community to the extent that it avoided the "normal" sexual practices of Caucasian human beings who resided in Europe or North America. Thus research interest was largely focused on "crazy sex, animal sex, and native sex" (p. 4).

Abnormal Sexual Practices

From the days of Krafft-Ebing (1886/1894) and Havelock Ellis (1899/1936), the categorization of abnormal practices and the descriptions of them in sometimes lurid case histories were major aspects of the study of sexuality. Some of the content was sufficiently shocking that vital portions of the text were presented in Latin in order to shield the unlearned from possible adverse and unwholesome effects. The scientist-scholar, however, was able to learn about the most titillating details of the way in which sexual excitement and fulfillment for some individuals were associated, for example, with giving or receiving pain, with consumption of urine-soaked bread, or with carnal knowledge of various farm animals.

One problem was that this approach to the field did not seem to lead anywhere. It was interesting to observe vicariously the "perversities" of others, and it might be comforting to find one's own proclivities omitted. Nevertheless, the end result was a panorama of sexual practices with little or no evidence as to the antecedents of this behavior and few valid ideas as to how to bring about behavioral change.

As the study of abnormality continued over a period of time, another problem became manifest. Society changed, values changed, and behavior changed. It may have seemed reasonable for Krafft-Ebing (1886/1894) to describe fellatio and cunnilingus as "horrible sexual acts" or for Walling (1912) to assert about masturbation that "this shameful and criminal act is the most frequent, as well as the most fatal, of all vices" (p. 34). When such pleasureable activities were eventually found not to be physically harmful and when they came to be practiced by most of us, the scientific treatises gradually shifted from proscription to prescription.

The more general problem of specifying what is meant by the "deviancy" of abnormal sexuality is value laden, as was demonstrated in 1974 when the American Psychiatric Association voted (by no means unanimously) that one who engaged in homosexual acts was no longer a "psychopathic personality with pathologic sexuality" (American Psychiatric Association, 1952). Instead, this behavior is now described in terms of object-choice or life-style and becomes a matter of psychiatric concern only to the extent that the individual is unhappy about it. Some definitions of abnormal sexuality seek to retain traditional values by assuming the normality of certain behaviors. For example, Suinn (1970) proposed that "the sexual deviations include all sexual behaviors in which gratification of sexual impulses is obtained by practices other than intercourse with a genitally mature person of the opposite sex who has reached the legal age of consent" (p. 311). Other definitions have shifted to a different set of values in an attempt to focus on the context, the affective responses of those involved, and the effects of the behavior rather than on who does what to whom with which bodily organ. For example, Byrne and Byrne (1977) proposed that "abnormal sexuality consists of any sex-related behavior that causes psychological distress or unwanted physical pain for the individual engaging in the act and/or for an unwitting or unwilling participant" (p. 345).

Whatever the definition and the behaviors described in whatever language, the categorization of sexual practices considered abnormal at a given time and place does not seem to provide us with much useful information with which to predict the sexual activities of ourselves and others.

The Sexual Behavior of Other Species

A different sort of descriptive approach to sexuality is the investigation of animal behavior. Other species provide an almost limitless array of sex acts with which to compare our own. Leaving aside the sexual activities of plants, we can examine the conditions under which members of other animal species become sexually aroused and the behavior that follows such arousal. Any similarities to human behavior provide fuel to spark sociobiological fires. Differences among other species and between another species and ours can be interpreted as evidence of either genetic or experiential diversity in determining sexual expression.

Such research has taught us a great deal about the physiological conditions necessary for an animal to be able to become sexually excited (arousability) and the necessary external conditions that actually elicit arousal. The former are primarily hormonal and depend on developmental changes, appropriate biological functioning (involving such things as diet and freedom from disease), and (in many species) seasonal changes that are associated with readiness to become aroused. The external stimuli that elicit excitement are most often related to sexual partners or potential partners. They include olfactory, visual, auditory, gustatory, and tactual cues.

The sexual behavior that ensues from such arousal ranges from the awesome charges of two amorous rhinoceroses across wide stretches of land to the scratching and clawing of minks that make their pelts unsuitable for furriers. Male rodents mount and dismount multiple times, bulls complete the act in a single thrust while cows placidly continue to munch grass, bees mate in mid-air, male elephants use their prehensile penises to persuasive effect, and kangaroos double their pleasure with bifurcated penises and vaginas. There are photographic records of the facial expression of stumptail monkeys at the moment of orgasm (Chevalier-Skolnikoff, 1975) and evidence that the female chimpanzee can obtain a climax with a Prelude 2 vibrator causing stomach contractions, pelvic thrusts, and the vocalization "Hoo-hoo-hoo" (Keller, 1981). The context in which such acts occur ranges from random and promiscuous matings among available strangers (e.g., dogs) to polygamy in which a dominant male has access to a well-defined harem (e.g., seals) to life-long monogamous pairings (e.g., grey-necked geese). Postcoital behavior includes the indifference of cats, the playfulness of dolphins, and the ingestion of the now useless male by female arachnids. The greatest similarity among species, by the way, is the use of the rear-entry position for intercourse.

Such research is interesting, and it adds to the store of sexual knowledge. Again, however, it does not tell us much that would increase our ability to predict any specific human sexual behavior except that we might be less likely to draft laws defining a given sexual practice as "an act against nature." Nature is the setting for practices that include sexual violence, masturbation, exposure of one's engorged genitalia to strangers, oral sex, and homosexuality. Other species do almost everything humans do except make obscene telephone calls.

An exception to the predictive nonutility of this research is, of course, the work of Harry Harlow and his associates. Their animal research is much more experimental and much more oriented toward seeking generalizations than most of the studies of animal sexuality. On the basis of Harlow's research, we know that in order to function as normal sexual adults, primates must have at least early tactual contact with a mothering figure and a chance to interact physically with peers. Without these early experiences, pubescent individuals show little inclination or ability to copulate with a sexually receptive partner (Erwin, Mitchell, & Maple, 1973; Harlow, 1975; Harlow, Harlow, Hansen, & Soumi, 1972; Mitchell, Raymond, Ruppenthal, & Harlow, 1966; Senko, 1966). When male rhesus monkeys are raised by punitive mothers, they are as likely to attack and even kill a potential female sex partner as to engage in intercourse with her (Arling & Harlow, 1967; Mitchell, Arling, & Moller, 1967). The possible parallels between the early experiences of an asexual, fearful, ineffective, and murderous monkey in Wisconsin and analogous human beings badly needs to be explored.

Cross-Cultural Studies of Human Sexuality

National Geographic could depict the unclothed bodies of the dark-skinned inhabitants of underdeveloped countries long before the white denizens of Western civilization could be so represented in *Playboy, Playgirl,* and all the rest. In a similar way, prior to the middle of this century describing the mating habits of aboriginal groups was generally more acceptable than describing those of one's neighbors.

The striking variations in the stimuli producing arousal, in the instrumental and goal-directed sexual behaviors, and in the interpersonal context of sexual interaction led to the inescapable conclusion that no widely shared and possibly genetically determined pattern of human sexuality exists. As the Ford and Beach (1951) compendium of such studies revealed, human beings vary from culture to culture in what they find exciting; such acts as kissing, breast play, oral sex, slapping, biting, dancing, and anal sex may or may not be an accepted part of the repertoire. Further, the frequency with which sexual interaction occurs, the positions of intercourse, the age at which intercourse is permitted, the reaction to same-gender interactions, and the allowable consanguinity between the two interactants all vary from group to group. "Natural" sexual behavior is no easier to define across cultures than it is across species.

Once again, there is an interesting body of descriptive knowledge about sexual behavior that does not serve a predictive function. Whether psychologists examine research on deviant sexuality, the sexual behavior of animals, of cross-cultural sex, we find ourselves overwhelmed by the diversity of what goes on out there and at the same time unable to use that information in an antecedent-consequent framework.

Descriptions of "Our Kind of People"

In addition to "acceptable" research on dissimilar others, other sex investigations produced data and speculations that were aimed at the normal residents of the investigators' societies. Perhaps for that reason, this research had greater popular impact (including widespread criticism) than the work previously described. The descriptive emphasis, however, was maintained.

Freudian concepts such as libido, the psychosexual stages of development, the Oedipus complex, castration anxiety, penis envy, and polymorphous perversity are obviously loaded with sexual meaning. Despite the dynamic aspects of psychoanalytic theory, the theory remains a descriptive (and even postdictive) rather than a predictive formulation, as undergraduates quickly discover when they inquire about the conditions under which one person becomes oral dependent and another anal retentive. When students are told that the antecedents of these characteristics can be excessive satisfaction or excessive frustration at a given stage, fixation at an ongoing developmental stage or regression to a previous one, and so forth, they get the idea that the theory tells one more about what has happened than about what will happen.

After Freud (1905/1962) shocked both the scientific community and the general public in the early part of this century, Kinsey and his colleagues in Bloomington underwent a similar experience in the post-World War II era. Surveys were not new to the field, and several earlier studies had appeared without exciting nearly as much interest and controversy as did the work at Indiana University (e.g., Davis, 1929; Hamilton, 1929; Terman, Buttenwieser, Ferguson, Johnson, & Wilson, 1938). The "Kinsey Reports" indicated what percentage of the population had engaged in masturbation, premarital intercourse, oral sex, extramarital intercourse, homosexual acts, and all the rest. This material was reported in relatively dry and presumably unexciting volumes that became best sellers for the W. B. Saunders Publishing Company (Kinsey, Pomeroy, & Martin, 1948; Kinsey, Pomeroy, Martin, & Gebhard, 1953). In addition to reading about specific acts, the reader could engage in a social comparison process with respect to frequency, duration, and coital positions for self versus the remainder of society. Again, the research had no predictive thrust, but voluminous data concerning the sexual activities of the average person were suddenly available. Criticisms about the adequacy of the sampling method or of the interview procedures did little to dampen the enthusiasm of either academics or lay persons.

Perhaps the ultimate step in the investigation of sexual behavior is the obvious one of directly observing the phenomena of interest. The problem, of course, is that sexuality has generally been, in custom and in legal statutes, a private activity. The pioneer in breaking this research barrier was John B. Watson (Magoun, 1981; McConnell, 1980). In World War I, Watson became interested in investigating the effects of venereal disease films on military audiences, and he extended this research after the war (Cohen, 1979). He was appalled when he discovered the prudish attitudes of physicians about sexually transmitted diseases and about sex itself (Watson & Lashley, 1919) and argued that human sexual behavior could best be studied by psychologists (Watson, 1929). Unfortunately for his academic career, the founder of behaviorism undertook this task as a participant-observer in an affair with a female graduate student at Johns Hopkins. In the subsequent divorce proceedings in 1919, his wife obtained and destroyed his laboratory data that consisted of physiological recordings of sexual arousal. Interestingly enough, Alfred Kinsey also desired to follow up his survey research with observational data, and he set aside space in the Institute for Sex Research for a physiological laboratory (Pomeroy, 1966, 1972). The laboratory was never operational, however, and the Bloomington group had to rely on motion pictures of heterosexual and homosexual behavior that had been obtained from various nonscientific sources.

After these two aborted attempts at direct observational research, success was achieved by Masters and Johnson (1960, 1961a, 1961b, 1962, 1963), who began their now familiar work with as little publicity as possible in St. Louis. By the mid-1960s, a much wider audience became aware that these scientists were obtaining detailed visual and physiological assessments of bodily changes that occurred during sexual activities such as masturbation and intercourse (Masters & Johnson, 1966). The resulting descriptions of the sexual response cycle and its four phases (see Figure 1) assumed a seemingly permanent place in conceptualizations of human sexuality. Such knowledge served as the background for their subsequent work on homosexuality and on the treatment of sexual dysfunctions (Masters and Johnson, 1970, 1979).

The therapeutic endeavors of Masters and Johnson (plus the growing interest in the treatment of such disorders by behavior modification techniques) represented one avenue by which prediction came to be of concern to sexologists. The other path to prediction was provided by the Commission on Obscenity and Pornography (1970). The Congress of the United States wanted this group to find out, among other things, the effect of erotica on subsequent behavior. That straightforward and seemingly elementary question led to (1) the realization that behavioral scientists did not know the answer because no such research had ever been conducted and (2) the funding of various investigations designed to provide the needed information. Among the consequences of that modest monetary expenditure were the initial involvement of a diverse group of psychologists (among others) in sex research, a quantum leap in the number of research designs involving antecedent-consequent relationships, the creation of a new and growing body of data that badly needed theoretical organization, and, to a growing extent, the legitimizing of scientific interest

MALES

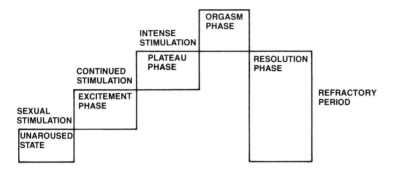

FEMALES

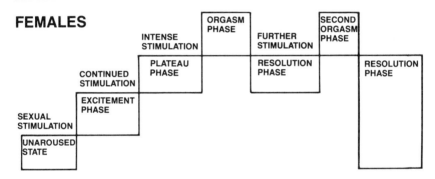

Figure 1. Masters and Johnson (1966) provided a description of the Sexual Response Cycle that involves four phases: excitement, plateau, orgasm, and resolution. These physiological processes are quite similar for males and females except that males tend to be unresponsive to further stimulation immediately after orgasm (the refractory period) whereas females remain responsive and are capable of subsequent orgasms. From R. A. Baron and D. Byrne, *Social Psychology: Understanding Human Interaction.* Boston: Allyn and Bacon, 1981, p. 547. Reprinted by permission.

in human sexuality among behavioral scientists. Where has this involvement and interest led us during the past decade?

A Theoretical Perspective:
The Sexual Behavior Sequence

Lewin's assertion that "Nothing is so practical as a good theory" used to be quoted frequently when psychologists wished to defend theory-building. It remains a valid assessment, and we should perhaps pause from time to time to remind ourselves of just why anyone bothers to attempt such a task.

The Utility of a Theory

Any enterprise from politics to science benefits from having a conceptual framework. At the very least, comprehensibility is enhanced when a person is able to fit isolated facts into a single higher order schema. This organizational process makes remembering, conceptualizing, and communicating the otherwise discrete bits and pieces of research data considerably easier. Hebb (1951) went so far as to say "that without theory of some kind, somewhere, psychological observation and description would at best be chaotic and meaningless" (p. 39). Thus even a relatively low-level theory adds meaning to the search for knowledge. Beyond that provision, a theoretical system can serve as a guide for recognizing what observations need to be made to "fill in the gaps." With luck and diligence, the theory becomes articulated as a collection of lawful empirical relations. Finally, at its highest level of functioning, a theory consists of an interconnected network of constructs held together in specified functional relationships. Such a theory makes possible predicting the probability of the occurrence of certain consequents in the presence of given antecedents. Further, fully developed theories allow one to make deductions that result in hypotheses about as yet unobserved phenomena.

Though physicists, astronomers, learning theorists, and others have given us samples of the joys of scientific theorizing, psychosexology is at a much earlier developmental stage. The history of sex research has been characterized by the accumulation of factual (and sometimes artifactual) information in various research approaches, each approach having a descriptive emphasis. Only in very recent years have there been attempts to construct the initial frameworks of such predictive formulations. Examples of these recent attempts include the role-script theory of Simon and Gagnon (1969), Mosher's (1980) account of the orgasmic experience, Storms' (1981) explanatory description of erotic orientation development, and the more inclusive constructions of Abramson (1982) and the present author (Byrne, 1977a). The general usefulness of any of these efforts cannot be known at the moment, but one of them will be put to heuristic duty

in the remainder of this chapter as an example of how such conceptualizations may help at least in organizing what we know.

Outlining the Variables in a Sequential Sexual Episode

One way to characterize behavior is to identify the responses one wishes to predict, the external stimuli that increase the probability of those responses, and the internal processes that mediate (and often initiate) the activity. Some psychologists find it reasonable to organize these events into "sequences" which have a beginning and an end. That statement does not mean that life actually consists of a series of starts and stops with pauses in-between to change reels. It does mean that such an organization makes possible observing and comprehending a phenomenon whose magnitude and complexity would otherwise defeat our best efforts. Besides, there is evidence that people in general find it most compatible to think of the behavior of themselves and others "as if" it were divided into precisely such sequences (Newtson, Engquist, & Bois, 1977).

In Figure 2 is a graphic depiction of the sexual behavior sequence more or less as it was initially presented (Byrne, 1977a). Within the stimulus-mediators-response paradigm, the model simply identifies the relevant constructs and suggests the relationships between and among them.

On the left are the external erotic stimuli, divided into those that constitute unconditioned stimuli and those to which a sexual response has been learned. On the right are the external responses, divided somewhat arbitrarily into instrumental acts and sexual goal responses. In between are the mediational variables—transitory affective responses to erotic cues, relatively stable evaluative responses, sexual information and beliefs, the expectancies based on those cognitions, imaginative fantasies, and the physiological responses associated with sexual arousal. Note that the latter biological aspects of the sequence include both internal and external processes. Finally, each sequence can potentially end in a rewarding or punishing outcome (or a mixture of the two). Such reinforcing events represent one way in which changes in the system are brought about, indicated in the figure as feedback.

I will now reassemble the various aspects of the model in order to examine what is currently known about predicting human sexual be-

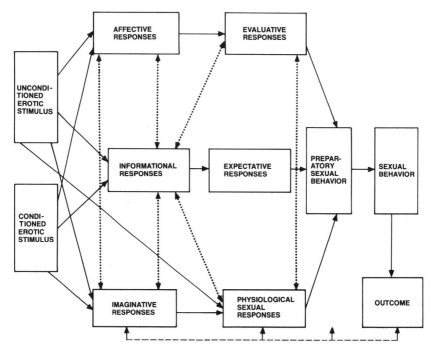

Figure 2. The Sexual Behavior Sequence is a conceptualization that provides a framework for studying human sexuality. This schema identifies the basic constructs as consisting of conditioned and unconditioned stimuli, six mediational variables, behavior that includes instrumental acts and goal responses, and outcome variables that are rewarding or punishing or both. The solid lines indicate the major antecedent-consequent relationships of the model, the dotted lines indicate secondary relationships, and the line made of dashes indicates a feedback process wherein the outcome associated with sexual acts influences subsequent functioning. From D. Byrne, "Social Psychology and the Study of Sexual Behavior," *Personality and Social Psychology Bulletin,* 1977, *3*, p. 14. Copyright © 1977 by The Society for Personality and Social Psychology, with permission of Sage Publications, Inc.

havior. First I will describe the three classes of variables that bring about sexual arousal, as depicted in Figure 3.

An assumption, consistent with existing data, is that the probability of sexual behavior increases as the level of sexual arousal increases. A further assumption is that the specific sexual behavior that takes place is determined by factors other than arousal, which is simply a motivational state that propels the individual toward an undesig-

AROUSAL

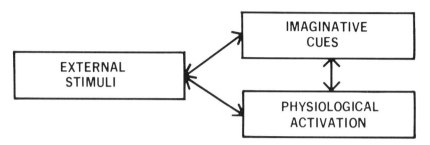

Figure 3. Within the Sexual Behavior Sequence, arousal is partially defined by physiological responses (and partially by subjective self-perceptions). It is proposed that arousal is a joint function of physiological factors, external cues, and internal imaginative cues.

nated sexual act. What do I mean by sexual arousal and what brings about this state?

Physiological Activation

Sexual arousal is defined in part by biological processes such as vaso-congestion, involving an increased supply of blood in the genitalia (and elsewhere) that is most obvious in the male's erection and the female's swollen labia and erect nipples. A result is a reddening of the tissues accompanied by higher temperature. There is also an increase in muscle tension (myotonia) and the secretion of lubricatory fluids in both males and females. In recent years numerous measuring devices have been developed to assess such changes and thus provide accurate indicators of physiological arousal (Kelley & Byrne, in press). These instruments include the penile plethysmograph (Abel & Blanchard, 1976; Rosen & Keefe, 1978) to measure erections in terms of changes in volume or circumference, the vaginal photoplethysmograph (Geer, 1975; Heiman, 1977; Sintchak & Geer, 1975) to measure changes in the blood supply of the vaginal walls by means of a light source and photosensitive receptor embedded in a tampon-like device, and the use of thermography (Seeley, Abramson, Perry, Rothblatt, & Seeley,

1980; Tordjman, Thierree, & Michel, 1980) to assess changes in temperature in specific areas of the genitalia.

Genital Changes and Sexual Arousal

The bodily changes described above sometimes serve as the operational definition of sexual arousal, but sometimes they are considered simply as the physical concomitants of subjectively defined arousal. Whichever approach is taken, research indicates that subjectively defined arousal as indicated on rating scales or by oral responses is highly correlated with the physiological measures for most normally functioning males and females *if* the appropriate methodology is used (Korff & Geer, Note 1). Appropriate methodology includes a sufficiently wide range of erotic stimuli and the assessment of both types of arousal at approximately the same time. Under these conditions, self-rated arousal and physiological arousal correlate in the .80s and .90s (Speiss, 1977; Korff & Geer, Note 1). When those conditions are not met, the correlations still tend to be significant but drop to the .40s, .50s, or below (Farkas, Sine, & Evans, 1979; Heiman, 1975, 1977; Osborn & Pollack, 1977; Wincze, Hoon, & Hoon, 1976, 1977). It is also generally found that the correlations are higher for males than for females (Hoon, 1978; Steinman, Wincze, Sakheim, Barlow, & Mavissakalian, 1981), possibly because males have learned to pay greater attention to genital-related physiological cues (Geer, 1979).

The relatively strong relationship between self-perceived arousal and various physiological indices can be taken as indicating validity (for both types of assessment) and as providing a unique opportunity in behavioral science to measure a motivational state in a way that does not depend either on the assumed effects of deprivation or on self-report. The magnitude of the subjective-physiological association is, without doubt, unusual and constitutes a welcome indication of where future research in this field may lead.

Another point to consider is that for some individuals little or no relation between perceived arousal and physiological arousal exists. What do these off-quadrant cases mean? To date, there has been more speculation than research on this topic. It is generally believed that maladjustment is associated with discrepancies between what an individual believes about his or her state of arousal and any genital changes that are or are not taking place. The impotent rapist would be an example of an individual high in self-perceived arousal who is low in physiological arousal. An anxious, sexually repressed individual might provide an example of low self-perceived arousal accompanied periodically by high physiological arousal that is mislabeled as disease, the work of the devil, or whatever. In either instance, one part of the treatment process would presumably involve learning to identify one's physiological state accurately (Heiman, 1975; Shapiro, 1977; Korff & Geer, Note 1). This would seem to be an extremely fruitful area for future research and application.

Physiological Processes as an Impetus to Arousal

From what has just been said, one can understand that a close association between subjective and physiological arousal suggests that any sign of genital excitement should be interpreted by the individual as an indication of his or her level of arousal. This sexual version of the James Lange theory exemplifies the idea, "If I have an erection, this must be lust." It follows that any event that has led to vasocongestion (e.g., a full bladder, a motorcycle ride, tight clothing, etc.) could result in the perception that one is sexually excited and hence ready for a sexual experience. The extent to which sexual behavior is motivated by such interpretations has not been investigated, but it seems probable that, for most individuals, cognitive attributions as to the source of arousal would strongly affect any resultant behavior.

Hormones and sexual behavior. There are other ways in which a physiological process could serve as the elicitor of arousal. A widely held belief is that differences in sex drive, in arousability, and in performance rest on hormonal variations. It follows that individual differences in sexual interest as well as age differences in sexual activity are the result of variations in hormone production. Is there anything wrong with that depiction?

As Rosen and Rosen (1981) point out, hormones unmistakably have a direct influence on one's male or female physical characteristics and on one's ability to reproduce. Secondary sexual characteristics, the menstrual cycle, the production of ova and sperm, the maintenance of pregnancy, and menopause are all under the direct influence of the level at which specific hormones are produced. When it comes to human *behavior*, however, hormonal variables do not provide predictive utility. How frequently an individual desires sexual outlet, the quality of his or her performance, preference among sexual activities, and object-choice are *not* hormonally determined.

Among lower mammals, female sexual activity is clearly associated with the presence of hormones at the appropriate levels, which in turn are associated with the ability to conceive. Among nonhuman primates, sexual activity is greatest and least selective when the estrogen level is high and reproduction possible, but intercourse also occurs, though more discriminatively, at other times in the cycle with a preferred partner or partners. Among human females, not only is sexuality not dependent on hormones and reproductive probability, there is actually a slight peak in sexual activity just before and just after menstruation—among the least likely times to conceive (McCauley & Ehrhardt, 1976). When female-initiated intercourse is separated from male-initiated intercourse, there does seem to be a tendency for female desire to show a slight increase at the time of ovulation (Adams, Gold, & Burt, 1978).

The sexual drive of males is often assumed to be based on the level of plasma testosterone in the system. Testosterone levels (and sexual interest) are much higher after puberty than before, suggesting the power of physiological processes. In contrast, castration after puberty may or may not affect sexual interest and performance, suggesting the power of psychological variables (Bremer, 1959). Differences in testosterone levels exist among individuals and within the same person from hour to hour, and these differences do not correspond to sexual drive. In addition, the amount of testosterone in the body is decreased by stress (Rosen & Rosen, 1981) and is positively correlated with hostile and anxious moods (Houser, 1979). With respect to sexual behavior, a high level of testosterone does not seem to lead to sexual arousal or sexual behavior, but the reverse is true. Both stimulation and orgasm are found to raise testosterone levels (Kaplan, 1974; Pirke, Kockott, & Dittmen, 1974; Purvis, Landgren, Cekan, & Diczfalusy, 1976; Rose, 1972). Thus a general conclusion is that one cannot predict male sexual behavior from the level of sex hormones, but hormone level can be predicted from sexual behavior.

Sex drive versus sex incentives. If hormones are not responsible for a strong internal push toward arousal and sexual behavior, is there any indication that sexual motivation fits a drive theory? Before turning to the central role of incentives with respect to human sexual motivation, I think it is worth noting the proposal by Luria and Rose (1979) that males may have a sex drive (in addition to being motivated by incentives), while females are motivated entirely by incentives. These authors suggest that in males a drive state is induced by the accumulation of fluid during the periods between ejaculations. As the seminal vesicles fill with their akaline secretion and the epididymis fills with matured sperm, the male feels "pushed" or "driven" toward sexual expression by these accumulated fluids. Despite recent research indicating the existence of a female prostate gland and evidence that stimulation of the Grafenberg spot elicits ejaculation in the female (Addiego, Belzer, Comolli, Moger, Perry, & Whipple, 1981; Belzer, 1981; Perry & Whipple, 1981; Sevely & Bennett, 1978; Weisberg, 1981), no one has yet proposed that females experience a build-up over time of ejaculate that produces a sexual drive. In the words of an Irish housewife explaining gender differences in sexuality to an American anthropologist, "Men can wait a long time before wanting it, but we can wait a lot longer" (Messenger, 1977, pp. 73–74).

If Luria and Rose are correct, it will be necessary to think of male sexuality as motivated by drive plus incentives and female sexuality as motivated by incentives alone. However accurate the hypothesis of gender differences in this respect, incentives are clearly of great importance to both sexes, and their role will now be examined.

External Sources of Sexual Arousal

As Figure 3 suggests, external factors play an important role in eliciting sexual arousal. External sexual incentives consist of three classes of variables—unconditioned stimuli, conditioned stimuli, and the sexual behavior of others.

Unconditioned Stimuli: Unlearned Human Arousers

It is well known that, in most species, sexually naive individuals will respond to specific stimuli by becoming aroused, approaching the source of stimulation, and engaging in sexual intercourse. The stimulus may involve any sense modality but is presumably effective only among members of a given species or a closely related species.

The most studied stimulus is the sexual pheromone (Hassett, 1978). Not only does female hormone level and sexual interest peak when fertility is optimal, but in many species the female also emits an odor that is strongly arousing and attractive to males of her kind. When an artificial version of this sexual attractant is placed on a spayed female dog, male dogs become aroused and try to mount her (Goodwin, Gooding, & Regnier, 1979). This phenomenon has been investigated in animals as diverse as mosquitoes, hamsters, dogs, and rhesus monkeys. In mammals, these excitatory secretions are labeled "copulins" by some investigators who reserve the term "pheromones" for the irresistible effect of smell on insect behavior (Keverne, 1977). Once again, the sexual behavior of human beings cannot be tied to such a straightforward physiological determinant. There is some evidence that the odor of vaginal secretions varies with the menstrual cycle (and hence hormone levels) and that these odors differ in how pleasantly they are rated by males (Doty, Ford, Preti, & Huggins, 1975). Nevertheless, attempts to relate the presence of these substances to sexual attractiveness or sexual activity have not been generally successful (Morris & Udry, 1978). A great deal of money is spent on artificial odors that are advertised, in effect, as attracting the opposite sex. When perfumes and after-shave lotions are marketed under such names as Pheromone and Musk, their desired effect seems obvious. Research suggests, however, that the interpersonal influence of a product such as perfume depends on additional factors including the wearer's style of dress and the other person's interpretation of the perfume-style combination (Baron 1981).

There have been some attempts to link other cues (e.g., the sight of breasts or buttocks) with human arousal, but cross-cultural studies provide little support for the universality of any such built-in stimulus-response connections. It nevertheless seems likely that the presence of a potential sex partner, involving whatever combination of sensory cues, elicits arousal (Griffitt, 1979). The only totally unambiguous unconditional stimulus for human sexual arousal appears to be a tactual one. Direct stimulation of the penis or clitoris (and to a lesser extent of other parts of the body) tends to be pleasant and is likely to result in some degree of arousal. The touch can be provided by oneself, another person, or objects in one's environment. This characteristic effect suggests the reason that Ford and Beach (1951) found genital caresses to be a world-wide component of foreplay despite enormous cultural differences in other practices such as kissing, breast play, or oral stimulation.

Conditioned Stimuli: Learning by Association

It has long been apparent from common experience, as well as from clinical case histories involving fetishism, sadomasochism, bestiality, "water sports," and other behavioral variations, that human beings can learn to become aroused in response to a wide variety of stimuli, including high heel shoes, pain, pigs, and reciprocal enemas.

Associational learning would seem to explain how these stimulus-response connections were acquired, but surprisingly little basic research has been directed at this aspect of sexual responsiveness. In the laboratory, it has been shown that when an erotic stimulus is repeatedly paired with a previously unarousing neutral stimulus such as a shoe or a geometric figure, the neutral stimulus acquires arousing properties as demonstrated in subsequent trials (McConaghy, 1970; Rachman, 1966; Rachman & Hodgson, 1968). Presumably, in real life, we learn in the same way to be sexually responsive to a particular perfume, a musical selection, an article of clothing, or whatever.

In a recent theoretical article, Storms (1981) has extended the conditioning model to explain the development of erotic orientation. Specifically, he deals with the way in which individuals learn heterosexual, bisexual, and homosexual orientations. In early adolescence, masturbation serves as an unconditional stimulus that permits pleasurable arousal to become paired with a wide variety of stimuli, including fantasized images. Orgasm provides a powerful reinforcement for these arousal-stimulus associations. Sexual orientation, then, depends simply on the nature of the conditioned stimuli (tangible and imagined) that are present during one's initial masturbatory experiences. Individual differences (and gender differences) along a homosexual-heterosexual dimension are thus based on such factors as the age at which masturbation begins in relation to the social development patterns of one's culture (Gagnon & Simon, 1973; Rook & Hammen, 1977).

Storms' theory provides a convincing explanation that ties together a number of divergent findings.[1] For example, sexual matura-

[1]It is not possible within the scope of this chapter to provide a thorough coverage of the antecedents of differential sexual preferences. With respect to a homosexual object choice, the etiological search began when such behavior was defined as a pathological condition, and it was deemed important to seek both "cause" and "cure." The search itself has become a matter of controversy, and the findings and interpretations are contradictory and the object of disputation. Theories abound and may roughly be di-

tion and masturbation at an early age are likely to occur prior to heterosexual socialization experiences and hence are more likely to involve conditioned stimuli of one's own gender. It follows that a homosexual orientation would involve early onset of sexual motivation (Goode & Haber, 1977; Manosevitz, 1970, 1972; Saghir & Robins, 1973). Since early maturing males excel in sports (Clausen, 1975), it is not surprising to find the incidence of homosexuality higher among college athletes than in the general college population (Garner & Smith, 1977). This conditioning theory also explains why male and female homosexuals develop in families with higher than average proportions of same-gender siblings (Gundlach, 1977; Schubert, Wagner, & Reiss, 1976).

The implications of the concept of conditioned sexual incentives have only begun to be explored.

Vicarious Excitement: The Real or Depicted Sexual Behavior of Others

Humans also become aroused when they witness the sexual activity of someone else. When people see erotic interactions or hear or read about them, they tend to find themselves responding physiologically as if they themselves were actually participating in the scene. Presumably, this response is one of the reasons that throughout recorded history sexual acts have been drawn, sculpted, written about, photographed, recorded, videotaped, and otherwise transmitted to others

vided into those that rest on biological determinism and those that stress experiential factors. Biological theories range from the suggestion that genetic factors are at work (Kallman, 1952; Pritchard, 1962; Slater, 1962) to those that rely on hormonal variations of multiple origins (Feldman & MacCulloch, 1971; Margolese, 1970). Experiential theories include psychodynamic postulations of the causal effects of specific family constellations such as a weak father and a strong mother for gay males and an inappropriately intimate father in the case of lesbians (Bieber, 1962; Kaye, 1972), social explanations based on the role demands of given cultures (Hoffman, 1968; McIntosh, 1968), the proposal that homosexuality is a by-product of heterosexual frustration that is based on gender differences in optimal reproduction strategies (Gallup & Suarez, Note 2), and learning-based situational formulations such as that of Storms (1981) discussed in the text and Green's (1974) hypothesis that some parents reinforce gender-inappropriate activities. It seems fair to say that there is no overwhelmingly convincing evidence from any of these theoretical camps. Perhaps the most curious recent contribution is that of Bell, Weinberg, and Hammersmith (1981) from the Alfred C. Kinsey Institute for Sex Research. They interviewed 979 homosexuals and 477 heterosexuals, found no specific family experiences that differentiated the two groups, and decided that sexual preference must therefore rest on biological differences! At the present time, we have little conclusive knowledge about the reasons for individual differences in the choice of same- or opposite-gender sexual objects.

by means of whatever technology humankind possessed at the time. Though the physical presence of other sexually engaged people is undoubtedly stimulating, the only evidence for this effect is in anecdotal accounts of group sex experiences and reports of reactions to stage performances involving "live sex acts." The vast majority of experimental sex research on humans has used erotic representations to elicit sexual arousal.

Countless studies have demonstrated that exposure to erotica in the form of drawings, photographs, films, audio tapes, and printed material elicits sexual arousal as measured either by self-reports of subjective excitement or by physiological indicators for both male and female subjects (e.g., Byrne & Lamberth, 1971; Fisher & Byrne, 1978b; Griffitt, 1973; Hatfield, Sprecher, & Traupman, 1978; Schmidt, 1975; Schmidt & Sigusch, 1970; Schmidt, Sigusch, & Schäfer, 1973; Kelley, Note 3, Note 4). In addition, sexual behavior has been found to show an increased probability of occurrence as a function of such exposure and arousal (e.g., Davis & Braucht, 1971; Fisher & Byrne, 1978a; Schmidt, Sigusch, & Meyberg, 1969). The specific behavior that occurs seems to be based on previous sexual experience and partner availability rather than on stimulus content. For example, after exposure to erotica consisting of photographic slides depicting petting, fellatio, cunnilingus, and intercourse, college students are likely to masturbate afterward (Amoroso, Brown, Pruesse, Ware, & Pilkey, 1971). After viewing erotica involving various sexual scenes such as a man with two women, married and cohabiting couples are likely to engage in simple coitus, especially if both members of the pair viewed the erotica (Kutchinsky, 1971). Differential arousal within such a laboratory experience has further been shown to predict differential sexual activity subsequently—the more arousal created in the experiment, the greater the probability of marital intercourse afterward (Cattell, Kawash, & DeYoung, 1972).

Analytic studies have made clear that erotic stimuli differ in how arousing they are to the average person (Brady & Levitt, 1965; Herrell, 1975; Levitt & Brady, 1965) and that individuals differ in their response to the same erotic depictions (Griffitt, 1975). With repeated exposure to such stimuli, both arousal and subsequent sexual activity show a tendency to decline (Howard, Reifler, & Liptzin, 1971; Mann, Berkowitz, Sidman, Starr, & West, 1974; Kelley, Note 5).

Given such extensive documentation of the effects of erotica on physiological responses and on behavior, it is surprising that only a limited amount of attention has been directed to the question, "Why?" That is, why should Person A undergo physiological activation leading to sexual activity simply because Person B has been depicted as being engaged in amorous interactions? The best answer at the moment is that such depictions are processed by the viewer in imaginative form (see the following section). The importance of cognitive activity in mediating the erotica-arousal effect has been shown by Geer and Fuhr (1976). They found that the effect of auditory erotica on the erectile response of males was inversely related to the complexity of sexually irrelevant cognitive activity occurring simultaneously. Further, the specific sensory modality is probably of importance in this respect. Cognition seems to interfere with the arousal properties of auditory erotica more than is true for visual erotica (Przybyla & Byrne, Note 6). This finding may mean that people respond primarily to visual images of sexuality and must translate verbal and auditory input into pictorial form. If so, direct visual stimulation would be less open to cognitive distraction. In any event, once those external stimuli are processed as part of the individual's internal imaginative activity, the person responds physiologically as though he or she were actually taking part in the visualized activity. The power of this imagination-arousal link will be discussed next.

Imaginative Cues to Arousal

In all probability, the uniquely human contribution to sexuality is the way in which internal images function to increase or decrease sexual arousal, to provide the opportunity to rehearse acts prior to their actual occurrence, to guide ongoing behavior, and to make it possible to take part imaginatively in activities that are unlikely to occur in real life (Byrne, 1977b; Byrne & Kelley, 1981; Kelley & Byrne, 1978; Przybyla, Byrne, & Kelley, in press). There are four types of imaginative cues that influence arousal and subsequent behavior—dreams, memories, imaginative play, and anticipatory fantasies.

Dreams

Dreams consist of images that are formed involuntarily during sleep. That dreams frequently contain sexual content has been generally accepted since Freud (1900/1953) made their interpretation an integral part of psychoanalysis. The erotic content of dreams seems to increase markedly at puberty, paralleling hormonal, ideational, and behavioral changes (Money & Clopper, 1978; Sarnoff, 1976).

Sexual dreams result in physiological arousal with the familiar bodily changes that comprise the sexual response cycle. Males who suffer from psychogenic impotence can be so diagnosed by the fact that they experience erections while they are asleep (Marshall, Surridge, & Delva, 1981). The strength of dream imagery is shown by the fact that the dreamer occasionally experiences orgasm, and this peak phase of the Masters and Johnson sequence is known as a wet dream, nocturnal emission, or nocturnal orgasm. In medieval Europe, the cause of such events was believed to be the action of incubi and succubi sent by the Devil to incite lust and unnatural passion by having carnal interactions with sleeping humans. Today, we have the less colorful belief that self-generated sexual images are responsible.

Incidentally, the drive theory of male sexuality (a hydraulic-like model) is supported by research by Brown, Amoroso, and Ware (1976) on nocturnal orgasms among young men who were exposed to erotic heterosexual slides in an experimental session. The subjects reported an increase in masturbation and a decrease in wet dreams during the subsequent 24 hours. In the week that followed, the reverse occurred—wet dreams increased as masturbation decreased. In the absence of comparable data for female subjects, such findings are at least consistent with the concept of a masculine sex drive that can be augmented by means of erotic incentives and reduced by alternative orgasmic outlets.

Memories

When individuals are asked to report their most exciting sexual fantasies, they frequently describe memories of previous sexual interactions in which they had been participants (Przybyla, Miller, & Byrne, Note 7). Because of their personal involvement, such recollections seem to be of special importance to the individual as sources of arousal (Kelley, 1979).

Various kinds of imagery, including memories, are used by most individuals to induce excitement prior to a sexual act and to guide and control excitement during the act up to and including orgasm (Kelley & Byrne, 1978). During both intercourse and masturbation, thoughts of previous sexual experiences are arousing to both genders, but somewhat more so for males than females (Crepault & Couture, 1980; McCauley & Swann, 1978, 1980; Sue, 1979).

Imaginative Play

The deliberate generation of fantasies to elicit and enhance excitement is not limited in content to memories of personal encounters. Most people's imagery seems to combine memories of their own experiences, memories of erotica to which they have been exposed, and original creations that constitute idiosyncratically arousing cues. Such fantasies occur not only in conjunction with sexual episodes but at other random times (daydreaming) as well (Giambra, 1979; Hariton & Singer, 1974; Hessellund, 1976; Wagman, 1967). Experimental subjects are easily able to fantasize on demand, and they subsequently report themselves to be more aroused than subjects exposed to explicit sexual pictures and stories (Byrne & Lamberth, 1971). Many individuals develop favorite fantasies or themes that are effectively arousing for themselves, and these frequently used images have been labeled "old friends" by Masters and Johnson (1979).

A number of investigators have reported sex differences in fantasy content and have found that male fantasies are more centered on the anatomical details of impersonal sex partners while female fantasies involve more emotional content and are more likely to have a plot; males also tend to fantasize themselves as dominant figures forcing sex on their partners while females have fantasies of submission and of being forced (Barclay, 1973; Hariton, 1972; Hunt, 1974; Sue, 1979). It should be noted once and for all that an emotionally exciting fantasy is not necessarily an indication of a desire to act out a comparable theme in real life (Byrne, 1977b). To believe, for example, that "rape" fantasies among females indicate a widespread desire to become victims of a criminal assault is analogous to assuming that the millions of individuals who spent money to view the movie *Jaws* secretly desire to be consumed by a great white shark. Gender differences in images of oral sex provide an example of the egocentrism of sexual fantasies—males imagine scenes of fellatio and females of cunnilingus (Przybyla, Miller, & Byrne, Note 7). Evidence that erotic fantasies are consistent with the individual's sexual orientation (Storms, 1980) also exists.

Anticipatory Fantasies

For the vast majority of individuals, sexual fantasies with or without masturbatory accompaniment are well established long before there have been any sexual interactions (Gagnon & Simon, 1973). Such fantasies often involve anticipations of future encounters of specific types. Such thought processes probably serve to motivate the individual, to define his or her sexual role, and to make possible trying out anticipated actions in private reverie.

That description may conjure up visions of Norman Rockwell adolescents visualizing the delights of their wedding day, but anticipatory imagery involves a variety of options. For example, the individual whose internal erotic scenes contain same-gender interactions should be more likely subsequently to seek homosexual than heterosexual partners (Storms, 1981). Quite possibly, repeated exposure to self-created exciting scenes of oral sex, anal sex, group sex, sadism, or whatever would similarly increase the probability of eventually engaging in such behavior (Byrne, 1977b). It is hoped that anticipatory fantasies will be the subject of a growing amount of future research. For example, fantasies of raping may be much more behaviorally predictive than fantasies of being raped.

It has been shown, then, that sexual arousal can be brought about by psychological factors, by various external cues, and by imaginative activity. The variables that influence whether arousal is expressed in overt behavior and how it is expressed will be discussed next.

Mediational Variables

As shown in Figure 4, four mediational constructs are specified as intervening between arousal and overt behavior: affective responses, evaluative responses, informational responses, and expectancies. Research to date indicates that such variables do not affect arousal once the individual is exposed to erotic stimulation, but they do affect voluntary exposure to arousal cues such as erotica and fantasies. They also determine how the individual reacts to the phenomenon of his or her own excitement.

MEDIATION

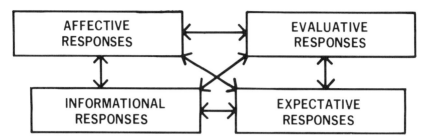

Figure 4. Within the Sexual Behavior Sequence, the effects of stimulation are assumed to be mediated by four emotional-cognitive variables involving affect, evaluation, information, and expectation. In addition, these variables influence approach-avoidance behavior in relation to specific stimuli.

Affective Responses

It has been shown (Byrne, Fisher, Lamberth, & Mitchell, 1974) that the immediate affective responses to erotic cues fall along orthogonal positive and negative dimensions. Different stimuli elicit different proportions of positive and negative affect (White, 1979), and different individuals characteristically respond to sexual stimuli with relatively positive, relatively negative, or ambivalent emotions or with an absence of affect (Baron & Byrne, 1977).

The relationship between these transitory affective responses and behavior has been the subject of only a few investigations. It has been found that the relative degree of positive versus negative affect elicited by an erotic stimulus leads, respectively, to approach versus avoidance behavior in response to either potential sex partners (Griffitt, May, & Veitch, 1974) or affect-inducing situations (Fisher, Fisher, & Byrne, 1977).

In studies of the effect of erotica on aggressive behavior, it has also been found that, when sexual cues elicit negative affect, there is a higher probability of subsequent aggressive acts (White, 1979). Positive affect is incompatible with aggression, so sexual cues that evoke positive affect decrease the probability of subsequent aggression (Baron, 1974, 1978; Baron & Bell, 1977; Zillmann, Bryant, Comisky, & Medoff, 1981; Zillmann & Sapolsky, 1977).

Evaluative Responses

The reinforcement-affect model of evaluative responses (Clore & Byrne 1974; Byrne, Note 8) specifies the way in which transitory affect is the basis for relatively stable evaluative responses such as attitudes. Very briefly, the proportion of positive versus negative affective responses (weighted to reflect differential magnitude) that are associated with a given stimulus determines the individual's evaluative assessment of that stimulus. Note that the affect may be elicited by the stimulus in question, by external events unrelated to the stimulus, or by an internal event such as mood state; whatever the source, all of the associated affective responses combine to determine the evaluative response. Finally, the two orthogonal dimensions of affect (pleasant and unpleasant) merge into a single evaluative dimension (like-dislike).

In the realm of sexuality, this affect-evaluative association has been demonstrated with respect to attitudinal judgments about pornography, censorship, contraception, and a variety of other sex-related issues (Byrne, Fisher, Lamberth, & Mitchell, 1974; Fisher, Fisher, & Byrne, 1977).

Most of the research has dealt with evaluative differences among individuals conceptualized as dispositional variables. Thus subjects are placed along a positive-negative dimension with respect to their attitudinal responses concerning a variety of sex-related topics such as masturbation, pornography, prostitution, homosexuality, or premarital sex. Individual differences have been designated as sexual liberalism-conservatism (Wallace & Wehmer, 1972), degree of guilt (Mosher, 1966, 1968), and erotophilia-erotophobia (Fisher, Byrne & White, 1982; Byrne, Note 8). Another approach has been to make the scale content relatively homogeneous; in such instances, the resulting dimension is more specific as with relatively positive versus negative attitudes about masturbation (Abramson, & Mosher, 1975; Mosher & Abramson, 1977), contraception (Parcel, 1975), homosexuality (Lumby, 1976), and rape (Burt, 1980).

Some of the work involving these variables has been directed at establishing the way in which evaluative differences influence the person's response to arousal and arousal cues. It has been established that erotic cues serve as rewards for those with positive attitudes about sex and as punishments for those with negative attitudes (Griffitt & Kaiser, 1978). Consistent with these findings, sexual liberals and conservatives report equal arousal when exposed to erotica, but liberals perceive the experience as positive and conservatives perceive it as negative (Wallace & Wehmer, 1972). In conjunction with these differential evaluations of arousal are the findings that erotophobes tend to have less contact with erotica than erotophiles (Fisher & Byrne, 1978a). Individuals high in sex guilt tend to prefer nonerotic to erotic magazines (Schill & Chapin, 1972), to spend less time viewing explicit sexual slides (Love, Sloan, & Schmidt, 1976), and to produce shorter and less explicit erotic fantasies than low-guilt individuals (Moreault & Follingstad, 1978). Sex guilt is also related to the tendency to perceive only the nonsexual meaning of double-entendre words (Galbraith & Mosher, 1968). Apparently, the negative evaluation of sexual cues leads to avoidance behavior that, in turn, reduces the incidence of arousal.

Behaviorally, an individual's relative positive-negative orientation to sex is found to play a pervasive role. As one might expect, those who respond with negative evaluations are found to dislike talking about sex (Fisher, Miller, Byrne, & White, 1980), to masturbate less frequently (Abramson & Mosher, 1975), to have less premarital sexual experience including breast play, oral sex, and intercourse (Mosher & Cross, 1971), to be less likely to take the steps necessary for effective contraception (Fisher, 1978; Fisher, Byrne, Edmunds, Miller, Kelley, & White, 1979), to become pregnant (Gerrard, 1977), to avoid sex-related medical procedures such as breast self-examination and gynecological examinations (Fisher, Byrne, & White, 1982), to perform less well in a college course on human sexuality despite comparable grades in other courses (Fisher, Note 9), and to draw less explicit nudes that depict smaller genitalia (Przybyla & Byrne, Note 10).

Thus individual differences in sexual evaluative responses influence the extent to which an individual purposefully encounters arousing stimuli, the frequency with which sexual behavior takes place, and a variety of approach-avoidant behaviors involving quite divergent activities that are sex-related.

Informational and Expectative Responses

There has been much less research dealing with the behavioral effects of what one knows or believes about sex than with the effects of feelings and attitudes. A specific behavioral example may be useful to show how such research would be incorporated within the model. If one wished to predict the masturbatory behavior of an adolescent male, the model suggests that one needs to take into account the person's physiological drive (e.g., time interval since last orgasm), any stimulation to which he is exposed (e.g., tactual contact, erotica, sexual fantasies), and the extent to which the stimuli or the behavior or both elicit positive or negative feelings and attitudes. How might the researcher include the informational-expectative influences? Perhaps the best approach is to follow the lead of such theorists as Rotter (e.g., Rotter & Hochreich, 1975) and Fishbein (e.g., Fishbein & Azjen, 1975) and deal with more than one variable at a time. One needs to know what the individual believes about masturbation, what probabilistic expectancies those beliefs engender as to the consequences of the behavior, and the value he places on attaining a given positive consequence and avoiding a given negative one. Let us say that the individual had been taught to believe that masturbation is a dangerous practice that brings about insanity. On the basis of experience, he also knows that masturbation is a pleasurable act that brings about orgasmic release. If those two belief systems were all that were operating in this sequence, it would be necessary to assess the person's perception of the probability of insanity and the probability of orgasm plus the value he places on avoiding insanity as a distant danger versus attaining orgasm as an immediate pleasure. Note that if the person's expectation and fear of insanity were greater than his expectation and enjoyment of orgasm, masturbation could still be predicted to occur *if* the arousal variables were sufficiently strong to overcome them. Whether the person sought to approach and attend to arousing stimuli would, in turn, be a function of the relative strength of positive versus negative elements of his affective-evaluative response system. Continued research should permit us to move from these generalizations toward specific mathematical formulations that permit precise behavioral prediction.

Some of the sex research on informational variables has been intraindividual in design. It has been found that those who are most attitudinally negative to sex report perceiving themselves as less knowledgeable on the topic (Byrne, Jazwinski, DeNinno, & Fisher, 1977), are more likely to believe in the truth of sexual myths (Mosher, 1979), are able to remember fewer details from a recorded lecture on birth control (Schwartz, 1973), and are more likely to communicate sexual misinformation to others (Mendelsohn & Mosher, 1979). A negative sexual orientation possibly leads the individual to avoid exposure to sexual information and to misperceive or forget that which *is* presented.

The sex research that has used some version of the belief-expectancy-valuation approach primarily involves contraceptive behavior, with the Fishbein group (e.g., Fishbein, 1972; Fishbein & Jaccard, 1973; Jaccard, Hand, Ku, Richardson, & Abella, 1982; McCarty, 1981) pioneering in this endeavor. Using a combination of the Fishbein and Byrne models, researchers have been able to demonstrate the predictive power of such an approach in studies of the use of university contraceptive services by female undergraduates (Fisher, Byrne, Edmunds, Miller, Kelley, & White, 1979) and of the use of condoms by male undergraduates (Fisher, 1978).

I hope that future sex research will be able to extend this multivariate approach beyond the realm of contraceptive behavior. In addition, this approach may prove useful to develop a taxonomy for categorizing informational variables. Presumably, there is information that has little effect on behavior (e.g., how to spell "fellatio") and information that has a very great effect (e.g., knowing that intercourse without contraception can result in an unwanted pregnancy). The latter type of information involves potential consequences and can be subdivided into positive and negative outcomes and into belief categories such as health, morality, normality, legality, or economics. In a contrasting approach, simply taking each behavior separately and obtaining the relevant beliefs of a specified population via open-ended response generation may prove more useful. For example, Fisher (1978) found that, with respect to condoms, male underguaduates hold a variety of positive (e.g., prevention of pregnancy, making the female feel less anxious) and negative (e.g., decreased sensitivity, embarrassing to use) beliefs, in different combinations for each specific individual.

Rewarded and Punished Sexual Behavior

In Figure 5 is shown the total sexual behavior sequence, as rearranged for the present exposition. The portion that remains to be discussed consists of the behaviors to be predicted and the rewarding and punishing consequences of those behaviors.

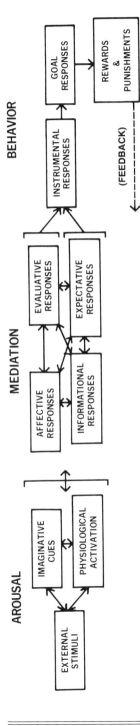

Figure 5. The Sexual Behavior Sequence allows prediction of human sexual response as a function of (1) motivational variables that influence arousal, (2) mediational variables that influence the behavioral expression of arousal, and (3) outcome variables that provide feedback and hence influence the probability of the responses occurring in subsequent sequences.

As has been shown in the preceding pages, the prediction of sexual behavior has included arousal-related behavior (e.g., reading pornography, creating sexual fantasies), instrumental acts (e.g., talking about sex, purchasing contraceptives), and goal responses (e.g., masturbation, intercourse). This range can be expanded to include behaviors as diverse as dating skills and pedophilia.

Although studying single behavior sequences may be of considerable value, a longer time span encompassing a series of such sequences permits us to examine the way in which sequences develop and change. For example, research has convincingly shown that exposure to a specific type of erotic scene does not lead to instantaneous modeling of the depicted behavior. Would the results be different, however, for repeated exposure over an extended period? My guess is that the likelihood of imitative behavior increases as the number of exposures increases. In another realm, we have seen that affective responses are pervasive in their influence, but affect can change over time. Individuals report engaging in a given act despite the fact that it elicits negative emotions and attitudes—then they find that they enjoy it. In subsequent sequences, the behavior should be much more likely to occur. There are also changes in informational responses. We know that beliefs and expectancies help determine behavior within a sequence, but what happens when an expectancy is not met and a belief is thus disconfirmed? It seems probable that the subsequent sequences would reveal changes as when one discovers that hair is not growing on one's palm after masturbation or that unprotected intercourse does not result in pregnancy. Note that the former example leads to a more accurate assessment and the latter to a more inaccurate assessment of reality; but the person's behavior should follow his or her beliefs, expectancies, and past experiences regardless of their veridicality.

The greatest source of behavioral change over time probably lies in the kinds of reinforcement that are associated with sex. Surprisingly little work has been directed at such variables. Some animal research has established that both intromission and orgasm function as rewards (Bolles, 1975; Larssen, 1956; Sachs & Marsan, 1972; Warden, 1931). Evidence with respect to the role of sexual rewards in human behavior is often indirect. For example, Kelley (1979) found much higher correlations for parent-offspring sexual attitudes among sexually inexperienced college students than among those who were sexually active. It seems reasonable to suppose that the parent-student divergence came about because the rewarding pleasures of sexual interactions reduced negative affective-evaluative reactions for the students involved but not for their parents back home. More directly, there is a great deal of therapeutic interest in using sexual pleasure (usually orgasm) to reinforce specific fantasies (Lobitz & LoPiccolo, 1972) or specific behaviors (Barlow, Reynolds, & Agras, 1973; Nemetz, Craig, & Reith, 1978).

Punishment has also been used to change sexual responses. In therapy, disgusting and otherwise unpleasant mental images are paired with specific undesirable sexual fantasies in order to eliminate them via aversive conditioning (Barlow, Leitenberg, & Agras, 1969; Brownell, Hayes, & Barlow, 1977; Levin, Barry, Gambaro, Wolfinsohn, & Smith, 1977). In analogous procedures, electric shock has been used to condition negative affect to an unacceptable arousing stimulus (Feldman & MacCulloch, 1971) and to deviant sexual acts (Blakemore, Thorpe, Barker, Conway, & Lavin, 1963). To date, such learning-oriented work has been conducted more frequently in clinical settings than in research laboratories.

One other line of outcome-oriented research has dealt with the effects of rape on the subsequent sexual responses of the victim. It has been found that those who have been forced to experience this criminal act report significantly less satisfaction in various types of sexual activities with their partners as long as two months after being attacked (Feldman-Summers, Gordon, & Meagher, 1979). Even 12 months following such an attack, affective responses are more negative among rape victims than among matched controls (Ellis, Atkeson, & Calhoun, 1981; Kilpatrick, Resick, & Veronen, 1981).

These various lines of research clearly indicate the importance of rewards and punishments in bringing about changes in the components of the sexual behavior sequence. It seems safe to conclude that reinforcement variables play a vital role in shaping, maintaining, and altering sexual behavior in the laboratory, in therapy, and in our everyday lives.

Conclusions

I hope that this overview of research on human sexual behavior demonstrates some of the possibilities that accrue when scientific activity is oriented toward prediction and is guided by a theoretical perspective. There is, of course, nothing sacrosanct about the particular model used in the present discussion; it was simply one example of the way in which an organizational schema can be useful.

It should also be noted that practical constraints forced the exclusion of a number of possible topics from extended discussion. Among the areas of sex research that deserve further attention are sexual development (Constantine & Martinson, 1981; Diamond, 1977; Morrison, Starks, Hyndman, & Ronzio, 1980), sexual dysfunctions (Kaplan, 1974), sexual crimes (Goldstein, Kant, & Hartman, 1974), and the interpersonal aspects of sex, love, and establishing relationships (Fisher & Byrne, 1981; Przybyla & Byrne, 1981).

Finally, I hope the message that sex research has finally come of age as a respectable topic for psychological inquiry (Bentler & Abramson, 1981) has become increasingly clear. Human sexuality is ubiquitous in its effects on our lives, and it involves impactful variables that can easily be manipulated in scientific research. As individuals and as scientists, we can look forward to a continuing expansion of knowledge concerning psychosexology in the decades ahead.

Reference Notes

1. Korff, J., & Geer, J. H. *The relationship between sexual arousal experience and genital response.* Paper presented at the meeting of the American Psychological Association, Montreal, September 1980.
2. Gallup, G. G., Jr., & Suarez, S. D. *Homosexuality as a byproduct of selection for optimal heterosexual strategies.* Unpublished manuscript, 1982. (Available from Department of Psychology, State University of New York at Albany, 1400 Washington Avenue, Albany, New York 12222).
3. Kelley, K. *The effects of gender, sex guilt, and authoritarianism on responses to heterosexual and masturbatory stimuli.* Unpublished manuscript, 1981. (Available from Department of Psychology, State University of New York at Albany, 1400 Washington Avenue, Albany, New York 12222).
4. Kelley, K. *Heterosexuals' homophobic attitudes and responses to mildly stimulating erotica.* Paper presented at the meeting of the Midwestern Psychological Association, Detroit, May 1981.
5. Kelley, K. *Familiarity with erotica breeds contempt: Effects of frequency of exposure and novelty of change stimulus.* Paper presented at the meeting of the Eastern Psychological Association, Baltimore, April 1982.
6. Przybyla, D. P. J., & Byrne, D. *The role of incompatible responses in the experience of cognitive sexual arousal.* Paper presented at the meeting of the Eastern Psychological Association, New York City, April 1981.
7. Przybyla, D. P. J., Miller, C. T., & Byrne, D. *Fantasy content in relation to gender and erotophobia-erotophilia.* Unpublished manuscript, 1982. (Available from Department of Psychology, State University of New York at Albany, 1400 Washington Avenue, Albany, New York 12222).
8. Byrne, D. *The antecedents, correlates, and consequents of erotophobia-erotophilia.* Paper presented at the meeting of the Society for the Scientific Study of Sex, New York City, November 1981.

9. Fisher, W. A. *Erotophobia-erotophilia and performance in a human sexuality course.* Unpublished manuscript, 1980. (Available from Department of Psychology, University of Western Ontario, London, Ontario, Canada N6A 5C2).

10. Przybyla, D. P. J., & Byrne, D. *Expressive behavior as a function of erotophobia-erotophilia.* Unpublished manuscript, 1982. (Available from Department of Psychology, State University of New York at Albany, 1400 Washington Avenue, Albany, New York 12222).

References

Abel, G. G., & Blanchard, E. The measurement and generation of sexual arousal in male sexual deviates. In M. Hersen, R. Eisler, and P. Miller (Eds.), *Progress in behavior modification,* 1976, *2,* 99–136.

Abramson, P. R. *The sexual system: A theory of human sexual behavior.* New York: Academic Press, 1982.

Abramson, P. R., & Mosher, D. L. Development of a measure of negative attitudes toward masturbation. *Journal of Consulting and Clinical Psychology,* 1975, *43,* 485–490.

Adams, D. B., Gold, A. R., & Burt, A. D. Rise in female-initiated sexual activity at ovulation. *New England Journal of Medicine,* 1978, *299,* 1145–1150.

Addiego, F., Belzer, E. G., Jr., Comolli, J., Moger, W., Perry, J. D., & Whipple, B. Female ejaculation: A case study. *Journal of Sex Research,* 1981, *17,* 13–21.

American Psychiatric Association. *Diagnostic and statistical manual: Mental disorders.* Washington, D.C.: American Psychiatric Association, 1952.

Amoroso, D. M., Brown, M., Pruesse, M., Ware, E. E., & Pilkey, D. W. An investigation of behavioral, psychological and physiological reactions to pornographic stimuli. In *Technical report of the Commission on Obscenity and Pornography* (Vol. 8). Washington, D.C.: U.S. Government Printing Office, 1971.

Arling, G. L., & Harlow, H. F. Effects of social deprivation on maternal behavior of rhesus monkeys. *Journal of Comparative and Physiological Psychology,* 1967, *64,* 371–377.

Barclay, A. M. Sexual fantasies in men and women. *Medical Aspects of Human Sexuality,* 1973, *7,* 205–216.

Barlow, D. H., Leitenberg, H., & Agras, W. S. Experimental control of sexual deviation through manipulation of the noxious scene in covert sensitization. *Journal of Abnormal Psychology,* 1969, *74,* 596–601.

Barlow, D. H., Reynolds, E. J., & Agras, W. S. Gender identity change in a transsexual. *Archives of General Psychiatry,* 1973, *28,* 569–576.

Baron, R. A. The aggression-inhibiting influence of heightened sexual arousal. *Journal of Personality and Social Psychology,* 1974, *30,* 318–322.

Baron, R. A. The aggression-inhibiting influence of sexual humor. *Journal of Personality and Social Psychology,* 1978, *36,* 189–197.

Baron, R. A. Olfaction and human social behavior: Effects of a pleasant scent on attraction and social perception. *Personality and Social Psychology Bulletin,* 1981, *7,* 611–616.

Baron, R. A., & Bell, P. A. Sexual arousal and aggression by males: Effects of type of erotic stimuli and prior provocation. *Journal of Personality and Social Psychology,* 1977, *35,* 79–87.

Baron, R. A., & Byrne, D. *Social psychology: Understanding human interaction* (2nd ed.). Boston: Allyn & Bacon, 1977.

Baron, R. A., & Byrne, D. *Social psychology: Understanding human interaction* (3rd ed.). Boston: Allyn & Bacon, 1981.

Bell, A. P., Weinberg, M. S., & Hammersmith, S. K. *Sexual preference: Its development in men and women.* Bloomington, Indiana: Indiana University Press, 1981.

Belzer, E. G., Jr. Orgasmic expulsions of women: A review and heuristic inquiry. *Journal of Sex Research,* 1981, *17,* 1–12.

Bentler, P. M., & Abramson, P. R. The science of sex research: Some methodological considerations. *Archives of Sexual Behavior,* 1981, *10,* 225–251.

Bieber, I. *Homosexuality: A psychoanalytic study.* New York: Basic Books, 1962.

Blakemore, C. G., Thorpe, J. G., Barker, J. C., Conway, C. G., & Lavin, N. L. The application of faradic aversion conditioning in a case of transvestism. *Behavior Research and Therapy,* 1963, *1,* 29–34.

Bolles, R. C. *Theory of motivation.* New York: Harper & Row, 1975.

Brady, J., & Levitt, E. E. The relation of sexual preferences to sexual experiences. *Psychological Record,* 1965, *15,* 377–384.

Bremer, J. *Asexualization: A follow-up study of 244 cases.* New York: Macmillan, 1959.

Brown, M., Amoroso, D. M., & Ware, E. E. Behavioral effects of viewing pornography. *Journal of Social Psychology,* 1976, *98,* 235–248.

Brownell, K. D., Hayes, S. C., & Barlow, D. H. Patterns of appropriate and deviant sexual arousal: The behavioral treatment of multiple sexual deviations. *Journal of Consulting and Clinical Psychology,* 1977, *45,* 1144–1155.

Burt, M. R. Cultural myths and supports for rape. *Journal of Personality and Social Psychology,* 1980, *38,* 217–230.

Byrne, D. Social psychology and the study of sexual behavior. *Personality and Social Psychology Bulletin,* 1977, *3,* 3–30. (a)

Byrne, D. The imagery of sex. In J. Money and H. Musaph (Eds.), *Handbook of sexology.* Amsterdam: Excerpta Medica, 1977. (b)

Byrne, D., & Byrne, L. A. *Exploring human sexuality.* New York: Harper & Row, 1977.

Byrne, D., Fisher, J. D., Lamberth, J., & Mitchell, H. E. Evaluations of erotica: Facts or feelings? *Journal of Personality and Social Psychology,* 1974, *29,* 111–116.

Byrne, D., Jazwinski, C., DeNinno, J. A., & Fisher, W. A. Negative sexual attitudes and contraception. In D. Byrne and L. A. Byrne (Eds.), *Exploring human sexuality.* New York: Harper & Row, 1977.

Byrne, D., & Kelley, K. *An introduction to personality* (3rd ed.). Englewood Cliffs, N.J.: Prentice-Hall, 1981.

Byrne, D., & Lamberth, J. The effect of erotic stimuli on sex arousal, evaluative responses, and subsequent behavior. In *Technical report of the commission on Obscenity and Pornography* (Vol. 8). Washington, D.C.: U.S. Government Printing Office, 1971.

Cattell, R. B., Kawash, G. F., & DeYoung, G. E. Validation of objective measures of ergic tension: Response of the sex erg to visual stimulation. *Journal of Experimental Research in Personality,* 1972, *6,* 76–83.

Chevalier-Skolnikoff, S. Heterosexual copulatory patterns in stumptail macaques *(Macaca arctoides)* and in other macaque species. *Archives of Sexual Behavior,* 1975, *4,* 199–220.

Clausen, J. The social meaning of differential physical and sexual maturation. In S. E. Dragastin and G. H. Elder (Eds.), *Adolescence and the life cycle.* New York: Hemisphere, 1975.

Clore, G. L., & Byrne, D. A reinforcement-affect model of attraction. In T. L. Huston (Ed.), *Foundations of interpersonal attraction.* New York: Academic Press, 1974.

Cohen, D. *J. B. Watson: The founder of behaviorism.* London: Routledge & Kegan Paul, 1979.

Commission on Obscenity and Pornography. *The report of the Commission on Obscenity and Pornography.* Washington, D.C.: U.S. Government Printing Office, 1970.

Constantine, L. L., & Martinson, F. M. (Eds.). *Children and sex: New findings, new perspectives.* Boston: Little, Brown, 1981.

Crépault, C., & Couture, M. Men's erotic fantasies. *Archives of Sexual Behavior,* 1980, *9,* 565–582.

Davis, K. B. *Factors in the sex life of 2,200 women.* New York: Harper & Row, 1929.

Davis, K. E., & Braucht, G. N. Reactions to viewing films of erotically realistic heterosexual behavior. In *Technical report of the Commission on Obscenity and Pornography* (Vol. 8). Washington, D.C.: U.S. Government Printing Office, 1971.

Diamond, M. Human sexual development: Biological foundations for social development. In F. A. Beach (Ed.), *Human sexuality in four perspectives.* Baltimore: The Johns Hopkins University Press, 1977.

Doty, R. L., Ford, M., Preti, G., & Huggins, G. R. Changes in the intensity and pleasantness of human vaginal odors during the menstrual cycle. *Science,* 1975, *190,* 1316–1318.

Ellis, E. M., Atkeson, B. M., & Calhoun, K. S. An assessment of long-term reaction to rape. *Journal of Abnormal Psychology,* 1981, *90,* 263–266.

Ellis, H. *Studies in the psychology of sex.* New York: Random House, 1936. (Originally published, 1899.)

Erwin, J., Mitchell, G., & Maple, T. Abnormal behavior in nonisolate-reared rhesus monkeys. *Psychological Reports,* 1973, *33,* 515–523.

Farkas, G. M., Sine, L. F., & Evans, I. M. The effects of distraction, performance demand, stimulus explicitness and personality on objective and subjective measures of male sexual arousal. *Behavior Research and Therapy,* 1979, *17,* 25–32.

Feldman, M. P., & MacCulloch, M. J. *Homosexual behavior: Therapy and assessment.* Oxford: Pergamon, 1971.

Feldman-Summers, S., Gordon, P. E., & Meagher, J. R. The impact of rape on sexual satisfaction. *Journal of Abnormal Psychology,* 1979, *88,* 101–105.

Fishbein, M. Toward an understanding of family planning behaviors. *Journal of Applied Social Psychology,* 1972, *2,* 214–227.

Fishbein, M., & Azjen, I. *Belief, attitude, intention, and behavior: An introduction to theory and research.* Reading, Mass.: Addison-Wesley, 1975.

Fishbein, M., & Jaccard, J. J. Theoretical and methodological considerations in the prediction of family planning intentions and behavior. *Representative Research in Social Psychology,* 1973, *4,* 37–51.

Fisher, W. A. *Affective, attitudinal, and normative determinants of contraceptive behavior among university men.* Unpublished doctoral dissertation, Purdue University, 1978.

Fisher, W. A., & Byrne. D. Individual differences in affective, evaluative, and behavioral responses to an erotic film. *Journal of Applied Social Psychology,* 1978, *8,* 355–365. (a)

Fisher, W. A., & Byrne, D. Sex differences in response to erotica? Love versus lust. *Journal of Personality and Social Psychology,* 1978, *36,* 119–125. (b)

Fisher, W. A., & Byrne, D. Social background, attitudes, and sexual attraction. In M. Cook (Ed.), *The bases of human sexual attraction.* London: Academic Press, 1981.

Fisher, W. A., & Byrne, D., Edmunds, M., Miller, C. T., Kelley, K., & White, L. A. Psychological and situation-specific correlates of contraceptive behavior among university women. *Journal of Sex Research,* 1979, *15,* 38–55.

Fisher, W. A., Byrne, D., & White, L. A. Emotional barriers to contraception. In D. Byrne and W. A. Fisher (Eds.), *Adolescents, sex, and contraception.* Hillsdale, N.J.: Erlbaum, 1982.

Fisher, W. A., Fisher, J. D., & Byrne, D. Consumer reactions to contraceptive purchasing. *Personality and Social Psychology Bulletin,* 1977, *3,* 293–296.

Fisher, W. A., Miller, C. T., Byrne, D., & White, L. A. Talking dirty: Responses to communicating a sexual message as a function of situational and personality factors. *Basic and Applied Social Psychology,* 1980, *1,* 115–126.

Ford, C. S., & Beach, F. A. *Patterns of sexual behavior.* New York: Harper, 1951.

Freud, S. *The interpretation of dreams.* London: Hogarth, 1953. (Originally published, 1900.)

Freud, S. *Three contributions to the theory of sex.* New York: Dutton, 1962. (Originally published, 1905.)

Gagnon, J. H., & Simon, W. *Sexual conduct: The social sources of human sexuality.* Chicago: Aldine, 1973.

Galbraith, G. G., & Mosher, D. L. Associative sexual response in relation to sexual arousal, guilt, and external approval contingencies. *Journal of Personality and Social Psychology,* 1968, *10,* 142–147.

Garner, B., & Smith, R. W. Are there really any gay male athletes? An empirical survey. *Journal of Sex Research,* 1977, *13,* 22–34.

Geer, J. H. Direct measurement of genital responding. *American Psychologist,* 1975, *30,* 415–418.

Geer, J. H. Biofeedback and the modification of sexual dysfunctions. In P. J. Gatchel and K. P. Price (Eds.), *Clinical applications of biofeedback: Appraisal and status.* New York: Pergamon, 1979.

Geer, J. H., & Fuhr, R. Cognitive factors in sexual arousal: The role of distraction. *Journal of Consulting and Clinical Psychology,* 1976, *44,* 238–243.

Gerrard, M. Sex guilt in abortion patients. *Journal of Consulting and Clinical Psychology,* 1977, *45,* 708.

Giambra, L. M. Sex differences in daydreaming and related mental activity from the late teens to the early nineties. *International Journal of Aging and Human Development,* 1979, *10*(1), 1–34.

Goldstein, M., Kant, H., & Hartman, J. J. *Pornography and sexual deviance.* Berkeley: University of Calfornia Press, 1974.

Goode, E., & Haber, L. Sexual correlates of homosexual experience: An exploratory study of college women. *Journal of Sex Research,* 1977, *13,* 12–21.

Goodwin, M., Gooding, K. M., & Regnier, F. Sex pheromone in the dog. *Science,* 1979, *203,* 559–561.

Green, R. Sexual identity conflict in children. New York: Basic Books, 1974.

Griffitt, W. Response to erotica and the projection of response to erotica in the opposite sex. *Journal of Experimental Research in Personality,* 1973, *6,* 330–338.

Griffitt, W. Sexual experience and sexual responsiveness: Sex differences. *Archives of Sexual Behavior,* 1975, *4,* 529–540.

Griffitt, W. Sexual stimulation and sociosexual behaviors. In M. Cook and G. Wilson (Eds.), *Love and attraction: An international conference.* New York: Pergamon, 1979.

Griffitt, W., & Kaiser, D. L. Affect, sex guilt, gender, and the rewarding-punishing effects of erotic stimuli. *Journal of Personality and Social Psychology,* 1978, *36,* 850–858.

Griffitt, W., May, J., & Veitch, R. Sexual stimulation and interpersonal behavior: Heterosexual evaluative responses, visual behavior, and physical proximity. *Journal of Personality and Social Psychology,* 1974, *30,* 367–377.

Gundlach, R. H. Sibship size, sibsex, and homosexuality among females. *Transnational Mental Health Research Newsletter,* 1977, *19,* 3–7.

Hamilton, G. V. *A study in marriage.* New York: Boni, 1929.

Hariton, B. E. *Women's fantasies during sexual intercourse with their husbands: A normative study with tests of personality and theoretical models.* Unpublished doctoral dissertation, City University of New York, 1972.

Hariton, B. E., & Singer, J. L. Women's fantasies during sexual intercourse: Normative and theoretical implications. *Journal of Consulting and Clinical Psychology,* 1974, *42,* 313–322.

Harlow, H. F. Lust, latency and love: Simian secrets of successful sex. *Journal of Sex Research,* 1975, *11,* 79–90.

Harlow, H. F., Harlow, M. K., Hansen, E. W., & Soumi, S. J. Infantile sexuality in monkeys. *Archives of Sexual Behavior,* 1972, *2,* 1–7.

Hassett, J. Sex and smell. *Psychology Today,* 1978, *11* (10), 40–42, 45.

Hatfield, E., Sprecher, S., & Traupmann, J. Men's and women's reactions to sexually explicit films. A serendipitous finding. *Archives of Sexual Behavior,* 1978, *7,* 583–592.

Hebb, D. O. The role of neurological ideas in psychology. *Journal of Personality,* 1951, *20,* 39–55.

Heiman, J. R. The physiology of erotica: Women's sexual arousal. *Psychology Today,* 1975, *8,* 91–94.

Heiman, J. R. A psychophysiological exploration of sexual arousal patterns in females and males. *Psychophysiology,* 1977, *14,* 266–274.

Herrell, J. M. Sex differences in emotional responses to "erotic literature." *Journal of Consulting and Clinical Psychology,* 1975, *43,* 921.

Hessellund, H. Masturbation and sexual fantasies in married couples. *Archives of Sexual Behavior,* 1976, *5,* 133–147.

Hoffman, M. *The gay world.* New York: Basic Books, 1968.

Hoon, P. The assessment of sexual arousal in women. In M. Hersen, R. M. Eisler, and P. M. Miller (Eds.), *Progress in behavior modification* (Vol. 7). New York: Academic Press, 1978.

Houser, B.B. An investigation of the correlation between hormonal levels in males and mood, behavior, and physical discomfort. *Hormones and Behavior,* 1979, *12,* 185–197.

Howard, J. L., Reifler, C. B., & Liptzin, M. B. Effects of exposure to pornography. In *Technical report of the Commission on Obscenity and Pornography* (Vol. 8). Washington, D.C.: U.S. Government Printing Office, 1971.

Hunt, M. *Sexual behavior in the 1970's.* Chicago: Playboy Press, 1974.

Jaccard, J., Hand, D., Ku, L., Richardson, K., & Abella, R. Attitudes toward male oral contraceptives: Implications for models of the relationship between beliefs and attitudes. *Journal of Applied Social Psychology,* 1981, *11,* 181–191.

Kallman, F. Twin and sibship study of overt male homosexuality. *American Journal of Human Genetics,* 1952, *4,* 136–146.

Kaplan, H. S. *The new sex therapy.* New York: Brunner/Mazel, 1974.

Kaye, H. E. Lesbian relationships. *Sexual Behavior,* April, 1972.

Keller, D. E. Quoted in *Playboy,* February 1981, p. 228.

Kelley, K. Socialization factors in contraceptive attitudes: Roles of affective responses, parental attitudes, and sexual experience. *Journal of Sex Research,* 1979, *15,* 6–20.

Kelley, K., & Byrne, D. The function of imaginative fantasy in sexual behavior. *Journal of Mental Imagery,* 1978, *2,* 139–146.

Kelley, K., & Byrne, D. Assessment of sexual responding: Arousal, affect, and behavior. In J. Cacioppo and R. Petty (Eds.), *Social psychophysiology.* New York: Guilford Press, in press.

Keverne, E. B. Pheromones and sexual behavior. In J. Money and H. Musaph (Eds.), *Handbook of sexology*. Amsterdam: Excerpta Medica, 1977.

Kilpatrick, D. G., Resick, P. A., & Veronen, L. J. Effects of a rape experience: A longitudinal study. *Journal of Social Issues*, 1981, *37*(4), 105–122.

Kinsey, A. C., Pomeroy, W., & Martin, C. *Sexual behavior in the human male*. Philadelphia: Saunders, 1948.

Kinsey, A. C., Pomeroy, W., & Martin, C., & Gebhard, P. *Sexual behavior in the human female*. Philadelphia: Saunders, 1953.

Krafft-Ebing, R. von. *Psychopathia sexualis*. Philadelphia: F. A. Davis, 1894. (Originally published, 1886).

Kutchinsky, B. The effect of pornography: A pilot experiment on perception, behavior, and attitudes. In *Technical report of the Commission on Obscenity and Pornography* (Vol. 8). Washington, D.C.: U.S. Government Printing Office, 1971.

Larssen, K. *Conditioning and sexual behavior in the male albino rat*. Stockholm: Almquist and Wiksell, 1956.

Levin, S. M., Barry, S. M., Gambaro, S., Wolfinsohn, L., & Smith, A. Variations of covert sensitization in the treatment of pedophilic behavior: A case study. *Journal of Consulting and Clinical Psychology*, 1977, *45*, 896–907.

Levitt, E. E., & Brady, J. P. Sexual preferences in young adult males and some correlates. *Journal of Clinical Psychology*, 1965, *21*, 347–354.

Lobitz, W. C., & LoPiccolo, J. New methods in the treatment of sexual dysfunction. *Journal of Behavior Therapy and Experimental Psychiatry*, 1972, *3*, 265–271.

Love, R. E., Sloan, L. R., & Schmidt, M. J. Viewing pornography and sex guilt: The priggish, the prudent, and the profligate. *Journal of Consulting and Clinical Psychology*, 1976, *44*, 624–629.

Lumby, M. E. Homophobia: The quest for a valid scale. *Journal of Homosexuality*, 1976, *2*, 39–47.

Luria, Z., & Rose, M. D. *Psychology of human sexuality*. New York: Wiley, 1979.

Magoun, H. W. John B. Watson and the study of human sexual behavior. *Journal of Sex Research*, 1981, *17*, 368–378.

Mann, J., Berkowitz, L., Sidman, J., Starr, S., & West, S. Satiation of the transient stimulating effect of erotic films. *Journal of Personality and Social Psychology*, 1974, *30*, 729–735.

Manosevitz, M. Early sexual behaviors in adult homosexual and heterosexual males. *Journal of Abnormal Psychology*, 1970, *76*, 396–402.

Manosevitz, M. The development of male homosexuality. *Journal of Sex Research*, 1972, *8*, 31–40.

Margolese, M. S. Homosexuality: A new endocrine correlate. *Hormones and Behavior*, 1970, *1*, 151–155.

Marshall, P., Surridge, D., & Delva, N. The role of nocturnal penile tumescence in differentiating between organic and psychogenic impotence: The first stage of validation. *Archives of Sexual Behavior*, 1981, *10*, 1–10.

Masters, W. H., & Johnson, V. E. The human female: Anatomy of sexual response. *Minnesota Medicine*, 1960, *43*, 31–36.

Masters, W. H., & Johnson, V. E. The physiology of the vaginal reproductive function. *Western Journal of Surgery*, 1961, *69*, 105–120. (a)

Masters, W. H., & Johnson, V. E. The artificial vagina: Anatomic, physiologic, psychosexual function. *Western Journal of Surgery*, 1961, *69*, 192–212. (b)

Masters, W. H., & Johnson, V. E. The sexual response cycle of the human female: III. The clitoris: Anatomic and clinical considerations. *Western Journal of Surgery*, 1962, *70*, 248–257.

Masters, W. H., & Johnson, V. E. The sexual response of the human male: I. Gross anatomic considerations. *Western Journal of Surgery*, 1963, *71*, 85–95.

Masters, W. H., & Johnson, V. E. *Human sexual response.* Boston: Little, Brown, 1966.

Masters, W. H., & Johnson, V. E. *Human sexual inadequacy.* Boston: Little, Brown, 1970.

Masters, W. H., & Johnson, V. E. *Homosexuality in perspective.* Boston: Little, Brown, 1979.

McCarty, D. Changing contraceptive usage intentions: A test of the Fishbein model of intention. *Journal of Applied Social Psychology*, 1981, *11*, 192–211.

McCauley, C., & Swann, C. P. Male-female differences in sexual fantasy. *Journal of Research in Personality*, 1978, *12*, 76–86.

McCauley, C., & Swann, C. P. Sex differences in the frequency and functions of fantasies during sexual activity. *Journal of Research in Personality*, 1980, *14*, 400–411.

McCauley, E., & Ehrhardt, A. A. Female sexual response: Hormonal and behavioral interactions. *Primary Care*, 1976, *3*, 455–476.

McConaghy, N. Penile response conditioning and its relationship to aversion therapy in homosexuals. *Behavioral Therapy*, 1970, *1*, 213–221.

McConnell, J. V. *Understanding human behavior: An introduction to psychology* (3rd ed.). New York: Holt, Rinehart, & Winston, 1980.

McIntosh, M. The homosexual role. *Social Problems*, 1968, *16*(2), 182–192.

Mendelsohn, M. J., & Mosher, D. L. Effects of sex guilt and premarital sexual permissiveness on role-played sex education and moral attitudes. *Journal of Sex Research*, 1979, *15*, 174–183.

Messenger, J. C. Sexual repression: Its manifestations. In D. Byrne and L. A. Byrne (Eds.), *Exploring human sexuality.* New York: Harper & Row, 1977.

Mitchell, G. D., Arling, G. L., & Moller, G. W. Long-term effects of maternal punishment on the behavior of monkeys. *Psychonomic Science*, 1967, *8*, 209–210.

Mitchell, G. D., Raymond, E. J., Ruppenthal, G. C., & Harlow, H. F. Long-term effects of total social isolation upon behavior of rhesus monkeys. *Psychological Reports*, 1966, *18*, 567–580.

Money, J., & Clopper, R. R. Psychosocial and psychosexual aspects of errors in pubertal onset and development. In M. Smart and R. Smart (Eds.), *Adolescents: Development and relationships.* New York: Macmillan, 1978.

Moreault, D., & Follingstad, D. R. Sexual fantasies of females as a function of sex guilt and experimental response cues. *Journal of Consulting and Clinical Psychology*, 1978, *46*, 1385–1393.

Morris, N. M., & Udry, J. R. Pheromonal influences on human sexual behavior: An experimental search. *Journal of Biosocial Science*, 1978, *10*, 147–157.

Morrison, E. S., Starks, K., Hyndman, C., & Ronzio, N. *Growing up sexual.* New York: Van Nostrand, 1980.

Mosher, D. L. The development and multitrait-multimethod matrix analysis of three measures of three aspects of guilt. *Journal of Consulting Psychology*, 1966, *30*, 25–29.

Mosher, D. L. Measurement of guilt in females by self report inventories. *Journal of Consulting and Clinical Psychology*, 1968, *32*, 690–695.

Mosher, D. L. Sex guilt and sex myths in college men and women. *Journal of Sex Research*, 1979, *15*, 224–234.

Mosher, D. L. Three dimensions of depth of involvement in human sexual response. *Journal of Sex Research*, 1980, *16*, 1–42.

Mosher, D. L., & Abramson, P. R. Subjective sexual arousal to films of masturbation. *Journal of Consulting and Clinical Psychology*, 1977, *45*, 796–807.

Mosher, D. L., & Cross, H. J. Sex guilt and premarital sexual experiences of college students. *Journal of Consulting and Clinical Psychology*, 1971, *36*, 27–32.

Nemetz, G. H., Craig, K. D., & Reith, G. Treatment of female sexual dysfunction through symbolic modeling. *Journal of Consulting and Clinical Psychology*, 1978, *46*, 62–73.

Newtson, D., Engquist, G., & Bois, J. The objective basis of behavior units. *Journal of Personality and Social Psychology*, 1977, *35*, 847–862.

Osborn, C. A., & Pollack, R. H. The effects of two types of erotic literature on physiological and verbal measures of female sexual arousal. *Journal of Sex Research*, 1977, *13*, 250–256.

Parcel, G. S. Development of an instrument to measure attitudes toward the personal use of premarital contraception. *Journal of School Health*, 1975, *45*, 157–160.

Perry, J. D., & Whipple, B. Pelvic muscle strength of female ejaculations: Evidence in support of a new theory of orgasm. *Journal of Sex Research*, 1981, *17*, 22–39.

Pirke, K. M., Kockott, G., & Dittmen, F. Psychosexual stimulation and plasma testosterone in men. *Archives of Sexual Behavior*, 1974, *3*, 577–584.

Pomeroy, W. B. The Masters-Johnson report and the Kinsey tradition. In R. Brecher and E. Brecher (Eds.), *An analysis of human sexual response*. Boston: Little, Brown, 1966.

Pomeroy, W. B. *Dr. Kinsey and the Institute for Sex Research*. New York: Harper & Row, 1972.

Pritchard, M. Homosexuality and genetic sex. *Journal of Mental Science*, 1962, *108*, 616–623.

Przybyla, D. P. J., & Byrne, D. Sexual relationships. In S. Duck and R. Gilmour (Eds.), *Personal relationships 1.: Studying personal relationships*. London: Academic Press, 1981.

Przybyla, D. P. J., Byrne, D., & Kelley, K. The role of imagery in sexual behavior. In A. A. Sheikh (Ed.), *Imagery: Current theory, research, and application*. New York: Wiley, in press.

Purvis, K., Landgren, B. M., Cekan, Z., & Diczfalusy, E. Endocrine effects of masturbation in men. *Journal of Endocrinology*, 1976, *70*, 439–444.

Rachman, S. Sexual fetishism: An experimental analogue. *Psychological Record*, 1966, *16*, 293–296.

Rachman, S., & Hodgson, R. J. Experimentally-induced "sexual fetishism": Replication and development. *Psychological Record*, 1968, *18*, 25–27.

Rook, K. S., & Hammen, C. L. A cognitive perspective on the experience of sexual arousal. *Journal of Social Issues*, 1977, *33*, 7–29,

Rose, R. M. Plasma testosterone levels in the male rhesus: Influences of sexual and social stimuli. *Science*, 1972, *178*, 643–645.

Rosen, R. C., & Keefe, F. J. The measurement of human penile tumescence. *Psychophysiology*, 1978, *15*, 366–376.

Rosen, R., & Rosen, L. R. *Human sexuality*. New York: Knopf, 1981.

Rotter, J. B., & Hochreich, D. J. *Personality*. Glenview, Ill.: Scott, Foresman, 1975.

Sachs, B. D., & Marsan, E. Male rats prefer sex to food after 6 days of food deprivation. *Psychonomic Science*, 1972, *28*, 47–49.

Saghir, M. T., & Robins, E. *Male and female homosexuality*. Baltimore: Williams & Wilkins, 1973.

Sarnoff, C. *Latency*. New York: Aronson, 1976.

Schill, T., & Chapin, J. Sex guilt and males' preference for reading erotic magazines. *Journal of Consulting and Clinical Psychology*, 1972, *39*, 516.

Schmidt, G. Male-female differences in sexual arousal and behavior during and after exposure to sexually explicit stimuli. *Archives of Sexual Behavior*, 1975, *4*, 353–363.

Schmidt, G., & Sigusch, V. Sex differences in responses to psychosexual stimulation by films and slides. *Journal of Sex Research*, 1970, *6*, 268–283.

Schmidt, G., Sigusch, V., & Meyberg, V. Psychosexual stimulation in men: Emotional reactions, changes of sex behavior, and measures of conservative attitudes. *Journal of Sex Research*, 1969, *5*, 199–217.

Schmidt, G., Sigusch, V., & Schäfer, S. Responses to reading erotic stories: Male-female differences. *Archives of Sexual Behavior*, 1973, *2*, 181–199.

Schubert, H. J., Wagner, M. E., & Reiss, B. F. Sibship size, sibsex, sibgap, and homosexuality among male outpatients. *Transnational Mental Health Research Newsletter*, 1976, *18*, 3–8.

Schwartz, S. Effects of sex guilt and sexual arousal on the retention of birth control information. *Journal of Consulting and Clinical Psychology*, 1973, *41*, 61–64.

Seeley, T. T., Abramson, P. R., Perry, L. B., Rothblatt, A. B., & Seeley, D. M. Thermographic measurement of sexual arousal: A methodological note. *Archives of Sexual Behavior*, 1980, *9*, 77–85.

Senko, M. G. *The effects of early, intermediate, and late experience upon adult macaque sexual behavior.* Unpublished master's thesis, University of Wisconsin, Madison, 1966.

Sevely, J. L., & Bennett, J. W. Concerning female ejaculation and the female prostate. *Journal of Sex Research*, 1978, *14*, 1–20.

Shapiro, D. A monologue on biofeedback and psychophysiology. *Psychophysiology*, 1977, *14*, 213–227.

Simon, W., & Gagnon, J. H. On psychosexual development. In D. A. Goslin (Ed.), *Handbook of socialization theory and research.* Chicago: Rand McNally, 1969.

Sintchak, G., & Geer, J. H. A vaginal plethysmographic system. *Psychophysiology*, 1975, *12*, 113–115.

Slater, E. Birth order and maternal age of homosexuals. *Lancet*, 1962, *1*, 69–71.

Speiss, W. F. J. *The psychophysiology of premature ejaculation.* Unpublished doctoral dissertation, State University of New York at Stony Brook, 1977.

Steinman, D. L., Wincze, J. P., Sakheim, D. K., Barlow, D. H., & Mavissakalian, M. A comparison of male and female patterns of sexual arousal. *Archives of Sexual Behavior*, 1981, *10*, 529–547.

Storms, M. D. Theories of sexual orientation. *Journal of Personality and Social Psychology*, 1980, *38*, 783–792.

Storms, M. D. A theory of erotic orientation development. *Psychological Review*, 1981, *88*, 340–353.

Sue, D. Erotic fantasies of college students during coitus. *Journal of Sex Research*, 1979, *15*, 299–305.

Suinn, R. M. *Fundamentals of behavior pathology.* New York: Wiley, 1970.

Terman, L. M., Buttenwieser, P., Ferguson, L. W., Johnson, W. B., & Wilson, D. P. *Psychological factors in marital happiness.* New York: McGraw-Hill, 1938.

Tordjman, G., Thierree, R., & Michel, J. R. Advances in the vascular pathology of male erectile dysfunction. *Archives of Sexual Behavior*, 1980, *9*, 391–398.

Wagman, M. Sex differences in types of daydreams. *Journal of Personality and Social Psychology*, 1967, *7*, 332.

Wallace, D. H., & Wehmer, G. Evaluation of visual erotica by sexual liberals and conservatives. *Journal of Sex Research*, 1972, *8*, 147–153.

Walling, W. H. *Sexology.* Philadelphia: Puritan, 1912.

Warden, C. J. *Animal motivation: Experimental studies on the albino rat.* New York: Columbia University Press, 1931.

Watson, J. B. Introduction. In G. V. Hamilton and K. Macgowan, *What is wrong with marriage?* New York: Boni, 1929.

Watson, J. B., & Lashley, K. S. The opinion of doctors regarding venereal disease. *Social Hygiene*, 1919, *4*, 769–847.

Weisberg, M. A note on female ejaculation. *Journal of Sex Research*, 1981, *17*, 90–91.

White, L. A. Erotica and aggression: The influence of sexual arousal, positive affect, and negative affect on aggressive behavior. *Journal of Personality and Social Psychology*, 1979, *37*, 591–601.

Wincze, J. P., Hoon, E. F., & Hoon, P. W. Psysiological responsivity of normal and sexually dysfunctional women during erotic stimulus exposure. *Journal of Psychosomatic Research*, 1976, *20*, 445–451.

Wincze, J. P., Hoon, P. W., & Hoon, E. F. Sexual arousal in women: A comparison of cognitive and physiological responses by continuous measurement. *Archives of Sexual Behavior*, 1977, *6*, 121–133.

Zillmann, D., Bryant, J., Comisky, P. W., & Medoff, N. J. Excitation and hedonic valence in the effect of erotica on motivated intermale aggression. *European Journal of Social Psychology*, 1981, *11*, 233–252.

Zillmann, D., & Sapolsky, B. S. What mediates the effect of mild erotica on annoyance and hostile behavior in males? *Journal of Personality and Social Psychology*, 1977, *35*, 587–596.